The Good Cook's
Guide to the
MICROWAVE

The Good Cook's Guide to the
MICROWAVE

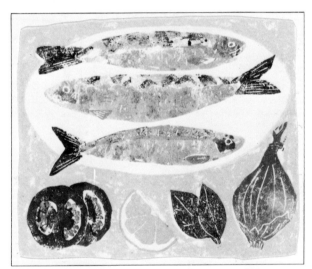

Sue Roberts

DORLING KINDERSLEY·LONDON

To Peter

A Jill Norman Book

First published in Great Britain in 1988
by Dorling Kindersley Limited,
9 Henrietta Street, London WC2E 8PS

Photography
Dave King
Illustrations
Nancy Anderson

British Library Cataloguing in Publication Data
Roberts, Sue
The Good Cook's Guide to the Microwave
1. Microwave cookery
I. Title   II. Series
641.5′882   TX832

ISBN 0 86318 284 4

Typesetting
Goodfellow & Egan, Cambridge
Colour reproduction
Scantrans, Singapore
Printed and bound by
Butler and Tanner, Frome, Somerset

CONTENTS

INTRODUCTION

The microwave oven is the most liberating and economical of modern kitchen appliances. Busy families, working mothers, single people, the disabled and the elderly, can all benefit from the many advantages that microwave cooking brings. The speed of cooking, reheating and defrosting is quite remarkable. A baked apple will cook in 2½ minutes, chicken takes 6–8 minutes per 1lb/500 g and a plated meal requires only 2–3 minutes to reheat. These ovens are highly energy efficient – the running costs are low, the oven requires no preheating and, because it is the food and not the surrounding space that is heated, very little energy is lost into the atmosphere. Microwave ovens are not, however, magical devices that require no skill of the cook. For the beginner there are new techniques to learn, so the manufacturer's handbook and the information in this book should be read carefully.

The beginner to microwave cooking has a number of factors to take account of:

size and shape of food
precise timing
composition of containers
new techniques
starting temperatures.

Advertising may have been misleading; food should not be abandoned to high technology. Although it cooks quickly by microwave, it often requires more attention during cooking. I have known people become disillusioned after their first mistakes, but once they begin to understand the basic techniques, cooking becomes much easier. Patience is necessary and if you start with simple tasks such as heating milk, defrosting and cooking smaller items, confidence will grow and accomplishment will follow.

WHAT ARE MICROWAVES?

Although electric cookers were introduced at the turn of the century, it was not until the late 1930s that their acceptance became widespread in the UK. Electricity as a cooking medium was treated with great suspicion and there was some fear of not being able to control the power source that could not be seen. Microwaves are being increasingly

ADVANTAGES AND LIMITATIONS

Advantages

Food retains more moisture, colour, flavour and, most importantly, nutrients.

No dry heat is produced so the oven interior stays fairly cool.

Containers never reach the high temperatures of conventional cooking (they will get hot if food is microwaved for a long time). Consequently, there are fewer accidents and, particularly for the disabled, the old and children, less likelihood of injury.

Many foods can be cooked in serving dishes and disposable microwave boiling bags and, unlike conventional cooking, food does not stick or burn on to containers. Time and effort are thus saved in washing up and cleaning.

Reheating is safe and quick; reheated food has the appearance of being freshly cooked.

Condensation caused by cooking is greatly reduced. There is very little steam with this method of cooking, so it is particularly suitable for badly ventilated kitchens. A microwave oven will not heat the kitchen as a conventional oven does; this is a great advantage during hot weather and kitchen decor will deteriorate less.

Special diets can be more conveniently catered for, especially when the diets are low fat or salt free. Diet cooking for a single member of a family often presents problems, but with a microwave oven the task is quickly and easily undertaken.

Lingering smells are eliminated after cooking fish or curry.

Ovens can be built into fitted kitchens or stand on a firm surface. They need a fused 13 amp plug and are then ready to use. They can be placed on a trolley and used in the dining room, sick room or outside as a back-up for a barbecue party. Portable models can be taken on holiday and are often used in caravans and on boats.

The microwave is useful for numerous little jobs such as melting chocolate, dissolving gelatine, softening brown sugar that has hardened in the packet, taking the chill off eggs for baking and softening butter for spreading or creaming.

Limitations

The microwave oven is best used in conjunction with the conventional oven and hob; it is not a complete replacement. Some foods benefit from conventional cooking methods and certain tasks should not be attempted with a microwave oven.

Deep fat frying is not possible as there is no way of controlling the temperature of the oil. It could ignite, causing a fire inside the oven cavity.

Eggs cannot be boiled; they would explode with the pressure that builds up inside the shell during cooking.

Pancakes, fritters and Yorkshire puddings turn out soggy and undercooked.

Double crust fruit pies should never be cooked from their raw state; the sweet filling heats up faster than the pastry, boils out and over the lid, resulting in a mass of raw pastry mixed with gooey filling and a very dirty oven. Cooked pies, however, do reheat successfully.

Christmas cakes and those requiring a stiff dropping consistency are best baked conventionally.

The cavity in most ovens is not large enough to accommodate a goose or turkey weighing over 12 lb/6 kg. These will have to be cooked conventionally.

Space is limited so that large amounts of food cannot be cooked at any one time, and as the quantity of food increases, so does the cooking time. A large number of baked potatoes or corn on the cob, for example, are more easily and rapidly cooked conventionally.

adapted for use in the home. Soon we will see the first 'microwave boilers' for central heating systems and microwave space heaters. No doubt, in 50 years or so, folk will wonder why there was such a commotion about microwaves for cooking.

Most people are not concerned about how their radios, refrigerators and televisions work, but, with microwave ovens this question is frequently raised.

The first microwave oven was used for making popcorn; borrowing radar technology, it was patented in 1945 by Dr Percy Spenser.

Microwaves occupy part of the radar band of the spectrum of electromagnetism and are used extensively in telecommunications. This spectrum includes extremely low frequencies (ELF) and ascends progressively through the radio frequencies (long, medium and short wave), TV, radar microwave, infra red, visible light, ultra violet, X rays, gamma rays and cosmic rays. The frequency of oscillation increases as one proceeds up this scale. The frequencies used in microwave cooking oscillate 2,450,000,000 times every second!

Although microwaves cause an increase in tissue temperature they are non-ionising, and do not build up in the body as do X rays and gamma rays.

How does the oven work?
When the oven is switched on the current passes through to the 'heart' of the oven, the magnetron. By means of resonant cavities in a vacuum tube this generates and then broadcasts the microwaves. A metal duct acts as the microwave guide into the oven chamber. So that the energy is dispersed evenly at this point, rotating metal blades stir the micro-waves into the chamber.

The food in the oven absorbs any microwaves that strike it directly. The remaining microwaves are repeatedly reflected by the oven walls and will bounce back and forth, until their passage is obstructed by the food which absorbs them, like a game of 3D snooker, with the food the pocket in the middle. This is really too mild a description since what occurs is a bombardment of electromagnetic energy, billions of pulses every second. All the polar molecules (such as water) in the food align themselves parallel to the electromagnetic field generated by the first pulse. At the next pulse the polarity is reversed, so all the molecules turn over 180° into reverse alignment. Such astounding alternations might be a jig and a jive too fast for cooks were it not that heat was the useful product of the friction of these excited molecules. The micro-waves penetrate to a depth of 1½ in/4 cm and the heat generated here is transmitted by conduction to the centre of the food.

FEATURES OF A MICROWAVE OVEN

Ovens can be very basic or sophisticated; as more features are included in the design, the cost will increase accordingly. Whatever type of oven is used the basic techniques of microwave cooking apply. For beginners, some ovens seem too high tech and bristle with as many probes and sensors as a space craft. Too much sophistication can complicate rather than simplify microwave cooking; an oven chosen from a medium price range will cook food just as well as one bearing the highest price tag.

All microwave ovens have the following features:

On/off control
Fan – to keep the oven cavity cool and extract steam.
Light
Magnetron – the generator of the microwaves.
Wave stirrer and guide – to assist the microwaves into the oven cavity and ensure their even distribution.
Timer
Power control
Metal oven lining – some are painted or covered in plastic.
Door – incorporating metal screen and safety catches.

Features on sophisticated ovens include:
Turntable – useful, as food does not have to be turned so frequently during cooking.
Rotating antennae – an alternative to a turntable; hidden beneath the floor of the oven, so food remains stationary during cooking.
Variable power control – gives greater flexibility in cooking. Power output can be lowered to slow down cooking; in microwave as in conventional cooking some dishes require long low heat, some medium and some a quick fierce blast.
Digital timer – you need to count the seconds during microwave cooking and this is the clearest presentation.

Shelf – useful, but cooking becomes complex when a number of dishes are being cooked at the same time.
Temperature probe – a microwave thermometer, attached by a special cord to the oven interior. It is inserted in the food, and instructs the oven to switch off when the food has reached a set temperature. However, it is best not to rely entirely on a probe. The probe reads the heat in its immediate vicinity. Fat splattering on the probe can give a false reading and the temperature of the food can be underestimated, resulting in undercooking.
Sensor – the oven calculates the total cooking time automatically from when the sensor detects the first puff of steam escaping from the covering. When cooking by sensor, the food must be covered with unpierced cling film. In order not to upset the calculation of time that elapses between the start of the programme and the first steam, the oven door must not be opened during this period.
Browning or grilling element – this is switched on after microwaving and browns food in the same way as a conventional grill.
Touch controls – easier to clean and better for disabled people or those with arthritis or multiple sclerosis. Some control panels can be converted to braille, or raised fluorescent studs can be placed over the touch control.
Memory bank – some ovens have pre-set programmes and spare cards for alternative programming so that favourite recipe instructions can be stored, readily located and loaded.
Combination ovens – combine convection and microwave modes. They will include many of the above features. They cook by microwave and convection in sequence, solo or simultaneously. More of this in chapter 9.

Denser foods, particularly meat, will continue to increase in temperature after the oven is switched off – from 5 to 15 minutes. This phenomenon is called standing time and is a result of the water molecules heating up faster than they are able to discharge the heat to surrounding cooler, non-polar molecules. See standing time (p.13) and particular requirements in the individual recipes for more information.

Are microwave ovens really safe?

Ovens are designed with a series of safety catches incorporated in the door so that when a cooking programme is interrupted, and the door is opened to stir, whisk or rearrange food, the generation of microwaves is instantly cut off. This fail-safe mechanism prevents you being harmed by the microwaves. The door is sealed and screened to keep the microwaves in the oven. Because of these safety mechanisms, it is important to treat the door with the utmost care. If the door becomes damaged, do not repair it yourself; the safety catches that switch off microwave generation might be intact while the screens and seals are failing, allowing microwave leakage. In the event of damage to the oven, particularly the door, or if you suspect that there is microwave leakage, contact a qualified microwave engineer. The majority of ovens will need checking once a year. Check with your own oven manufacturer's instructions and keep to this recommendation, even if the oven appears to be working efficiently. The recommendation takes account of heavy and light usage. Caterers and restaurants making heavy use of a domestic oven are advised to have checks more frequently – every 6–9 months.

Two types of detector are available for checking microwave leakage. The cheaper, at about £5, is not very accurate. The professional type can be depended on but costs over £60. This detector is easily used; all that is required after setting the device is to cast a slow sweep around the door's perimeter while the oven is switched on. It registers the presence or absence of microwaves.

Timing and power levels

There is a very wide range of power controls among the various makes of microwave ovens and calculating cooking times would be much easier if there was a 'standard' microwave oven. Timing can only be approximate and no two ovens cook the same. This is particularly noticeable with delicate foods. In conventional cooking a specific time and setting can be given, say, gas 4/180°C/350°F and once preheated, there is only a slight variation between different ovens. With microwave ovens there are variations in calibrations of power output, total outputs and in size of oven cavities.

The power controls on a microwave oven can be as simple as defrost/cook. Others are numbered and power levels can range from 1–5, 1–9, 1–10, and 1–12. One of the latest combination ovens has over 100 settings. In addition, the oven's power output (wattage) varies. Domestic models may have an output of 500, 550, 600, 650, 700 or 750 watts. The higher the wattage the faster the oven cooks.

When a recipe states 'microwave on high', the cooking time will vary according to the type of oven used. The power output of a 500 watt oven set on high will obviously be lower than that of a 750 watt oven, and 5 minutes cooking time at each of these power levels will reflect 50% advantage possessed by the more powerful oven. In this book, all the recipes have been tested in a 650 watt oven. When high is referred to it means the full power output, namely 650 watts. Medium is approximately 60% of total power output, defrost is approximately 30% of total power output. The majority of domestic microwave ovens are between 600 and 700 watts. There is very little difference in the timings for ovens in this range.

◆ 11

In an oven with a wattage of 750 watts, the cooking time need only be decreased by 5 seconds for each minute of cooking required by the recipe. However, there is a significant difference in cooking times when a 500 watt oven is used. Timing must be increased by 15–20 seconds for each minute of cooking.

Another factor to consider is that if the cavity of a 600 watt oven is small, food will cook faster than in an oven of the same wattage with a larger cavity. Although the power output is the same, the microwave signal weakens with the task of filling a greater volume.

It is also worth noting that food cooks faster when it is placed on a trivet or on the shelf (if the oven has one). In most ovens the microwaves enter the cavity through the top and the microwave signals are stronger here.

Always cook for the minimum time stated in any recipe, and if in doubt, allow the food to stand and then return to the oven if any further cooking is required. Foods will not be spoiled – even light sponge cakes can be returned to the oven after standing time.

Hot spots

'Hot spots' are areas in the oven where the microwave energy is more concentrated (higher). It is useful to know exactly where the 'hot spots' are in your own oven. For example, a leg of lamb has a thick and a thin end and will cook more evenly when the thick end is positioned in a

COOKING TECHNIQUES

Stirring and whisking

These enable heat to be evenly distributed throughout the food during cooking, reheating and defrosting; wherever possible, foods must be stirred once or twice during this time. Sauces will need whisking more frequently to prevent lumps forming. Details are given in the individual recipes when appropriate.

Turning

Thicker pieces of food require turning at least once during cooking and defrosting, e.g. fish steaks, baked potatoes, pieces of chicken.

Positioning and rearranging

Arrange foods so that the thicker parts are positioned towards the outside of the container where there is more microwave energy, and thinner parts to the centre, where there is less. Items such as meatballs will need to be rearranged twice and turned over once during cooking; first move those in the centre of the container to the outside edges and vice versa. Food arranged in a circle will cook better, since the microwaves will be able to penetrate from all angles.

Piercing

Foods encased in their own skin or membrane, e.g. baked potatoes, apples, tomatoes, chicken livers and chestnuts, need pricking several times or scoring before cooking, to prevent their skins from bursting as pressure inside increases. Egg yolks need lightly piercing with the tip of a sharp knife or with a cocktail stick otherwise they may explode.

Starting temperatures

The temperature of the food before cooking affects the overall cooking time. For example, a plated meal reheated straight from the refrigerator will take longer than one at room temperature.

Quantities

Small quantities of food cook more quickly than larger amounts. As the quantity of food being cooked, defrosted or reheated is increased, the time must be adjusted accordingly.

Liquids

Getting the liquids right is crucial for success.

Cake and pudding mixtures should have a very soft, dropping consistency and, in some recipes, resemble a batter. When converting a conventional cake recipe to the microwave method, remember to increase the quantity of liquid. Consider, also, that a mixture rich in fruit is likely to be unsuccessful – the fruit could settle in the base of the container if the consistency is too slack.

Casseroles, soups and vegetables require less liquid when cooked by microwave. Large quantities (1 pt/600 ml upwards) take some time to reach boiling point, whereas smaller quantities heat rapidly. Reduce the amount of liquid to speed cooking, then dilute soups and casseroles at the end.

Vegetables require very little or no liquid at all as there is less evaporation during cooking. 4 tablespoons water is fine for 1 lb/500 g carrots, while watery vegetables such as courgettes need no additional liquid.

Obviously, when the quantity is above ½ pt/300 ml, starting with boiling water will speed up the cooking process.

Shape of food

As with conventional cooking, small pieces of food cook more quickly than large pieces. Vegetables sliced thinly will cook more quickly and evenly than those chopped roughly. One large potato will take longer to cook than two medium

COOKING TECHNIQUES

ones; a large potato will require turning more than once during cooking, and to enable the centre to cook through evenly, the power will need to be reduced from high to medium during the latter part of cooking. 1 lb/500 g grated carrots will cook faster than the same quantity roughly chopped.

Ingredients
Always use good quality ingredients; the microwave cannot transform an old, tough cut of meat into a prime succulent one.

Weigh ingredients out carefully, especially for cake and pudding mixtures. If this advice is ignored then failure is more likely than success. As the cooking time is so short and the moist microwave method differs from the dry heat of a conventional oven, there is insufficient time and opportunity to rectify mistakes. Unfortunately, they only become apparent towards the end of cooking time.

Standing time
When food is removed from the oven it continues to cook by conduction of heat from the superheated polar molecules, i.e. the intense heat which is generated in the outside edges during cooking equalizes itself throughout the food, and the internal temperature of covered food rises. This is referred to as standing time. Dense food such as joints of meat require a long standing time; a leg of lamb needs to stand, tented under foil, shiny side in, for 20 minutes, whereas airy sponge mixtures require only 5–10 minutes standing time.

Food should never be eaten until standing time is complete because you could burn your mouth. A reheated mince pie might feel warm as it is removed from the microwave, yet the sweet filling is likely to be boiling hot.

Tests for doneness appear in the recipes, although for many people unfamiliar with the cooked appearance of microwaved food, it can be difficult to judge at first. As a general rule, always undercook food and test before and after standing time. Food can always be returned to the oven for extra cooking whereas overcooked food is spoiled and wasted.

Also, during and after defrosting, food needs to stand for a short time to encourage even thawing. Fish, for example, if thawed too quickly will feel warm on the outside while the centre is still icy; these warm areas denote that cooking has begun. The fish is then likely to cook unevenly, some parts becoming dried out while the centre or thicker areas remain slightly raw.

FEEDING BABIES
Extra care must be taken when heating food and liquids for babies.

Bottles When reheating bottles of milk remember to remove the teat so that pressure does not build up inside the bottle. Teats can burn and melt. Reheat for the minimum time and remember that milk will heat up faster in a plastic bottle. Shake the bottle well and test the temperature before feeding the baby.

Solids Pour contents from cans and jars into a cereal bowl. Stir once during reheating and test before feeding the baby. Small quantities of food can reach very high temperatures after 1 minute on high, especially when sugars (processed or natural quantities contained in fruits) are among the ingredients.

◆ 13

'hot spot'. If a cup of coffee or a scrambled egg is microwaved, cooking or heating will be faster when these are situated in 'hot spots'. Nothing can be done to alter any hotter areas in an oven, as the pattern the microwaves follow is determined by the individual oven design.

The microwave pattern in many of the more recently manufactured ovens is much more even than in ovens 5–10 years old, though I would still recommend testing for 'hot spots'. Here is an excellent test that Cecilia Norman recommends.

Ovens without a turntable Fill 9 identical tumblers ¼ full with cold water and arrange in an even pattern on the oven floor. Microwave on high and watch to see which tumblers reach boiling point first. If there is only a few seconds difference then the microwave pattern can be considered even. If 30 seconds or more, remember to arrange foods and liquids in the oven so that they can benefit from being microwaved in the 'hotter' areas.

Ovens with a turntable The coolest part on all turntables, is always in the centre. Fill 6 identical tumblers ¼ full with cold water. Arrange around the edges of the turntable. Microwave on high and watch closely. You may find that as the tumblers pass through a certain area the water boils furiously and then subsides. This is why it is necessary to turn containers even when the oven has a turntable, in order to promote even cooking, especially when the food is solid, e.g. cakes and pâtés. My oven does have one 'hot spot' and if I don't give my cake container a half turn once during cooking, then a section overcooks.

Fats and sugars have complex molecular structures with some swivelling dipolar groups that respond strongly to microwaves. Since microwaves are attracted to fats and sugars, food containing large quantities of either will always cook and reheat rapidly.

EQUIPMENT

A variety of dishes can be used in the microwave and food can be cooked and served in the same container.

Metal

Microwaves cannot penetrate metal and containers made of this material should never be used.

Most people will occasionally have observed blue sparks or heard a crackling noise when certain containers are placed in the microwave. This is known as arcing – the microwaves have taken a short cut from the regular reflective pattern and have left an electrically luminous trace of their tracks. Switch off the oven to prevent fire, damage to the magnetron or pitting of the oven lining.

Metal is used in the manufacture of certain items and cannot always be seen, but whether seen or unseen, all metals should be avoided. Beware of ironstone and some earthenware vessels since they sometimes contain 'spots' of impurities that can cause sparking. The glazes in some ceramics may contain the metallic element cobalt which is used to create a blue colour; this too should be avoided.

Metals that can be seen include metallic rims, enamelled paint, metallic inscriptions on the underside of dishes, tiny screws holding handles on teapots and jugs. However, small pieces of foil can be used safely in most ovens – check the oven manufacturer's instructions before shielding foods in this way.

Plastics

There is often confusion over which type of plastic can be used in a microwave oven. Generally, flexible plastics such as ordinary Tupperware are unsuitable and can melt with prolonged use. Boilable plastics such as polypropylene are suitable although these should not be used for melting fats or heating sugary jams or syrups. Many types of plastic containers are made specially for microwave ovens, and the microwaves pass through these materials efficiently, which speeds up the cooking process. Some are very versatile and can be used in the conventional oven, freezer and microwave. Sometimes, plastics absorb food colours and odours but these can be removed easily by soaking in a solution of sterilizing fluid (the type used for sterilizing babies' bottles).

◆ 15

Glass

Ovenproof glass is ideal as food can be observed during cooking. Ordinary glass can be used if the foods or liquids do not have a high fat or sugar content. Ovenproof glass and ordinary glass are not flameproof and should never be placed under a microwave browning element or a conventional grill. Ceramic glass is an excellent material and can be used in microwave, conventional oven and freezer. It is flameproof and can safely be placed under the grill. These dishes are attractive and food can be served straight from them.

Ceramics

Ordinary ceramic and china dishes are suitable for microwave use but check underneath for metallic inscriptions. Don't use cracked or chipped containers because microwaves do cause vibrations and a plate with a small crack could break completely during cooking. Avoid using items that have handles repaired with glue as this could melt and the handles detach.

Wooden bowls and wickerware

These can be used for brief periods but prolonged use will dry them out. Check wicker baskets for metal staples. Don't leave wooden spoons in containers during cooking; the handles get hot, food odours will cling and the wood will eventually crack.

Paper and polystyrene

White paper napkins and absorbent kitchen paper can be used for reheating pastry and bread. Use white not coloured or patterned paper as the dyes can transfer to the food. Cups and shallow trays made from polystyrene are not recommended because they will melt when the food inside reaches a high temperature.

Paper cups and plates can be used and are very convenient for reheating. Don't leave waxed paperware in the oven for more than a couple of minutes, however; as the heat rises, the coating will melt and amalgamate with the contents. Plastic cups can be used to reheat liquids briefly, but never allow them to boil as the plastic will melt.

Roasting and boiling bags

Disposable microwave roasting and boiling bags are perfect for meat and vegetables.

Roasting bags encourage natural browning, especially when larger joints of meat and poultry are placed inside the bag for the whole of the cooking time. They also help to keep the oven interior clean.

Boiling bags are used mainly for vegetables and promote quick and even cooking. Never use the metal ties that are sometimes supplied with them. Secure the top loosely with an elastic band, or cut a piece from the top of the bag to use as a tie. Stand boiling bags in a container so that they remain upright and are easier to remove from the oven. Do not overfill the bags, as the food will not cook evenly.

It is not a good idea to slash bags; hands and wrists may get scalded when removing the hot bags from the oven. Instead, leave a largish gap and secure the top loosely. Ordinary polythene bags should not be used.

TESTING CONTAINERS FOR MICROWAVE USE

Here is a simple way of testing (non-metallic) containers for microwave use. Stand a tumbler, half filled with cold water, inside the dish you wish to test. Microwave on high for a few minutes. Then check:
a. If the dish is cool and the water is hot, then the water has absorbed the microwaves and the dish is suitable.
b. If the dish feels warm it has absorbed some of the microwaves and can be used safely for reheating and defrosting.
c. If the dish feels warm and the water has not heated up after a few minutes it is unsuitable for microwave cooking.

Browning dishes

The browning dish is preheated in the microwave before foods are added and this is the only type of container that can safely be placed empty into the oven cavity without damaging the magnetron. Two types of browning dish are available: one is shallow, without a lid and is called a 'sizzler' or 'griddle'; the other is deeper and has a lid, which makes it more versatile. They come in round and rectangular shapes; check with the individual manufacturer's instructions before use as preheating times vary. If the dish is preheated beyond the recommended time, the turntable or oven floor could become damaged.

These dishes have a special impregnated base which absorbs the microwaves and the surface of the dish becomes red hot, like a griddle. Meat can be seared and items such as rissoles and chops will crisp and brown and the quantity of fat required is minimal. Food cooked in the browning dish has a fried or grilled appearance and is a healthier alternative to conventionally fried food.

If you cook any of the following dishes regularly you will find a browning dish an invaluable piece of microwave equipment and the cost (from £12–£25) justified: liver, bacon, sausages, steak, chops, small joints, fish cakes, rissoles, sauté potatoes, beefburgers. Alternatively cook in an ordinary dish and brown under a preheated grill afterwards.

The largest browning dish can just about accommodate 4 chicken quarters, so if you cook for a large number of people it would be more practical to use a frying pan or the grill. The average preheating time for a browning dish is approximately 7 minutes and if bacon is required for one or two people only, then it would be quicker to use the grill.

Care must be taken when cleaning the browning dish. Abrasive powders and creams should never be used on the surface as it must not become scratched in any way. Some 'sizzler' dishes cannot be completely immersed in water, and if the food has cooked onto the surface, cleaning can be difficult. Both types of dishes are best cleaned while they are still warm. Make a paste from water and bicarbonate of soda, spread over the warm dishes and leave to soak for a little while. This will loosen any stubborn bits of food without damaging the dish.

Trivets or roasting racks

A rectangular or round trivet is an essential piece of microware. Stand joints and whole poultry on a trivet to prevent them from stewing in their own juices.

When reheating pastries and bread, line the trivet with a double layer of white kitchen paper to prevent the bases turning soggy. The centre of a cake will set and cook more quickly and evenly if it stands on a trivet during cooking. Air is able to circulate freely underneath and the microwaves are able to penetrate from more angles, thus cooking more efficiently.

Shape and thickness of containers

Round containers generally give the best results as the microwaves are able to penetrate food from more angles efficiently. They should be straight-sided and the diameter should be no more than 9 in/23 cm. If a wider container is used, the outside edges will cook long before the centre is done.

A ring mould is perfect since the absence of a centre allows the microwaves to penetrate from all directions and angles. It can be used to cook denser mixtures such as pâtés and meat loaves, as well as cakes and vegetables.

Square or oblong containers should have rounded corners to prevent the concentration of microwaves overcooking the food in these areas. With longer loaf dishes it will be necessary to shield the corners with foil for half of the cooking time to prevent these parts from drying out.

Oval dishes are ideal when fish or corn on the cob are being cooked. Rearrange the foods halfway through cooking for even results.

The thickness of the container affects the overall cooking time. Light plastic microware allows food to cook quicker than heavier ovenproof glass or ceramic containers. Overall cooking time will require some adjustment to take account of this and allowances appear in all the recipes.

When food is spread out in shallow containers it cooks more quickly and evenly. Narrow, deep containers slow down the cooking and the food requires a lot of turning or stirring.

COVERINGS

To retain moisture in foods, in most cases, a covering is necessary. This can be cling film, greaseproof paper, paper towels, casserole lids (loose fitting), or plates. Foil is used in small amounts, to shield certain parts to prevent overcooking. It is wise to overwrap the shielding with cling film or fasten it to the food with wooden cocktail sticks so that it does not become detached during cooking; foil should never touch the sides of the oven or the door.

Similarly, when using greaseproof paper or paper towels to cover food, secure with wooden cocktail sticks or the fan inside the oven will lift the paper during cooking. Absorbent paper is a useful covering when fat, from sausages for example, is splattering. Heavier paper towels do not stick to bacon as kitchen paper does sometimes, and these coverings should be removed immediately after cooking. A complete covering allows the food to cook by steam as well as microwave energy and the finished dish will always be more moist.

Casserole lids can be used but must be loose enough for a little steam to escape during cooking. A lot of pressure builds up inside containers and if lids are too tight they could be forced off during cooking. Plates can be used to cover bowls, but it is as well to remember that both plates and lids are thicker than cling film and paper coverings so the overall cooking time will need to be slightly increased to allow for this.

Cling film

Cling film is an excellent cover, trapping steam inside the containers which speeds up the cooking process and allows the food to be easily observed, but there is much controversy over the use of cling film in microwave cooking. Some countries have banned its use because the chemicals used to create stretchability may be carcinogenic. It is said that the chemicals can transfer or migrate, particularly if the film is in direct contact with fatty foods. However, a non-pvc cling wrap which does not contain harmful chemicals is now available and it works well in the microwave and for general use.

♦ 19

In the ordinary microwave oven, cling film must be pierced, otherwise it will balloon up and burst, creating a vacuum which results in the cling film sticking to the food. Some microwave ovens have a sensor, and it is in these ovens only that the covering must be unpierced cling film.

With a sensor, the overall cooking time is calculated from the moment that the first steam escapes as the cover is lifted. It is important that the cooking is not disturbed in any way until this happens, so any stirring or rearranging must be done after this time.

SPECIAL USES FOR YOUR MICROWAVE

The microwave oven is useful for many little tasks and I have listed a number of these here. A glass or small bowl of water is used in some of the methods when the natural moisture level is low in some ingredients. The microwaves need this additional moisture to protect the magnetron from damage and prevent the absorbent kitchen paper from igniting.

To crisp breakfast cereals Line a shallow dish with white kitchen paper and stand a tumbler half filled with cold water in the centre. Spread a good handful of cereal around the edge of the dish. Microwave uncovered on high for 30 seconds. Stir and continue to cook for a further 30 seconds–1 minute until the cereal is crisp.

To dry fresh herbs Line a shallow dish with white kitchen paper and stand a tumbler half filled with cold water in the centre. Remove the leaves from the stalks and arrange around the edge of the dish. Microwave uncovered on high for 1 minute. Stir. Continue to cook in this way until the leaves are just dry. Stand for 10 minutes then cool completely. Remove any remaining stalks then crush the herbs and store in airtight containers away from strong light. Top up the water if it boils dry. 1 oz/25 g will take approximately 6 minutes on high. Bay leaves, marjoram, tarragon and chives take a bit longer. Be careful with delicate basil leaves – these can burn.

To refresh pot pourri Line a plate with white kitchen paper and stand a tumbler half filled with water in the centre. Spread a good handful of pot pourri around the edge of the dish. Microwave on high for 30 seconds–1 minute. Stand for 2 minutes.

To dry citrus rinds Try to buy unsprayed citrus fruit. Wash fruit thoroughly then pat dry. Line a plate or shallow dish with white kitchen paper and place a tumbler half filled with cold water in the centre. Arrange the finely grated zest of 2 or 3 lemons, oranges or limes around the edges of the dish. Microwave uncovered on high for 30 seconds. Rub the zest with your fingertips and continue to cook for a further 30 seconds. Check, and if not completely dry continue to cook for a further 30 seconds. Remove from the microwave when almost dry. Stand at room temperature for about 1 hour until completely dried. Store in an airtight container for up to 2 months.

To dissolve gelatine Put 4 tablespoons cold water into a cup. Sprinkle on ½ oz/15 g gelatine. Microwave uncovered on high for 30 seconds, or until dissolved. Do not allow to boil – watch carefully.

To melt chocolate Break up 2 oz/50 g chocolate into an ovenproof glass or ceramic bowl (not plastic). Microwave uncovered on medium for 2–3 minutes until chocolate pieces are just losing their shape. Stir once during this time. Stir until completely melted during standing time. Watch carefully as chocolate can overcook and become gritty.

To dissolve jelly cubes Place the cubes in a medium bowl or jug with ¼ pt/150 ml cold water. Microwave on high until almost melted. Stir until completely dissolved.

To soften butter Use a high setting when melting butter or margarine. Defrost setting is used for softening. Place 4 oz/125 g butter or block margarine, without wrappings, in a small bowl. Microwave on defrost for 15 seconds, turning the bowl once. Stand for 2–3 minutes.

To soften brown sugar that has become hard Place 8 oz/250 g sugar into a microwave boiling bag or medium bowl. Sprinkle 1 tablespoon water over sugar. Either fold the top of the bag over loosely or cover the bowl. Microwave on high for 30 seconds–1 minute. Stand for 5 minutes. Watch carefully – do not allow the sugar to melt.

To soften ice cream before serving straight from the freezer Microwave on medium for up to 1 minute per 2 pt/1.2 litres. Stand for 1 minute before serving.

To soften hard pâté Pâté taken straight from the refrigerator may be hard. To soften 1 lb/500 g, microwave on medium for 30 seconds– 1 minute. Stand for 1 minute before serving.

To cook poppodoms Spread 3 average sized poppodoms over the turntable or oven floor. Microwave uncovered on high for 1–1½ minutes until they puff up. Stand for 30 seconds for crisping to complete. Poppodoms can be lightly brushed with oil before microwaving.

To toast coconut Spread 4 oz/125 g desiccated coconut on a shallow dish or plate. Microwave uncovered on high for 3 minutes or until lightly browned. Stir twice during this time. Coconut continues to brown during standing time of 2–3 minutes.

◆ 21

To roast nuts Spread 2 oz/50 g nuts on a shallow dish, leaving the centre of the dish empty. Microwave uncovered on high for approximately 3 minutes. Stir once during this time. Remove the nuts from the microwave when they become lightly browned. Whole almonds will need splitting to check the exact timing. Nuts will burn in the centre if they are microwaved too long. Stand for 3 minutes, when they will brown further.

To take the chill off eggs for baking It is dangerous to place whole eggs in the microwave as they can easily explode. However, the chill can be taken off an egg by microwaving on high for 3 seconds. Remove the egg from the microwave after this time – count to three if your microwave oven does not have a digital timer.

To extract the maximum juice from citrus fruits Microwave 1 orange or lemon on high for 15–25 seconds – no longer, otherwise the fruit will explode. Every drop of juice can then be extracted from the fruit.

To extract the last bit of honey, syrup or jam from glass jars Not metal cans or plastic jars. Remove the lids and microwave on high for 10 seconds or a few seconds more. Don't allow the ingredients to boil otherwise the jars may crack.

To reheat coffee Don't throw away ground coffee that has gone cold as this reheats perfectly in the microwave. Stale coffee beans can be refreshed by spreading 2 oz/50 g beans over a shallow dish. Microwave uncovered on high for 10–20 seconds.

To make dried breadcrumbs Place a thick slice of bread on a plate. Microwave uncovered on high for 2 minutes. If the bread is still soft microwave for a further 30 seconds or until just dry. Stand for 2 minutes then process in a blender or food processor. Alternatively place in a plastic bag and beat with a rolling pin.

To mull wine Quantities over 2 pt/1.2 litres are best prepared conventionally. Combine all ingredients, except any spirit, in a large jug or bowl. Microwave uncovered on high for 5–6 minutes until hot and steaming but not boiling. Stir twice during cooking. Stir in any spirit, then stand for 3 minutes before serving.

To plump up dried fruits *Small fruits* – currants, raisins, sultanas. Spread the fruit out in a shallow dish and add 4 tablespoons cold water or fruit juice to 4 oz/125 g dried fruit. Cover and microwave on high for 2–3 minutes until well plumped and softened. Stir once during cooking. Watch carefully – burning can occur if overcooked. Cover and stand for 3–5 minutes.

Larger dried fruits – see Figs Benedicte recipe on page 176.

To chambre red wine I would not use this method for expensive wine but for wine under £5.00 a bottle it is perfectly all right. If the oven cavity is high enough to accommodate the bottle, remove any foil and cork and microwave on high for 30 seconds. Stand for 5 minutes. Alternatively, decant the wine into a large microwave jug. Microwave uncovered on high for 30 seconds. Stand for 5 minutes.

To ripen cheeses *Camembert, Brie and other semi-soft cheeses.* Remove the wrappings and stand 8 oz/250 g cheese on a plate. Microwave uncovered on defrost for 15–30 seconds. Watch closely and check once or twice during this time. Stand for 5–10 minutes before serving.

Hard cheeses. The flavour is best when these are served at room temperature rather than chilled. Remove the wrappings and stand the cheese on a plate. Microwave uncovered on defrost for approximately 30 seconds per 8 oz/250 g. Turn the cheese over once. Stand for 5 minutes before serving.

To warm flour for breadmaking Place 3 lb/1.5 kg flour in a large plastic mixing bowl. Microwave uncovered on high for 1 minute or until warmed through. Stir before adding other ingredients.

SENSIBLE PRECAUTIONS

Never
- Slam the oven door, lean on it or hang tea towels over it. These actions could cause misalignment of the door.
- Block the air vents. Ensure that the minimum space required is allowed around the oven, especially when built in.
- Stand anything on top of the oven.
- Operate without the turntable unless the manufacturer recommends this.
- Operate the oven empty – this will damage the magnetron.
- Allow foil to touch the oven lining or door.
- Use metal containers.

Other precautions
- The most frequent accidents with microwave cooking are caused by food that explodes, burns from containers and liquids boiling over.

- Foods encased in a membrane or skin, e.g. fruit, eggs, chicken livers etc, must be pierced to prevent them exploding as pressure builds up during cooking.
- Although the oven interior remains relatively cool during cooking, some containers can become very hot indeed, because heat is transferred from the food to the container. Ovenproof glass and ceramic containers can reach high temperatures and oven gloves must be used when removing them.
- Plastic containers can get hot, especially if the food inside them contains a high proportion of fat or sugar.
- Liquids should always be cooked in containers large enough to prevent them boiling over.
- Cling film coverings and lids should always be removed carefully so that the steam is directed away from the body.

OVEN CARE

- Microwave ovens are easy to clean as food does not get burned on them as it does in a conventional oven. Before cleaning switch off the power.
- Any spills must be removed immediately since the microwaves will continue to cook this food/liquid. Spills that remain inside the oven will also affect the cooking time on other dishes.
- Never scour or use abrasive powders or creams as these will scratch the lining. When the lining is scratched, arcing occurs, the food will not cook properly and the magnetron will eventually become damaged. Use a soft cloth and a mild solution of washing-up liquid for cleaning the oven cavity and door.
- Never use any sharp object to clean around the door seals.
- If spills don't respond to light cleaning, place a bowl with 1 pt/600 ml cold water in the oven. Bring to the boil and allow it to stand with the door closed for 5–10 minutes. During this time the oven cavity will fill with steam and

condensation will loosen any cooked-on food which can then be easily wiped off.

Use this method also for removing lingering odours from the oven after pungent foods such as curry have been cooked; if smells persist, freshen by adding the juice of a lemon to the cold water and proceeding as above.
- The oven exterior is easy to clean with a soft cloth and mild soapy liquid. Wipe over the air vents carefully and take care that no water drips through.

Note:
The power output can be affected during peak power times and cooking times will need to be increased slightly. Also, when other appliances are being run off the same circuit, some adjustment to timing will be necessary.

If the oven has been used continuously for a couple of hours the cavity and turntable will be warm. Further dishes will cook slightly faster, so remember to take account of this by decreasing the cooking time.

STOCKS, SOUPS AND ACCOMPANIMENTS

STOCKS

Home-made stocks are superior to any of the commercial stock cubes available. They are better flavoured, additive free, salt free, and of course, very nutritious. Making stocks conventionally can be a lengthy business, and the microwave reduces the time considerably. Vegetable, chicken and fish stocks can all be made in the microwave. However, stocks using tougher cuts of meat (like oxtail) are better cooked in the usual way, because long, slow cooking tenderizes the meat fibres. To make a more concentrated stock use less water and freeze in ice cube trays to give you 'natural' stock cubes to hand. Dissolve them in boiling water before use.

24 ◆

CHICKEN STOCK

Makes 1 PT/600 ML

Never throw away a chicken carcass – chicken stock is no trouble to make with a microwave.

INGREDIENTS	
1 chicken carcass, broken into 4 pieces	2 in/5 cm piece carrot, thinly sliced
1 pt/600 ml cold water	sprig of fresh thyme or
1 bay leaf	good pinch of dried
6 black peppercorns	**Container**
sprig of parsley	5 pt/2.8 litre plastic microware bowl.
1 small onion, quartered, or	Increase timing by 5 minutes if using
1 small leek, finely sliced	ovenproof glass or ceramic container.
2 in/5 cm piece celery, thinly sliced	

1 Place all the ingredients in the bowl. Cover and microwave on high until boiling point is reached. Stir well.
2 Reduce the power setting to medium, cover and microwave for a further 20 minutes. For ovens without a variable power control, use the defrost setting and cook for 40 minutes.
3 Strain, cool and remove fat.

FISH STOCK

Makes 1 PT/600 ML

I have found that this deteriorates when frozen for more than 6 weeks so use up before this time.

INGREDIENTS

1 pt/600 ml cold water	6 black peppercorns
8 oz/250 g fish trimmings (head, skin, bones)	sprig of parsley
2 in/5 cm piece celery, thinly sliced	**Container** 3½ pt/2 litre plastic microware jug. Increase timing by 2 minutes when using ovenproof glass or ceramic container.
2 in/5 cm piece carrot, thinly sliced	
1 small onion, finely chopped	
1 bay leaf	

1 Place all the ingredients in the jug. Cover and microwave on high until boiling point is reached. Stir well.
2 Reduce the power setting to medium, cover and microwave for 10 minutes. For ovens without a variable power control, use the defrost setting and cook for 20 minutes.
3 Stand, covered, for 5 minutes, then strain.

◆ 25

VEGETABLE STOCK

Makes 1 PT/600 ML

Other vegetables can be used such as celery, outer leaves of cabbage, Brussels sprouts and even potato peelings.

INGREDIENTS

1 small carrot, finely sliced	6 black peppercorns
1 small leek, finely sliced	1 pt/600 ml cold water
1 small onion, finely chopped	**Container** 5 pt/2.8 litre plastic microware bowl. Increase timing by 4 minutes when using ovenproof glass or ceramic container.
1 small turnip, finely chopped	
bouquet garni	
1 clove garlic, crushed (optional)	

1 Place all the ingredients in the bowl. Cover and microwave on high until boiling point is reached. Stir well.
2 Reduce the power setting to medium and microwave for 15 minutes. For ovens without a variable power control, use the defrost setting and cook for 30 minutes. Stir 2 or 3 times during cooking.
3 Strain.

SOUPS

There is nothing quite like a flavoursome bowl of home-made soup during the colder months. Microwaved soups have good, fresh flavours, vibrant colours, a pleasant texture and cook very quickly. They can be made in individual portions or larger quantities. Always start off with hot stock or water. While ¼ pt/150 ml of liquid heats up quickly, larger amounts take some time to reach boiling point. Cook soups in concentrated form and dilute with more hot stock or water towards the end of cooking time. Most soups freeze well, and it is convenient to freeze individual portions for future use. These take only 5 minutes on high to reheat from their frozen state, though it is more practical and much faster to reheat large quantities of frozen soup in the conventional way.

CARROT AND ORANGE SOUP

26 ◆

Serves 4

A fresh tasting and delicately spiced soup which can be served hot or chilled.
If serving chilled, reduce the oil to 1 teaspoon.
Use hot water rather than stock for a more subtle flavour.

INGREDIENTS	
8 oz/250 g carrots, grated	1 teaspoon ground coriander
1 small onion, finely chopped	herb salt, black pepper
1 tablespoon sunflower oil	1 tablespoon finely chopped fresh coriander leaves
¼ pt/150 ml pure orange juice	
¾ pt/450 ml boiling water	**Container**
1 bay leaf	5 pt/2.8 litre plastic microware bowl. Increase timing by 4 minutes when using ovenproof glass or ceramic container.
2 teaspoons arrowroot dissolved in 4 teaspoons cold water	

1 Place the grated carrots, onion and oil in the bowl. Cover and microwave on high for 5 minutes. Stir once during cooking.
2 Stir in the orange juice, boiling water, bay leaf and ground coriander.
3 Cover and microwave on high for 8 minutes. Stir twice during cooking.
4 Stand for 5 minutes. Remove the bay leaf and liquidize until smooth.
5 Return to the cleaned bowl and stir in the dissolved arrowroot.
6 Microwave uncovered on high for 3–4 minutes, until thickened and just boiling. Stir once during cooking. Adjust seasoning to taste.
7 To serve, sprinkle with the chopped coriander leaves.
Reheat: uncovered on high for 4–5 minutes. Stir once during this time. Don't allow it to boil.

CHICKEN AND VEGETABLE SOUP

Serves 4

An ideal way of using up leftover chicken or turkey.
The meat should be in fairly large chunks.

INGREDIENTS

4 oz/125 g leeks, finely sliced	2 teaspoons cornflour dissolved in a little cold water
4 oz/125 g potato, finely diced	¼ pt/150 ml skimmed milk
2 oz/50 g carrots, finely chopped	salt
1 oz/25 g sunflower margarine	
1 pt/600 ml chicken stock or boiling water	**Container**
1 bay leaf	5 pt/2.8 litre plastic microware bowl. Increase timing by 2 minutes when using ovenproof glass or ceramic container.
black pepper	
8 oz/250 g cooked chicken, cut into chunks	

1 Place the leeks, potato, carrots and margarine in the bowl. Cover and microwave on high for 5 minutes. Stir once during cooking.
2 Add the boiling stock or water, bay leaf and black pepper. Cover and microwave on high for 5 minutes. Stir once during cooking.
3 Add the chicken, cover and microwave on high for 3 minutes.
4 Stir in the dissolved cornflour and microwave uncovered on high for 2 minutes. Stir once during cooking.
5 Remove the bay leaf, stir in the milk and adjust seasoning to taste.
Reheat: uncovered on high for 5–6 minutes. Stir once during this time.

◆ 27

CREAM OF CAULIFLOWER SOUP

Serves 4

Light and creamy, delicately flavoured. Use only florets as the green leaves spoil the colour and impart a bitter flavour. Potato is used to thicken this and many of the soups that follow.

INGREDIENTS

12 oz/375 g cauliflower florets, chopped	black pepper
1 small onion, finely chopped	¼ pt/150 ml skimmed milk
4 oz/125 g potato, grated	salt
1 pt/600 ml boiling chicken or vegetable stock	**Container**
1 oz/25 g sunflower margarine	5 pt/2.8 litre plastic microware bowl. Increase timing by 3–4 minutes when using ovenproof glass or ceramic container.
1 bay leaf	

1 Put the cauliflower, onion, potato, stock, margarine, bay leaf and black pepper in the bowl.
2 Cover and microwave on high for 20 minutes. Stir 3 times during cooking.
3 Remove the bay leaf and stir in the milk. Liquidize until smooth and adjust seasoning to taste.
Reheat: uncovered on high for 4–5 minutes. Stir twice during this time.

Cream of broccoli soup
Substitute 12 oz/375 g broccoli (calabrese) for the cauliflower florets. Peel the stalks and chop finely. Use florets, leaves and stalks.

FRESH TOMATO SOUP

Serves 4–6

The wonderful fresh flavour of tomatoes is emphasized by microwaving:
I consider this to be the very best way of cooking fresh tomato soup.

INGREDIENTS	
1 medium onion, finely chopped	1 pt/600 ml boiling chicken or vegetable stock
4 oz/125 g potato, finely diced	
1 oz/25 g sunflower margarine	black pepper
2 lb/1 kg fresh ripe tomatoes, roughly chopped	salt
	milk or cream for garnish
1 teaspoon chopped fresh basil or ½ teaspoon dried	**Container**
	5 pt/2.8 litre plastic microware bowl.
1 bay leaf	Increase timing by 3 minutes when using ovenproof glass or ceramic container.
1 teaspoon clear honey	
2 tablespoons passata (p.209)	

28 ◆

1 Place the onion, potato and margarine in the bowl. Cover and microwave on high for 4 minutes. Stir once during cooking.
2 Add the tomatoes, dried basil (add fresh basil towards the end of cooking), bay leaf, honey, passata, boiling stock and a little black pepper. Stir the ingredients together well.
3 Cover and microwave on high for 15 minutes. Stir 3 times during cooking.
4 Remove the bay leaf, cool slightly, then liquidize until smooth. Sieve and adjust the seasoning to taste.
5 To garnish swirl in a little milk or cream.
Reheat: uncovered on high for approximately 5 minutes. Stir once during this time.

GOLDEN TROUT SOUP

Serves 4 as a main course, 6 as a starter

This soup makes a bright and warming lunch or supper, accompanied by hunks of bread and a crunchy salad.

INGREDIENTS

8 oz/250 g trout, cleaned	½ teaspoon paprika
1 medium onion, finely chopped	black pepper
1 clove garlic, crushed	1–2 teaspoons natural soy sauce (shoya is the best available)
1 teaspoon finely grated fresh root ginger	
1 medium carrot, finely chopped	**Containers**
6 oz/175 g potato, diced	5 pt/2.8 litre plastic microware bowl. Increase timing by 3–4 minutes when using ovenproof glass or ceramic container. 3½ pt/2 litre plastic microware jug. Increase timing by 1 minute when using ovenproof glass or ceramic jug. Dinner plate.
1 teaspoon sunflower oil	
1½ pt/900 ml boiling water	
½ teaspoon ground coriander	
½ teaspoon turmeric	

1 Wash the trout and pat dry. Slash the skin twice on each side to prevent bursting during cooking. Position towards one side of the plate.

2 Cover and microwave on high for 1½ minutes or until just cooked. Stand for 5 minutes then remove head, skin and bones. Put these into the jug. Flake the fish and put to one side.

3 Place the onion, garlic, ginger, carrot, potato and oil in the bowl.

4 Cover and microwave on high for 6 minutes. Stir twice during cooking.

5 Pour 1 pt/600 ml boiling water over the fish skin and bones. Cover and microwave on high for 3 minutes. Strain over the vegetables.

6 Stir in the coriander, turmeric, paprika and black pepper. Cover and microwave on high for 6 minutes. Stir once during cooking.

7 Stir in the flaked fish. Cover and microwave on high for 2 minutes.

8 Stir in the remaining boiling water and season with soy sauce to taste.

Reheat: uncovered on high for 6–8 minutes. Stir twice during this time.

◆ 29

GREEN PEA SOUP

Serves 4

This soup has a fresh flavour and bright colour. I like to add about a teaspoon of finely chopped fresh mint. Don't use dried mint – this often has a rather musty taste and could spoil the soup. Fresh peas can be used when available.

INGREDIENTS	
4 oz/125 g potato, finely diced	1 teaspoon finely chopped mint
1 medium onion, finely chopped	herb salt, black pepper
1 tablespoon sunflower oil	1 tablespoon natural yoghurt
1 clove garlic, crushed	1 tablespoon snipped fresh chives
8 oz/250 g peas	**Container**
1 pt/600 ml boiling chicken or vegetable stock	5 pt/2.8 litre plastic microware bowl. Increase timing by 2 minutes when using ovenproof glass or ceramic container.
1 bay leaf	

1 Place the potato, onion, oil and garlic in the bowl. Cover and microwave on high for 5 minutes. Stir twice during cooking.
2 Stir in the peas, boiling stock and the bay leaf. Cover and microwave on high for 10 minutes if using frozen peas, 12 minutes if fresh. Stir twice during cooking.
3 Cool slightly, then remove the bay leaf, add the mint, if using, and liquidize until smooth. Adjust seasoning to taste.
4 To garnish, swirl in the yoghurt and sprinkle with snipped chives.
Reheat: before adding the yoghurt and chives, uncovered on high for 4–5 minutes. Stir once during this time.

JAPANESE MISO SOUP

Serves 4–6

A traditional soup from Japan – light, and highly nutritious. Wakame is a mild flavoured sea vegetable, and miso is a naturally fermented soy bean product; both are available from health food shops (see p.208). Never allow liquids to return to the boil after miso has been added.

INGREDIENTS	
2 in/5 cm strip of wakame seaweed, washed quickly in cold water then soaked in ½ pt/300 ml cold water for 15 minutes	2 oz/50 g mooli (white radish), cut in half lengthways then sliced into thin half-moon shapes
	1 small onion, sliced thinly
1 medium carrot, cut into thin matchsticks	1¼ pt/750 ml boiling vegetable or chicken stock

◆

	Container
4 oz/125 g firm tofu, cut into ½ in/1 cm dice	5 pt/2.8 litre plastic microware bowl. Increase timing by 3 minutes when using ovenproof glass or ceramic container.
4–6 teaspoons miso, mixed with a little cold water	

1 Slice the soaked wakame finely and place in the bowl with the soaking water (this contains valuable minerals). Add the remaining vegetables and 1 pt/600 ml boiling stock.
2 Cover and microwave on high for 25 minutes. Stir 3 times during cooking. Add the cubed tofu during the last 3 minutes of cooking time.
3 Dilute the soup with the remaining boiling stock.
4 To serve, miso is stirred into each individual bowl, to taste, at the table.
Reheat: without the miso, uncovered on high for 5 minutes. Stir once during this time.

LEEK AND POTATO SOUP

Serves 4–6

I like to serve this filling soup with matzo balls (p.35) and grated cheese; it is a substantial dish for lunch or supper.

INGREDIENTS	
1 small carrot, grated	¼ pt/150 ml skimmed milk
4 oz/125 g leeks, finely sliced	salt, black pepper
12 oz/375 g potatoes, finely diced	paprika
1 clove garlic, crushed	**Container**
1 oz/25 g sunflower margarine	5 pt/2.8 litre plastic microware bowl. Increase timing by 3 minutes when using ovenproof glass or ceramic container.
1 pt/600 ml boiling chicken or vegetable stock	
1 bay leaf	

1 Put the carrot, leeks, potatoes, garlic and margarine in the bowl. Cover and microwave on high for 8 minutes. Stir twice during cooking.
2 Add the boiling stock and bay leaf. Cover and microwave on high for 6 minutes. Stir once during cooking.
3 Remove the bay leaf, stir in the milk and liquidize until smooth. Adjust seasoning to taste.
4 To serve, sprinkle with paprika.
Reheat: uncovered on high for 5 minutes. Stir once during this time.

MINESTRONE

Serves 4–6

A meal in itself. Serve with extra Parmesan and hot crusty bread.
If possible, use freshly grated Parmesan which has a much finer flavour
than the powdery variety sold in tubs or packets.

INGREDIENTS

1½ pt/900 ml boiling beef, chicken or vegetable stock	2 teaspoons chopped fresh basil or 1 teaspoon dried
4 oz/125 g turnips, finely diced	1 bay leaf
4 oz/125 g carrots, finely diced	1 tablespoon olive oil
2 sticks of celery, finely sliced on diagonal	2 tablespoons grated Parmesan cheese
4 oz/125 g potato, finely diced	1 tablespoon finely chopped fresh parsley
4 oz/125 g leeks, shredded	salt, black pepper
2 oz/50 g wholewheat macaroni	**Container**
4 tablespoons passata (p.209)	5 pt/2.8 litre plastic microware bowl. Increase timing by 5–7 minutes when using ovenproof glass or ceramic container.
7 oz/225 g can red kidney beans, drained	
8 oz/250 g can tomatoes	
2 cloves garlic, crushed	

32 ◆

1 Place the boiling stock, all the vegetables, macaroni, passata, drained red kidney beans, tomatoes, garlic, basil, bay leaf and oil in the bowl. Mix thoroughly.
2 Cover and microwave on high for 25–30 minutes, until the vegetables are just tender. Stir 3 times during cooking.
3 Stir in 1 tablespoon Parmesan cheese and most of the parsley. Adjust seasoning to taste.
4 To serve, sprinkle with the remaining Parmesan and parsley.
Reheat: before garnishing, uncovered on high for 8 minutes. Stir twice during this time.

SPICED LENTIL AND TOMATO SOUP

Serves 4–6

Lightly spiced and very warming on cold winter nights.
Liquidize the soup for a short time only, to give a rough and more
interesting texture.

INGREDIENTS

6 oz/175 g orange split lentils, soaked in cold water overnight, then rinsed and drained (this shortens the cooking time and prevents them boiling over during cooking)	2 oz/50 g carrots, grated
	4 oz/125 g onion, finely chopped
	14 oz/400 g can tomatoes, crushed with their juice
	1 clove garlic, crushed

4 in/10 cm piece celery, finely chopped	1½ pt/900 ml boiling chicken or vegetable stock or water
1 bay leaf	
½ teaspoon curry paste	salt
1 teaspoon finely grated fresh ginger root	black pepper
	1 tablespoon finely chopped fresh coriander leaves
½ teaspoon turmeric	
1 teaspoon ground coriander	**Container**
½ teaspoon ground cumin	5 pt/2.8 litre plastic microware bowl. Increase timing by 3–5 minutes when using ovenproof glass or ceramic container.
1 teaspoon garam masala	

1 Place the drained lentils, carrots, onion, tomatoes, garlic, celery, bay leaf, curry paste, ginger, turmeric, coriander, cumin, garam masala and 1¼ pt/750 ml boiling stock or water in the bowl. Mix well.
2 Cover and microwave on high for 25 minutes. Stir 4 times during cooking.
3 Remove the bay leaf and stir in the remaining boiling stock. Liquidize and adjust seasoning to taste.
4 To serve, sprinkle with the chopped coriander leaves.
Reheat: before garnishing, uncovered on high for 5–6 minutes. Stir twice during this time.

◆ 33

VEGETABLE BORTSCH

Serves 6

Extremely filling, with full flavour and vibrant colour.
Use a strong stock for this soup.

INGREDIENTS

8 oz/250 g raw beetroot, cut into thin matchsticks	black pepper
	2 tablespoons arrowroot dissolved in 2 tablespoons cold water
4 oz/125 g red cabbage, finely shredded	
4 oz/125 g carrots, grated	2–3 tablespoons finely chopped fresh parsley
1 small onion, finely chopped	
4 oz/125 g potato, finely diced	herb salt
1 clove garlic, crushed	¼ pt/150ml natural yoghurt
1 tablespoon sunflower oil	snipped chives
1 teaspoon brown sugar	**Container**
1 tablespoon red wine vinegar	5 pt/2.8 litre plastic microware bowl. Increase timing by 4–5 minutes when using ovenproof glass or ceramic container.
2 pt/1.2 litre boiling vegetable, chicken or beef stock	
1 bay leaf	
8 oz/250 g beefsteak tomato, peeled and chopped	

1 Put the beetroot, cabbage, carrots, onion, potato, garlic, oil, vinegar and sugar in the bowl. Mix well.
2 Cover and microwave on high for 10 minutes. Stir 3 times during cooking.
3 Add 1 pt/600 ml boiling stock, the bay leaf, tomato purée and black pepper.
4 Cover and microwave on high for 20–25 minutes, until the vegetables are just tender.
5 Stir in the remaining boiling stock and dissolved arrowroot.
6 Microwave uncovered on high for a further 2–3 minutes until thickened. Stir once during cooking.
7 Stir in the parsley and adjust seasoning to taste.
8 To serve, swirl in the yoghurt and sprinkle with snipped chives.
Reheat: without the yoghurt and chives, uncovered on high for 6–8 minutes. Stir twice during this time.

PLAIN CROUTONS

Serves 4

Croûtons can be made quickly in the microwave. Watch them closely as they easily overcook. Croûtons made with white bread will cook faster than those made with wholemeal.
Once cooled, store in an airtight container.

INGREDIENTS
4 slices wholemeal bread, crusts removed

1 Cut each slice of bread into twelve ½ in/1 cm cubes.
2 Lay a piece of white kitchen paper on the turntable or oven floor.
3 Arrange the bread cubes in a wide circle on the paper.
4 Microwave uncovered on high for 3½–4 minutes until dry.
5 Stand for 2 minutes.

GARLIC CROUTONS

Serves 4

Watch these carefully to avoid burning. Don't be alarmed when they collapse and appear to be soggy, they will crisp up during the second part of cooking. Once cooled, store them in an airtight container.

INGREDIENTS

	Container
4 slices wholemeal bread, crusts removed	Medium plastic microware bowl. Increase timing by 1–2 minutes when using ovenproof glass or ceramic container.
1½ oz/40 g sunflower margarine	
1 clove garlic, crushed	
1 teaspoon papriha	
herb salt, black pepper	

1 Cut each slice of bread into twelve ½ in/1 cm cubes.
2 Place the margarine in the bowl and microwave uncovered on high until melted.
3 Stir in the garlic, paprika and seasoning. Add the bread and toss the cubes to coat with the mixture.
4 Microwave uncovered on high for 2 minutes. Stir well. Continue to cook for a further 1½–2 minutes until just crisp.
5 Stand for 2 minutes.

◆ 35

MATZO BALLS

Serves 6

Traditionally served with chicken soup, light matzo balls are every bit as good with many of the other soups in this chapter. Matzo meal is available from most supermarkets.

INGREDIENTS

	Container
1 small egg	Medium plastic microware bowl. Increase timing by 3–5 minutes when using ovenproof glass or ceramic container.
4 oz/125 g fine matzo meal	
½ teaspoon baking powder	
½ teaspoon salt	
a little black pepper	
¼ pt/150 ml cold water	
1 pt/600 ml boiling water	

1 Put all the ingredients in a bowl and mix together thoroughly. Add a little extra cold water if necessary until the mixture resembles a soft dough.
2 Roll into 30 tiny balls.

3 Pour the boiling water into the microware bowl and microwave uncovered on high until the water returns to a rolling boil.

4 Drop 15 of the balls into the water and microwave uncovered on high for 2½ minutes. The balls will swell and turn over towards the end of cooking time.

5 Remove with a slotted spoon and repeat with the remaining batch.

6 Add to the soup and serve immediately.

DUMPLINGS

Serves 4–6

Dumplings are great in soups, stews and casseroles. Vegetable suet, obtainable from large supermarkets, makes nice light dumplings, but sunflower margarine is a good substitute. Add variety to your dumplings by altering the seasonings and flavourings.

For this recipe the dumplings were cooked in a medium bowl containing 1 pt/600 ml boiling water. Ensure that the water returns to a rolling boil before adding the dumplings.

Results are just as good when the dumplings are added to casseroles or stews towards the end of cooking time. Cook covered, arranging the dumplings around the edge of the container, and increase the timing slightly for this method.

36 ◆

INGREDIENTS

1½ oz/40 g vegetable suet	1 teaspoon finely chopped fresh parsley
4 oz/125 g self-raising flour or 4 oz/125 g plain flour and ½ teaspoon baking powder	1 teaspoon finely chopped fresh sage or thyme 1 tablespoon freshly grated Parmesan cheese
½ teaspoon salt	
black pepper	**Container**
7–8 tablespoons cold water to mix	Medium plastic microware bowl. Increase timing by 2–3 minutes when using ovenproof glass or ceramic container.
Optional extras – use one of the following: 1 teaspoon mixed dried herbs	

1 Put all the ingredients in a bowl. Mix thoroughly and knead lightly.

2 Divide into 8 and roll into balls (smaller dumplings can be made if preferred).

3 Drop into boiling water in the microware bowl and microwave uncovered on high for 6–8 minutes until cooked. Stir once during cooking. The dumplings are cooked when they rise and double in size. Stand, covered, for 3 minutes.

Alternatively, add to casseroles and microwave covered on high for 8–10 minutes. Turn and rearrange once during cooking. Stand, covered, for 3 minutes.

SAUCES

Anyone who has experienced difficulty with sticking and lumping when making sauces, will be delighted at the ease with which these can be microwaved. There are also no sticky pans or double boilers to wash up afterwards. Once you have microwaved a simple roux-based sauce you will never want to use the conventional method again. There is no chance of the sauce burning, and you won't have to stand over a pan, constantly stirring.

I find a large, wide, microware jug the most practical container to use. This gives ample space for whisking and for the sauce to rise, as it reaches boiling point. A balloon whisk is essential as sauces require frequent, vigorous whisking to prevent lumping during cooking.

Roux-based sauces are always cooked on high, but when reheating, and particularly if the sauce is covering other food, it is better to reheat on a medium setting. If a high setting is used, the sauce may boil before the food is properly reheated, because of its high fat content.

Sauces thickened with eggs need to be cooked and reheated on a low setting, otherwise they may curdle and become rubbery.

When thickening with cornflour or arrowroot, mix these with a little cold water until they are dissolved, before adding the main quantity of liquid. Take great care when using yoghurt and cream since a sauce with these ingredients will spoil if it reaches boiling point. Remove the sauce from the oven, and leave to continue cooking during standing time. Care must be taken during reheating, which must be on a low setting.

When reducing a sauce, leave the container uncovered and stir frequently, or transfer to a pan and reduce conventionally. I have found that reducing the conventional way is much quicker, especially when the liquid is ½ pt/300 ml and above. A sauce thickened in this way is a healthier alternative to those thickened with starch and fats.

◆ 37

BECHAMEL SAUCE

Makes 1 PT/600 ML

Basic roux sauces thicken on cooling and freeze well. For a heavier sauce use ¾ pt/450 ml milk to 1½ oz/40 g of flour and fat. Whisk vigorously during cooking, and stir in additional seasonings and flavourings once the sauce has reached boiling point.

Reheat on a medium setting when the sauce is covering other foods. This prevents the sauce evaporating and boiling furiously whilst the food underneath is still reheating.

I have used skimmed milk in all the following recipes, but any type of milk can be used. The richer the milk, the richer the sauce will be. Unsweetened soy milk will give a slightly nutty flavour to the sauce.

INGREDIENTS	
1 pt/600 ml skimmed milk	1½ oz/40 g sunflower margarine
1 oz/25 g carrot, thinly sliced	1½ oz/40 g plain flour
2 in/5 cm piece celery, thinly sliced	herb salt, black pepper
1 oz/25 g onion, chopped	**Container**
a little grated nutmeg	3½ pt/2 litre plastic microware jug.
1 bay leaf	Increase timing by 1–2 minutes if using
sprig of fresh parsley and thyme	ovenproof glass or ceramic jug.

1 Place the milk in the jug with all the vegetables, nutmeg and herbs.
2 Cover and microwave on high for 4 minutes. Stir well, cover and stand for 1 hour for the full flavours to develop.
3 Strain into a bowl.
4 Place the margarine in the jug and microwave uncovered on high until melted. Stir in the flour and microwave for 1 minute.
5 Gradually whisk in the flavoured milk and microwave on high for 1 minute. Whisk well. Continue to microwave on high, whisking every 30 seconds, until the sauce reaches boiling point. Adjust seasoning to taste.
Reheat: uncovered on high for 3–4 minutes. Stir twice during this time.

Béchamel sauce can be flavoured with many things; here are two suggestions.
Cheese sauce
At the end of cooking stir in 3 oz/75 g grated cheese, a little grated nutmeg, ½ teaspoon mustard powder and season to taste with salt and pepper. Stir well, until cheese is melted, and all the ingredients are well blended together.
Parsley sauce
At the end of cooking, stir in 2 tablespoons finely chopped fresh parsley and season to taste.

PIMENTO SAUCE

Serves 4

This has a bright, fresh yellow colour and can be served over vegetables, fish or chicken. All roux-based sauces thicken on cooling and a couple of tablespoons of cream may be added towards the end of cooking/reheating time if liked. The sauce can be sharpened with a little mustard powder or creamed horseradish – stir either of these into the béchamel before combining with the other ingredients.

INGREDIENTS

2 medium yellow peppers	**Container**
½ pt/300 ml béchamel sauce (p.38)	3½ pt/2 litre plastic microware jug.
salt, black pepper	Increase timing by 2 minutes when using ovenproof glass or ceramic jug.
1 small red pepper, peeled thinly with a vegetable peeler then chopped into tiny dice	

1 Immerse the yellow peppers in boiling water for 2 minutes. Cool, then remove the stalks, seeds and white membrane. Liquidize until smooth, then sieve, pressing as much through as possible.
2 Put the béchamel into the jug and stir in the puréed peppers.
3 Microwave uncovered on high for 2½–3 minutes until boiling. Stir well after each minute of cooking time.
4 Adjust seasoning to taste and stir in the diced red pepper.
5 Microwave uncovered on high for 30 seconds.
Reheat: uncovered on high for 3 minutes. Stir once during this time.

◆ 39

GINGER AND SHOYU SAUCE

Makes 1 PT/600 ML

Wonderful served over fish, vegetables or chicken. Shoyu is a light, naturally fermented soy sauce and should be used moderately, allowing the fresh flavours of the other ingredients to predominate.

INGREDIENTS

1 small onion, finely chopped	4 teaspoons arrowroot dissolved in 4 teaspoons cold water
1 small clove garlic, crushed	
1 teaspoon finely grated fresh root ginger	2 teaspoons finely chopped fresh parsley
	2–3 teaspoons shoyu
1 pt/600 ml boiling water, vegetable or chicken stock	**Container**
	3½ pt/2 litre plastic microware jug.
2 oz/50 g mushrooms, finely chopped	Increase timing by 4–5 minutes when using ovenproof glass or ceramic jug.
black pepper	

1 Place the onion and garlic in the jug. Cover and microwave on high for 3 minutes. Stir once during cooking.
2 Stir in the ginger, boiling water or stock, mushrooms and black pepper. Cover and microwave on high for 3 minutes, stirring once during cooking.
3 Stir in the dissolved arrowroot, parsley and shoyu.
4 Microwave uncovered on high for 1 minute. Stir well. Continue to cook in this way until sauce reaches boiling point.
5 Cover and stand for 3 minutes. Adjust seasoning to taste.
Reheat: uncovered on high for 4–5 minutes. Stir twice during this time.

CAPER SAUCE

Serves 4

This has a rich, savoury flavour and is excellent with fish or vegetables (especially cauliflower). When serving with fish, it is best to reheat the sauce separately, and to cook the fish just before serving.
Mix a few tablespoons of the sauce with the flesh of baked potatoes, then sprinkle with grated cheese for a quick supper dish.
Chopped gherkins could be used instead of capers.

40 ◆

INGREDIENTS	
1½ oz/40 g butter	**Container**
1 large onion, finely chopped	3½ pt/2 litre plastic microware jug.
¾ pt/450 ml béchamel sauce (p.38)	Increase timing by 2 minutes when using ovenproof glass or ceramic jug.
salt, pepper	
3 tablespoons single cream	
2 tablespoons capers, chopped	

1 Cut the butter into small pieces and put in the jug with the onion. Cover and microwave on high for 5–6 minutes until the onion has softened. Stir once during cooking.
2 Transfer to a food processor and blend until smooth.
3 Rinse out the jug. Put the puréed onion and béchamel in the jug. Mix together thoroughly and adjust seasoning to taste.
4 Microwave uncovered on high for 2–3 minutes until boiling (total cooking time will depend on the temperature of the béchamel. If it is hot, it will cook quickly. When it has been made well in advance, then chilled, it will take longer than the time specified.)
5 Stir in the single cream and capers. Microwave uncovered on high for 30 seconds. Stir well and serve.
Reheat: uncovered on high for 3 minutes. Stir once during this time.

FISH VELOUTE

Serves 4

This is a good basic sauce for fish which should be made from home-made fish stock and NOT stock cubes. Cream can be stirred in at the end of cooking and additional flavourings, e.g. wine, finely grated cheese or chopped hard-boiled eggs, may be added.

INGREDIENTS

	Container
1 oz/25 g unsalted or slightly salted butter	3½ pt/2 litre plastic microware jug. Increase timing by 2 minutes when using ovenproof glass or ceramic jug.
1 oz/25 g plain flour	
¾ pt/450 ml warm fish stock (p.25)	
salt, pepper	

1 Put the butter into the jug and microwave uncovered on high for 45 seconds or until melted.
2 Stir in the flour. Microwave uncovered on high for up to 1 minute or until the mixture puffs up.
3 Whisk in the warm fish stock. Microwave uncovered on high for approximately 3 minutes, until boiling. Whisk well after each minute of cooking time. Adjust seasoning to taste.
Reheat: uncovered on high for 3 minutes. Stir once during this time.

◆ 41

RICH TOMATO SAUCE

Serves 4

Cherry tomatoes and beefsteak tomatoes form the basis of this sauce which has a good fresh flavour and strong orange colour. Fresh plum tomatoes are now appearing in some of the larger supermarkets during the early weeks of autumn and can be used wholly or in part in this sauce; when these are used, the sauce will be bright red.

INGREDIENTS	
1 clove garlic, crushed	good pinch of sugar
1 medium onion, finely chopped	2 tablespoons passata (p. 209)
1 shallot, finely chopped	black pepper
1 tablespoon olive oil	squeeze of lemon juice
8 oz/250 g beefsteak tomatoes, chopped	salt
8 oz/250 g cherry tomatoes, each pricked with the tip of a sharp knife	**Container**
6 tablespoons dry red wine or 6 tablespoons vegetable stock	3½ pt/2 litre plastic microware jug. Increase timing by 2 minutes when using ovenproof glass or ceramic jug.
1 bay leaf	
2 teaspoons shredded fresh basil leaves or ½ teaspoon dried basil	

1 Put the garlic, onion, shallot and olive oil into the jug. Cover and microwave on high for 3 minutes.
2 Add the tomatoes, wine or stock, bay leaf, dried basil (add fresh basil later), sugar, passata, black pepper and a squeeze of lemon juice.
3 Microwave uncovered on high for 8–10 minutes until the sauce has boiled and all ingredients are softened. Stir once during cooking.
4 Discard the bay leaf. Add the fresh basil if using. Liquidize until smooth, sieve and adjust seasoning to taste.
5 Reheat briefly on high if ingredients have cooled down slightly.
Reheat: uncovered on high for 4 minutes. Stir once during this time.

EGGS AND CHEESE

Eggs and cheese can present problems to those just beginning microwave cooking, because the results can be stringy and rubbery. It is so easy to overcook eggs and apart from scrambled eggs, which can be cooked on a high setting, most egg dishes are best cooked on medium. The egg yolk contains a high proportion of fat, to which the microwaves are attracted, and which will therefore cook before the white. When a high setting is used, the yolk can turn rubbery, while the white remains half cooked. So watch these egg dishes carefully during cooking.

It is not possible to boil eggs in the microwave as they would explode from the pressure that builds up inside the shell. However, the chill can be taken off a cold egg by microwaving for no longer than 3 seconds. This is useful if eggs which have been refrigerated are required for baking. Fried eggs are best cooked in a browning dish; only cook for the minimum time and cover during standing time. If you are frying a number of eggs it is probably quicker and more practical to cook them conventionally. Poached and baked eggs are simple and these both require a cover during cooking, so that moisture is retained. When frying, poaching or baking eggs, lightly prick the yolk with a cocktail stick before microwaving to prevent it from exploding.

Scrambled eggs are whisked during cooking, and, as the yolks and whites are beaten together, a high setting can be used. There is less evaporation during cooking, and none of the egg sticks to the pan, therefore the quantity of scrambled egg is increased, when microwaved.

Dishes containing a high proportion of eggs and dairy foods are best reheated on a medium setting. If your oven does not have a variable power control, reheat these on the defrost setting. The only exception to this rule is when the total power output of the oven is between 500 and 550 watts. These ovens are smaller and the high power setting is equivalent to a medium setting on an oven with a total power output of 650 to 750 watts.

POACHED EGGS

For 1

It is essential that the yolk is pierced before cooking otherwise the eggs could explode. The water must be returned to a rolling boil before the eggs are added, otherwise the overall cooking time will need to be increased. Remove from the oven when the whites are just set. Standing time is as long as the cooking time, sometimes longer. Different sized eggs will vary slightly in overall cooking time.

INGREDIENTS

	Container
8 tablespoons boiling water	Plastic microware bowl.
1 size 3 egg	Increase timing by a few seconds only if using
½ teaspoon vinegar	ovenproof glass or ceramic bowl.

1 Place the boiling water in the bowl and microwave uncovered on high until the water returns to a rolling boil.
2 Break the egg onto a saucer and prick the yolk with a cocktail stick. Slide into the water, together with the vinegar.
3 Cover and microwave on medium for 1 minute or until the white is just set.
4 Stand, covered, for 1–1½ minutes.

For a larger number of eggs increase quantities and cooking times as follows:
For 2
¼ pint/150 ml boiling water
Cook on medium for 1 minute 45 seconds or until the whites are just set.
Stand, covered, for 2–2½ minutes.
For 4
¾ pint/450 ml boiling water
1 teaspoon of vinegar
Cook on medium for 3 minutes or until the whites are just set.
Stand, covered, for 2½–3 minutes.

These timings are for cooking in a plastic microware bowl. If using an ovenproof glass or ceramic bowl increase the timing by up to a further 1½ minutes for 4 eggs. The key to success is to watch the eggs carefully and remove them when the whites are only just set, they will continue to cook while they are standing.

44 ◆

SCRAMBLED EGGS

For 1

This dish can be cooked on high but take care not to overcook the eggs; remove from the microwave just as they begin to thicken. Season after cooking as salt will toughen eggs if it is added at the beginning.

INGREDIENTS

	Container
small knob of sunflower margarine	Plastic microware bowl.
1 size 3 egg	Increase timing by a few seconds only when
2 tablespoons milk	using ovenproof glass or ceramic bowl.

1 Place the margarine in the bowl and microwave on high until melted.
2 Whisk the egg and milk lightly together and pour into the bowl.
3 Microwave uncovered on high for 1 minute. After 30 seconds stir with a fork, drawing the outside edges to the centre.
4 Stand, covered, for 30 seconds. Season to taste.

For a larger number of eggs increase quantities and cooking times as follows:
For 2
4 tablespoons milk
Microwave uncovered on high for approximately 1 minute 45 seconds, stirring with a fork every 30 seconds. Stand covered for 1 minute.
For 4
8 tablespoons milk
Microwave uncovered on high for approximately 3 minutes, stirring with a fork every 30 seconds. Stand covered for 2 minutes.

Use a large container as the eggs will increase in volume; a large plastic microwave jug is ideal. You will need to increase cooking times if you are using an ovenproof glass or ceramic bowl.

MICRO BAKED EGGS

For 1

The whites in this recipe have a firmer texture than microwaved poached eggs. Remove from the oven as soon as the whites are set.

INGREDIENTS

	Container
knob of sunflower margarine	Plastic microware ramekins.
1 size 3 egg	Increase timings by approximately
	10 seconds per egg when using
	ovenproof glass or ceramic containers.

1 Place the margarine in a ramekin dish. Microwave uncovered on high until melted.
2 Break the egg into the ramekin and prick the yolk with a cocktail stick.
3 Cover and microwave on medium for 1 minute or so until the white is just set. Stand, covered, for 30 seconds.
For a larger number of eggs increase cooking times as follows:
For 2
Cover and microwave on medium for 1¾–2 minutes, until the whites are just set.
Stand, covered, for 1 minute.
For 4
Cover and microwave on medium for 3–3½ minutes. Arrange the containers around the edge of the turntable or in a circle on the oven floor. Give each container a half turn once during cooking.
Stand, covered, for 1½–2 minutes.

SPANISH OMELETTE

Serves 1 to 2

A substantial omelette, good served with a simple salad.
The recipe is for one or possibly two; cooking larger omelettes can be difficult as the centre does not set well, and the power setting would need to be medium. When I cook this type of omelette for 4 or 6 people I microwave the vegetables first and then complete the recipe conventionally. This is the quickest and most practical way.

INGREDIENTS	
2 teaspoons olive oil	1 oz/25 g cooked potato, sliced
1 oz/25 g onion, finely chopped	1 medium tomato, thinly sliced
1 clove garlic, crushed	salt and black pepper
1 rasher bacon, derind and cut into small pieces	parsley for garnish
2 size 3 eggs, beaten lightly with 1 tablespoon cold water	**Container** 7½ in/19 cm shallow ovenproof glass flan dish. Plastic is unsuitable for this recipe.

1 Put the oil, onion, garlic and bacon in the flan dish. Cover and microwave on high for 3 minutes. Stir once during cooking.
2 Add the eggs, cover and microwave on high for 30 seconds. Add the potato, cover and microwave on high for 30 seconds.
3 If the flan dish is not flameproof carefully slide the omelette onto a flameproof plate.
4 Top with the tomato slices and sprinkle grated cheese over the top. Season.
5 Place under a preheated grill until lightly browned and bubbling.
6 Sprinkle with fresh parsley to serve.
Reheat: unsuitable.

LEEK AND PEPPER QUICHE

Serves 4–6 (see colour plate 1)

Low fat yoghurt is used here as a healthier alternative to cream. The top can be browned after cooking under a preheated grill when a flameproof container is used. Don't worry if the quiche looks a little wobbly in the centre at the end of cooking time – it will set completely as it stands and cools. The filled quiche is cooked on a medium setting to prevent the outside edges turning tough and rubbery before the centre is cooked.

INGREDIENTS

Pastry:	2 oz/50 g Cheddar cheese, grated
2 oz/50 g plain Farmhouse flour (p.207)	1 tablespoon finely chopped fresh parsley
2 oz/50 g plain white flour	salt, black pepper
pinch of salt	**Containers**
1½ oz/40 g sunflower margarine	8 in/20 cm ovenproof glass flan dish (glass/ceramic dish is probably more suitable as you may wish to brown the flan under the grill).
cold water to mix	Trivet.
Filling:	Medium plastic microware bowl.
8 oz/250 g leeks, finely sliced	Reduce the timing by 30 seconds for pastry and 1 minute for filling when using plastic microware containers.
1 medium red pepper, stalk, seeds and white membrane removed, diced	
2 teaspoons sunflower oil	
¼ pt/150 ml thick natural yoghurt	
2 size 1 eggs, beaten	

♦ 47

1 Mix the flour and salt together in a mixing bowl. Rub in the margarine lightly with the fingertips and add just enough cold water to mix to a soft dough. Use the blade of a palette knife for mixing.

2 Wrap the pastry in polythene and chill for 15 minutes or more in the refrigerator.

3 Roll out on a lightly floured board, then brush off excess flour from both sides of the pastry. Line the flan dish, pressing firmly into the base and sides of the dish. Try not to stretch the pastry as it will shrink more during cooking. Trim the edges and prick the base regularly with a fork.

4 Stand the flan dish on the trivet and microwave uncovered on high for 4½ minutes, turning the dish once during cooking. If the pastry begins to rise up out of the dish, press it back lightly with a fork.

5 Place the leeks, red pepper and oil in the microware bowl. Cover and microwave on high for 4 minutes. Stir once during cooking. Drain off excess liquid. If the juices are included, the filling won't set.

6 In a large mixing bowl beat the yoghurt until smooth, then gradually beat in the eggs. Stir in the grated cheese and cooked vegetables. Stir in most of the parsley, salt and black pepper to taste, and mix together thoroughly. Spoon into the pastry case.

7 Stand the dish on the trivet and microwave uncovered on medium for 10–12 minutes until almost set. Take care not to overcook. Turn the dish

3 times during cooking.

8 If you wish, brown the top under a preheated grill. Stand, uncovered, for 5–10 minutes. Sprinkle with the remaining parsley.

Reheat: remove the quiche from the dish. Line a trivet or plate with a double layer of white kitchen paper and stand the quiche on this. Microwave uncovered on medium for 6 minutes or until heated through. Turn twice during this time.

CHEESE AND LEEK PUDDING

Serves 4

An economical supper dish that is quick and easy to make.
Serve with a salad or lightly cooked green vegetables.

INGREDIENTS	
4 tablespoons natural yoghurt	4 oz/125 g leeks, finely shredded
2 size 3 eggs, beaten	4 oz/125 g fresh wholewheat breadcrumbs
½ pt/300 ml skimmed milk	
good grating of nutmeg	2 medium tomatoes, sliced thinly
4 oz/125 g Cheddar cheese, grated	**Containers**
½ teaspoon mustard powder	Small plastic microwave bowl.
2 tablespoons finely chopped fresh parsley	1¾ pt/1 litre plastic microware ring mould. Increase timing by 2 minutes when using ovenproof glass or ceramic container.
salt, black pepper	Plastic trivet.

1 Put the yoghurt in the bowl and beat until smooth. Gradually beat in the eggs and milk. Stir in the nutmeg, cheese, mustard powder, 1½ tablespoons parsley, black pepper and a little salt. Stand for 5 minutes.

2 Add the leeks to the small bowl. Cover and microwave on high for 3 minutes. Stir once during cooking.

3 Mix in the breadcrumbs thoroughly and spoon into the lightly greased ring mould.

4 Stand the container on a trivet, cover and microwave on medium for 12 minutes. Remove the covering after 10 minutes. Turn the dish 3 times during cooking.

5 Stand, uncovered, for 5 minutes.

6 Place the slices of tomato around the outside edge of a dinner plate. Microwave uncovered on high for 1 minute.

7 Turn the pudding out onto a plate and top with the tomato slices, then sprinkle with black pepper and the remaining parsley.

Reheat: stand the ring mould on a trivet, cover and microwave on medium for 5–6 minutes. Turn once during this time.

PASTA AND GRAINS

Pasta, rice and other grains microwave well; pasta cooks perfectly 'al dente' and rice has a good flavour, with tender separate grains. There is no time saved when microwaving these, but there is much less steam in the kitchen and no sticky pan to scour afterwards.

Pasta is best cooked in a large bowl so that there is ample room for expansion during cooking. Water must be boiling before the pasta is added, and always mix in a teaspoon of oil to prevent the pasta from sticking together. Pasta should always be fully immersed in water – any protruding bits will not cook. Pasta is cooked uncovered, covered during standing time, then drained before serving.

White rice, except the 'easy cook' variety, needs washing thoroughly before cooking. Place in a strainer and wash under cold, running water to remove any loose gritty bits and excess starch. Brown rice needs rinsing several times in a large bowl of cold water, changing the water until all the grit and loose bits of husk are washed away. When the water is clear, drain. If the rice is not washed properly a grey scum will form which will affect the flavour of the cooked rice.

Both white and brown rice are available in several varieties:

slim, long grained basmati rice
fatter, long grained Patna or American rice
medium grained Italian arborio or risotto rice
round, short grained Carolina or pudding rice
glutinous rice, otherwise known as sweet or sticky rice.
This is available in long grains from Thailand or short, plump grains from China, and can be bought in oriental stores or from the Clearspring Grocer (p.209).

The cooking times for all these varies. The slim, long grained variety cooks the fastest – 15 minutes for white rice, 30 for brown. An extra 5–15 minutes will need to be allowed for the other varieties; test after the minimum time and increase timing as necessary. Pudding rice will take longer to cook and, once the water (or milk) has boiled, it should be cooked on the defrost setting.

All the varieties can be used in savoury dishes, although short grained rice is stickier and is best for rissoles and puddings. As with pasta, always cook in a large container to prevent the rice from boiling over.

Millet, buckwheat, bulgar wheat, barley and couscous adapt well to the microwave. Again, there is no great saving on cooking time, but they cook well, are very moist and the flavours are more pronounced. If barley is to be used in casseroles or soups, it helps if the grain is first soaked for a few hours, or overnight, before cooking. This will shorten the cooking time considerably. Try and use whole (pot) barley rather than the polished pearl barley, because it retains its natural fibres, but pearl barley does not need to be soaked. Whole grains are becoming more popular and can be bought in many supermarkets and health food shops. For a change, try substituting buckwheat and millet for rice in savoury dishes.

Pasta and grains all reheat quickly and successfully on a high setting. Cover, and stir or shake the container from time to time.

PASTA

Always use a large bowl which allows plenty of room for expansion during cooking. It is possible to cook up to 1 lb/500 g short cut macaroni or pasta shapes at one time, but don't cook more than 8 oz/250 g long spaghetti. It is therefore more practical to cook larger amounts conventionally. Always allow the water to return to a rolling boil before adding the pasta, otherwise it will cook unevenly.
It is preferable to use a plastic microware bowl, because water can take ages to return to a rolling boil in ovenproof glass.

INGREDIENTS	
3½ pts/2 litres boiling water	**Container**
1 teaspoon oil	5 pt/2.8 litre plastic microware bowl.
½ teaspoon salt	Increase timing by as much as 5 minutes when using ovenproof glass.
8 oz/250 g dried pasta	

1 Pour the boiling water into the bowl. Microwave uncovered on high for 2 minutes or until the water returns to a rolling boil.
2 Stir in the oil, salt and pasta.
3 Microwave uncovered on high for 5 minutes.
4 Stir well. Cover and stand for the following times: spaghetti – 5 minutes; tagliatelle – 3–5 minutes; macaroni and pasta shapes – 5–8 minutes. Wholewheat spaghetti needs a slightly longer standing time than white. Drain after standing time is completed and cover until ready to serve.
Reheat: covered on high for 3 minutes for 8 oz/250 g pasta. Stir once during this time. Pasta must have been kept covered for reheating to be successful.
Egg noodles and fresh pasta
Microwave on high uncovered for 1 minute. Egg noodles have no standing time. Fresh pasta needs 2–3 minutes standing time, depending on the thickness of the pasta.

VEGETABLE MACARONI AU GRATIN

Serves 4

A substantial main course, serve with a mixed green salad or lightly cooked green vegetables. Vary the vegetables according to season and personal taste – courgettes, onion, sweetcorn or finely sliced celery all give splendid results. The pasta can be cooked conventionally while the vegetables and sauce are being microwaved.
Vegetarians could omit the bacon and reduce the cooking time in step 1 by 1 minute.

INGREDIENTS

2 slices bacon, derind and cut into small pieces (optional)	2 oz/50 g fresh wholewheat breadcrumbs
8 oz/250 g leeks, finely sliced	salt and black pepper
8 oz/250 g mushrooms, thinly sliced	**Containers**
1 pt/600 ml béchamel sauce (see p.00)	Medium plastic microware bowl. Increase timing by 2 minutes when using ovenproof glass or ceramic container. Flameproof oval gratin dish.
6 oz/175 g cooked short cut macaroni or other pasta shapes (see p.00)	
4 oz/125 g Cheddar cheese, grated	

◆ 51

1 Put the bacon and leeks in the bowl. Cover and microwave on high for 5 minutes. Stir once during cooking.
2 Add the mushrooms, cover and microwave on high for 3 minutes or until all the ingredients are tender. Stir once during cooking.
3 Combine the béchamel sauce, cooked pasta, vegetables and 2 oz/50 g grated cheese; adjust seasoning to taste.
4 Transfer to the flameproof gratin dish. Cover and microwave on high for approximately 4–5 minutes, until the ingredients are well heated through. Stir once during cooking. The overall cooking time will depend upon the temperature of the pasta and sauce. If these are freshly cooked and quite warm then the above timing will be correct. If the sauce has been made well in advance, then the timing will need to be adjusted.
5 Mix the remaining cheese with the breadcrumbs and sprinkle over the pasta and vegetables.
6 Brown under a preheated grill until golden and crisp.
Reheat: uncovered on a medium setting for approximately 12 minutes. Turn the dish three times during this time.

FARFALLE WITH PESTO, ANCHOVIES AND OLIVES

Serves 4

One of my favourite quick supper dishes, satisfying and full of flavour.
The pasta can be microwaved (see p.50), but if the meal is required in
a hurry, cook the pasta conventionally while you microwave the sauce.
Green courgettes or small custard marrows, sliced lengthways into small
pieces, can be used when yellow courgettes are unobtainable, and if you
can't find chestnut mushrooms, use button mushrooms. Choose a good
quality commercial pesto if you don't have time to make your own.
I have cooked this sauce in a wok and the cooking time is similar
although the resulting sauce does not have quite such a good flavour
and the yield is smaller. There is less evaporation in microwaving
and every last bit can be scraped from the cooking container.

INGREDIENTS	
1 tablespoon olive oil	about 15 calamata olives stoned and halved
1–2 cloves garlic, crushed	
12 oz/375 g yellow courgettes, halved lengthways, then cut into ½ in/1 cm half-moon slices	1 small can anchovies, rinsed in cold water, drained and chopped
8 oz/250 g chestnut mushrooms thinly sliced	8 oz/250 g farfalle (pasta bows), cooked
	a few fresh basil leaves, torn into shreds
bunch of spring onions, trimmed and finely chopped	**Container** Large plastic microware bowl. Increase timing by 3 minutes when using ovenproof glass or ceramic container.
2 heaped tablespoons pesto	
black pepper	

1 Put the olive oil, garlic and courgettes into the bowl. Cover and microwave
on high for 3 minutes. Shake the bowl once during cooking.
2 Stir in the mushrooms. Cover and microwave on high for 2 minutes.
3 Stir in the spring onions and pesto and season with plenty of black pepper.
4 Cover and microwave on high for 3 minutes.
5 Add the olives and chopped anchovies. Cover and microwave on high for
2 minutes.
6 Combine the sauce with the cooked pasta and sprinkle with the shredded
basil leaves.
Reheat: covered on high for 4½ minutes. Stir once during this time.

SPAGHETTI NAPOLITANA

Serves 4

Serve this filling dish for lunch or supper with a mixed green salad.
I suggest that you cook the spaghetti conventionally while the sauce is
prepared in the microwave – it will taste better if freshly made.

INGREDIENTS

1 large onion, finely chopped	black pepper
1 clove garlic, crushed	2 tablespoons finely chopped fresh parsley
2 teaspoons chopped fresh basil or 1 teaspoon dried	salt
1 tablespoon olive oil	8 oz/250 g wholewheat spaghetti, cooked
14 oz/425 g can tomatoes, crushed with their juice	grated Parmesan cheese
4 tablespoons passata (p.209)	**Container**
2 tablespoons tomato purée	Medium plastic microware bowl. Increase timing by 3 minutes when using ovenproof glass or ceramic container.
4 tablespoons red wine	

1 Place the onion, garlic, basil and oil in the bowl. Cover and microwave on high for 5 minutes. Stir once during cooking.
2 Stir in the tomatoes, passata, tomato purée, red wine and black pepper.
3 Cover and microwave on high for 8 minutes. Stir 3 times during cooking.
4 Stir in 1 tablespoon parsley. Cover and stand for 5 minutes. Adjust seasoning to taste.
5 Combine the sauce with the cooked spaghetti and sprinkle with Parmesan and extra parsley.
Reheat: covered on high for 6–8 minutes. Stir once during this time.

◆ 53

PORRIDGE

Serves 4

Porridge is creamier and has a better flavour when microwaved –
and there's no messy pan to wash up afterwards.
Use a large bowl, to allow enough space for ingredients to rise up when
boiling point is reached.
For a hearty breakfast, serve with yoghurt and top with fresh fruit or
plumped-up dried fruit.

INGREDIENTS

4 oz/125 g porridge oats	**Container**
¼ pt/150 ml cold water	5 pt/2.8 litre plastic microware bowl.
1 pt/600 ml boiling water	Increase timing by 2–3 minutes when using ovenproof glass or ceramic container.
pinch of salt	

1 Place the porridge oats and cold water in the bowl. Mix together, then stir in the boiling water and salt.
2 Microwave uncovered on high for approximately 6 minutes, or until boiling point is reached. Whisk well after each minute of cooking.
3 Stand, covered, for 3 minutes.
4 To serve, stir in milk or yoghurt, fresh or dried fruit, sugar or honey. Or add 2 oz/50 g raisins to the porridge after 4 minutes of cooking time. They sweeten the porridge and plump up nicely.

WHITE RICE

Serves 4

Basmati rice is the one I prefer above all others when long grained white rice is called for. Microwaving draws out its delicate flavour and the cooked grains are tender and separate.

Place basmati rice in a strainer and wash under cold running water before cooking.

Use a deep container to prevent the rice from boiling over.

INGREDIENTS	
8 oz/250 g basmati rice, washed and drained	**Container** 3½ pt/2 litre ovenproof glass casserole. Decrease timing by 1–2 minutes when using a plastic microware container.
1 pt/600 ml boiling water	
½ teaspoon salt	

1 Place the rice, water and salt in the casserole dish. Cover and microwave on high for 15 minutes. Turn the dish 3 times during cooking.
2 Stand, covered, for 10 minutes, then fluff up with a fork.
Reheat: covered on high for 3 minutes. Stir once during this time.

Saffron rice
Add a few strands of saffron to the rice at the beginning of cooking.

BROWN RICE

Serves 4

Brown rice should be washed thoroughly in a bowl, in several changes
of cold water, then drained before cooking.
Use a large container as the rice needs space to expand and boil up
during cooking.

INGREDIENTS

8 oz/250 g brown rice, washed and drained	**Container**
1¼ pt/750 ml boiling water	5 pt/2.8 litre plastic microware bowl. Increase timing by 3 minutes when using ovenproof glass or ceramic container.
a good pinch of salt	

1 Place the rice, water and salt in the bowl. Cover and microwave on high for
10 minutes.
2 Reduce the setting to medium and microwave, covered, for 20 minutes.
Test to see if the grains are tender, if not recover and microwave for a further
10–15 minutes.
3 Stand, covered, for 10 minutes, then fluff up with a fork.
Reheat: covered on high for 4 minutes. Stir once during this time.

◆ 55

BROWN RICE WITH HERB SALAD

Serves 4

I like to serve this with poached salmon steaks or chicken.

INGREDIENTS

8 oz/250 g easy cook brown rice	2 teaspoons finely chopped fresh parsley
1¼ pt/750 ml boiling water	1 teaspoon finely chopped fresh oregano
½ teaspoon salt	about 6 fresh basil leaves, torn into fine shreds
1 tablespoon olive oil	
2 tablespoons sunflower oil	½ cucumber cut into ½ in/1 cm dice
2 tablespoons lemon juice	zest of 1 lemon
1 teaspoon wholegrain mustard	**Container**
black pepper	5 pt/2.8 litre plastic microware bowl. Increase timing by 4 minutes when using ovenproof glass container.
4 spring onions, sliced thinly on diagonal	

1 Place the rice, boiling water and salt into the bowl. Cover and microwave
on high for 10 minutes.
2 Reduce to medium setting and microwave for 20 minutes, or until the rice
is tender and all the liquid is absorbed. Stand, covered, for 5 minutes.
3 Place the olive oil, sunflower oil, lemon juice, mustard and a little salt and

pepper in a screw top jar. Shake until all the ingredients are well mixed.
4 Pour the dressing over the hot rice, after standing time. Mix with a fork until well combined. Cover the bowl with a clean teatowel and allow to cool.
5 Once cooled, stir in the spring onions, fresh herbs and cucumber. Garnish with the lemon zest.

BROWN RICE RISOTTO

Serves 4

Sweet brown rice is stickier than other varieties and has a marvellous flavour. It can be difficult to find but can be purchased by mail order from the Clearspring Grocer (p.209). However, the recipe works well with brown round grain rice.

INGREDIENTS

½ red pepper, finely chopped	¼ teaspoon salt
½ green pepper, finely chopped	1 teaspoon turmeric
4 oz/125 g mushrooms, finely chopped	1 tablespoon finely chopped fresh parsley
1 tablespoon olive oil	black pepper
1 oz/25 g sunflower margarine	**Containers**
1 medium onion, finely chopped	Medium microware bowl.
8 oz/250 g sweet brown rice, washed and drained	5 pt/2.8 litre plastic microware bowl. Increase timing by 1 minute for the peppers and 3 minutes for the rice when
4 oz/125 g cashew nuts	using ovenproof glass or ceramic containers.
1½ pt/900 ml boiling chicken or vegetable stock or water	

1 Place the peppers and mushrooms in the medium bowl. Cover and microwave on high for 3 minutes. Stir once during cooking. Put to one side covered.
2 Place the oil and margarine in the large bowl. Microwave on high until the margarine has melted.
3 Stir in the onion and microwave uncovered on high for 2 minutes.
4 Stir in the rice and nuts. Microwave uncovered on high for 5 minutes. Stir once during cooking.
5 Stir in 1¼ pt/750ml boiling stock or water, salt and turmeric. Microwave uncovered on high for 10 minutes. Stir twice during cooking.
6 Reduce the setting to medium and continue to microwave uncovered for 10 minutes. Stir 3 times during cooking.
7 Add the remaining boiling stock or water and stir well. Microwave uncovered on medium for 15 minutes. Stir 3 times during cooking.
8 Add the cooked vegetables together with their juices and stir well.
9 Cover and microwave on high for 8 minutes. Stir once during cooking.
10 Stir in the parsley.
11 Stand, covered, for 10 minutes. Stir and adjust seasoning to taste.
Reheat: covered on high for 6 minutes. Stir once during this time.

SAFFRON RISOTTO

Serves 4

Italian arborio rice is traditionally used for risottos.
It has a wonderful flavour and texture and can be bought in larger
supermarkets and delicatessens. Risotto is cooked uncovered and needs
stirring frequently during cooking.
Turmeric can be substituted for the saffron in this recipe; it will taste quite
different, but will produce an equally attractive colour. For a really splendid
flavour, replace 6 tablespoons of the stock with dry white wine.
Serve as a first course, main course or accompaniment to meat, poultry, fish
and many vegetable dishes.

INGREDIENTS

1 medium onion, finely chopped	¼ teaspoon salt
1 oz/25 g sunflower margarine	black pepper
1 tablespoon olive oil	2 tablespoons finely chopped fresh parsley
8 oz/250 g arborio rice, washed and drained	
	3 tablespoons grated Parmesan cheese
1½ pt/900 ml boiling chicken or vegetable stock or water	**Container**
½ teaspoon powdered saffron or 1 teaspoon turmeric	5 pt/2.8 litre plastic microware bowl. Increase the timing by 2–3 minutes when using ovenproof glass or ceramic container.

◆ 57

1 Place the onion, margarine and olive oil in the bowl.
2 Microwave uncovered on high for 3 minutes. Stir once during cooking.
3 Stir in the rice. Microwave uncovered on high for 4 minutes. Stir once
during cooking.
4 Stir in 1¼ pt/750 ml boiling stock or water, saffron or turmeric and salt
and pepper.
5 Microwave uncovered on high for 10 minutes. Stir 3 times during cooking.
6 Stir in the remaining boiling stock or water. Microwave uncovered on high
for 5 minutes. Stir twice during cooking.
7 Stir in 1 tablespoon parsley and the Parmesan cheese.
8 Cover and stand for 10 minutes. Adjust seasoning before serving and
sprinkle with remaining parsley.
Reheat: covered on high for 4–5 minutes. Stir once during this time.

MILLET

Serves 4   Cooked weight: 1lb 4oz/625 g

Millet is a small compact yellow grain which fluffs up during a short cooking time. Millet contains useful quantities of calcium and protein, is said to have an alkalizing effect on digestion and is beneficial for disorders of the stomach, spleen and pancreas.

Millet has a nutty flavour; it can be dry roasted in a frying pan before microwaving which will enhance its flavour.

Replace rice with millet in savoury dishes and as a base for rissoles and savoury loaves. It is essential to serve a sauce or moist foods with millet; a topping of ratatouille makes an excellent accompaniment.

INGREDIENTS

6 oz/175 g millet, washed in a strainer under cold running water, then drained	**Container** 5 pt/2.8 litre plastic microware bowl.
1¼ pt/750 ml boiling water	Increase timing by 2 minutes when using ovenproof glass or ceramic container.
½ teaspoon salt	

1 Place all the ingredients in the bowl. Cover and microwave on high for 20 minutes.

2 Stir. Stand, covered, for 5 minutes. Fluff up with a fork before serving.

Reheat: sprinkle 2 tablespoons cold water over the millet, cover and microwave on high for 3–4 minutes. Turn the bowl once during this time.

MILLET AND VEGETABLE TURBAN

Serves 4

A light and well balanced main course. Serve hot or cold, accompanied by soup and salads.

INGREDIENTS

4 oz/125 g carrots, grated	salt, pepper
1 medium onion, finely chopped	**Garnish** ½ cucumber, thinly sliced
1 tablespoon sunflower oil	
½ red pepper, diced	bunch of watercress
4 oz/125 g courgettes, cut into ½ in/1 cm dice	**Containers** Medium microware bowl. 4 pt/2.3 litre plastic microware ring mould.
1 egg, beaten	Increase timing slightly when using a smaller
8 oz/250 g fromage frais or other low fat soft cheese	ring mould or an ovenproof glass mould. Trivet.
10 oz/300 g cooked millet	

1 Place the carrots, onion and oil in the bowl. Cover and microwave on high for 4 minutes. Stir once during cooking.
2 Stir in the red pepper and courgettes. Cover and microwave on high for 3 minutes. Stir once during cooking.
3 In a large bowl beat the egg and cheese together. Beat in the millet until the mixture is smooth. Stir in the cooked vegetables and mix together thoroughly. Season to taste.
4 Spoon into the lightly greased ring mould, pressing the mixture down well.
5 Cover and stand the container on a trivet. Microwave on high for 7 minutes, turning once during cooking. Stand, covered, for 10 minutes.
6 Turn out on to a plate. Garnish the top with thinly sliced cucumber and fill the centre with watercress.
Reheat: stand the container on a trivet, cover and microwave on medium for 5–6 minutes. Turn once during this time.

BUCKWHEAT

Serves 4   Cooked weight: 1 lb 6 oz/675 g

Buckwheat is a traditional staple grain eaten in Russia, Poland and Central Asia. It has a warming effect on the body in the same way as porridge oats. It cooks quickly and can be used instead of rice in many savoury dishes. Purchase roasted buckwheat otherwise you will need to dry roast it in a frying pan before microwaving.
Buckwheat contains rutin which is beneficial for circulatory disorders and in eliminating excess water from the body.

◆ 59

INGREDIENTS

6 oz/175 g roasted buckwheat, washed briefly in a strainer under cold water, then drained	**Container** 5 pt/2.8 litre plastic microware bowl. Increase timing by 3 minutes when using ovenproof glass or ceramic container.
1¼ pt/750 ml boiling water	
½ teaspoon salt	

1 Place all the ingredients in the bowl.
2 Cover and microwave on high for 15 minutes. Stir well, cover and stand for 5 minutes. Fluff up with a fork before serving.
Reheat: sprinkle 2 tablespoons cold water over the buckwheat. Cover and microwave on high for 3–4 minutes.

BUCKWHEAT MUSHROOMS AND ONIONS

Serves 4

Serve as an accompaniment to bean casseroles and vegetable dishes
or as a stuffing for pancakes and pies. Buckwheat can be dry and requires
a sauce or topping with moist foods. The shiitake mushrooms and onions
add a sweet flavour and moistness to the buckwheat in this recipe.

INGREDIENTS	
1 medium onion, finely chopped	1 lb 6 oz/675 g cooked buckwheat (p.59)
1 teaspoon mixed dried herbs	
1 tablespoon sunflower oil	3 tablespoons finely chopped fresh parsley
8 oz/250 g shiitake mushrooms (p.209), thinly sliced	
2–3 teaspoons natural soy sauce (shoyu)	**Containers** Medium plastic microware bowl. Increase timing by 2 minutes when using ovenproof glass or ceramic container. Microwave serving dish.
black pepper	

1 Place the onion, mixed dried herbs and oil in the bowl.
2 Cover and microwave on high for 4 minutes. Stir once during cooking.
3 Add the mushrooms. Cover and microwave on high for 3 minutes. Stir
once during cooking.
4 Stir in the soy sauce and black pepper to taste.
5 Mix the cooked buckwheat and parsley with the vegetables. Spoon into a
serving dish.
6 Cover and microwave on high for 3 minutes or until heated through. Stir
once during this time.
Reheat: covered on high for 4–5 minutes. Stir once during this time.

BULGAR WHEAT

Serves 4   Cooked weight: 1 lb 12 oz/875 g

Bulgar is a processed wholewheat product. The wheat is cracked and then
steamed. It cooks quickly, is light in texture and has a wonderful flavour.

INGREDIENTS	
8 oz/250 g bulgar wheat	**Container** 5 pt/2.8 litre plastic microware bowl. Increase timing by 2–3 minutes when using ovenproof glass or ceramic container.
1½ pt/1 litre boiling water	
½ teaspoon salt	

1 Place all the ingredients in the bowl.
2 Cover and microwave on high for 8 minutes.
3 Stir, then stand, covered, for 5 minutes. Fluff up with a fork before serving.
Reheat: covered on high for 3–4 minutes. Stir once during this time.

NUTTY BULGAR PILAU

Serves 4

Light, filling and delicately flavoured.
Serve with fish, chicken and salad dishes.

INGREDIENTS

4 sticks celery, finely sliced	2 tablespoons finely chopped parsley
1 medium onion, finely chopped	2 tablespoons lemon juice
½ teaspoon ground cinnamon	**Garnish**
2 tablespoons olive oil	quartered tomatoes
1 oz/25 g sunflower margarine	green olives
2 oz/50 g almonds, slivered or flaked	lemon slices
1 teaspoon natural soy sauce (shoyu)	**Containers**
1 lb 12 oz/875 g cooked bulgar wheat (p.60)	Medium plastic microware bowl. Small plastic microware bowl.
2 oz/50 g raisins	Increase timing by 3 minutes for the celery and onion, and 30 seconds for the almonds
salt, pepper	when using ovenproof glass or ceramic
3 tablespoons finely chopped celery leaves	container.

◆ 61

1 Place the celery, onion, cinnamon and olive oil in the medium bowl.
2 Cover and microwave on high for 6 minutes. Stir once during cooking.
3 Place the margarine in the small bowl and microwave uncovered on high for 45 seconds or until melted. Stir in the almonds. Microwave uncovered on high for 2½ minutes. Stir once during cooking.
4 Stir in the soy sauce.
5 Mix the bulgar wheat, almonds, vegetables and raisins together. Season to taste.
6 Cover and microwave on high for 3 minutes. Stir once during cooking.
7 Stir in the celery leaves, parsley and lemon juice. Cover and microwave on high for 2 minutes. Garnish before serving.
Reheat: covered on high for 4–5 minutes. Stir once during this time.

BARLEY

Serves 4   Cooked weight: 1 lb 4 oz/625 g

Barley has an excellent flavour when microwaved and can be used as
a substitute for rice in many savoury dishes. A mixture of half brown rice
and half barley is perhaps the best way of serving this chewy textured grain
to those who are unfamiliar with its earthy taste. Pot barley contains the
nutritious outer husk – pearl barley has had this removed, which is why
it cooks faster. Reduce the cooking time for pot barley by soaking in
cold water overnight.
I often make a rich vegetable, lentil and barley casserole in the winter.
It seems to have a tranquillizing effect on rowdy toddlers or children
who don't seem to feel the need for sleep.

INGREDIENTS

6 oz/175 g pot barley, soaked in cold water overnight and drained	**Container**
1¼ pt/750 ml boiling water	3½ pt/2 litre ovenproof glass casserole dish or bowl.
½ teaspoon salt	Decrease timing by 2 minutes when using a plastic microware container.
	The container must be deep to prevent the barley boiling over during cooking.

1 Put the barley, boiling water and salt in the casserole dish or bowl.
2 Cover and microwave on high for 6 minutes.
3 Reduce the setting to medium and microwave, covered, for 6 minutes.
4 Reduce the setting to defrost and microwave, covered, for 30 minutes.
5 Stand, covered, for 10 minutes. Drain and reserve any liquid for soups and
sauces.
Reheat: sprinkle 2 tablespoons cold water over the barley. Cover and
microwave on high for 4–5 minutes. Stir once during this time.

MUSHROOM, RICE AND BARLEY TURBAN

Serves 4

An extremely filling and highly nutritious main course.
Serve with broccoli or Brussels sprouts and a rich vegetable sauce.

INGREDIENTS

8 oz/250 g mushrooms, finely chopped	1 tablespoon natural soy sauce (shoyu)
1 medium onion, finely chopped	black pepper
2 tablespoons sunflower oil	**Containers**
12oz/375 g cooked brown rice	Medium plastic microware bowl.
12 oz/375 g cooked pot barley	4 pt/2.3 litre plastic microware ring mould.
3 tablespoons finely chopped fresh parsley	Increase timing by 2 minutes when using ovenproof glass or ceramic container.
1 large egg, beaten	Trivet.

1 Place the mushrooms, onion and oil in the bowl. Cover and microwave on high for 4–5 minutes until just softened. Stir once during cooking.
2 Drain the vegetables and reserve the juices for the sauce.
3 Place the cooked vegetables in a large bowl, using a fork mix thoroughly with all the remaining ingredients.
4 Spoon into the lightly greased ring mould and press the mixture down firmly.
5 Cover, stand the container on a trivet and microwave on high for 8 minutes. Turn the dish twice during cooking.
6 Stand, covered, for 10 minutes.
7 Invert on to a plate, fill the centre with lightly cooked vegetables and serve with a good sauce.
Reheat: stand the container on a trivet, cover and microwave on high for 6 minutes. Turn twice during this time.

◆ 63

VEGETABLES

Vegetables will play a more prominent part in your menus once you have savoured the fresh flavours, intensified colours and excellent texture of microwave cooking.

Remove vegetables from the oven when just fork tender and slightly crisp; prolonged cooking will toughen them. At the end of cooking, taste before seasoning; you will discover that very little or no additional salt is required. Vegetables contain natural mineral salts; these remain in the microwaved vegetables, and are not lost in the cooking water. Use good quality, fresh produce; the microwave cannot magically transform end of season woody carrots into tender young things.

Frozen vegetables can be cooked straight from the freezer, and don't usually require any additional water. Blanching vegetables for the freezer saves time and is less trouble in the microwave; use just a few tablespoons of water to each 1 lb/500 g vegetables and leave out the salt. Canned vegetables simply need draining, covering and heating. Shake or stir once or twice, so that heat is evenly distributed.

Even when reheated, vegetables have the appearance of being just cooked. They reheat rapidly so keep an eye on them to prevent them cooking further and toughening. You can get an indication of how hot they are by feeling the underneath of the container. Stir once or twice to distribute heat evenly.

From the nutritional point of view, microwaves score high, because very little liquid is required for cooking, therefore more nutrients are retained. Vegetables with a high water content, like peppers, courgettes, spinach and marrows need no additional liquid. Little or no fat or oil is required. A good example of this is ratatouille (p.74), which requires ¼ pt/150 ml oil when conventionally cooked compared with 2 tablespoons when microwaved.

Vegetables should be cooked in a shallow dish so that they can be spread out. Deep dishes are especially unsuitable for dense vegetables like carrots, Brussels sprouts and cauliflower, because they will not cook evenly, will require a lot of stirring during cooking, and overall cooking time will be increased. I often use special microwave boiling bags, and find that these give the very best results for potatoes and cauliflower. Boiling bags are much cheaper than roasting bags, and can be bought from supermarkets, freezer centres and specialist cook shops. The microwaves are able to penetrate these very efficiently,

TRIVET

1·Leek and Pepper Quiche. See recipe on page 47

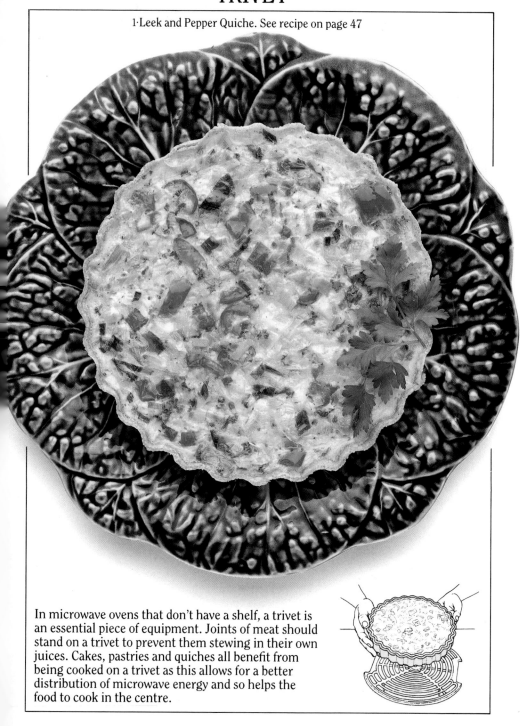

In microwave ovens that don't have a shelf, a trivet is an essential piece of equipment. Joints of meat should stand on a trivet to prevent them stewing in their own juices. Cakes, pastries and quiches all benefit from being cooked on a trivet as this allows for a better distribution of microwave energy and so helps the food to cook in the centre.

PIERCING

2·Stuffed Aubergine. See recipe on page 67

Foods encased
in their own skin,
such as whole fruit or
vegetables, or encased in a
membrane, such as chicken livers, must
be pierced or slashed with a fork or the tip of a
sharp knife, to prevent them from exploding during
cooking. Egg yolks must be pierced with a cocktail stick.

SHIELDING

3·Sea Bass, Sake and Shitake. See recipe on page 122

Thin or delicate parts of food can be protected by small pieces of aluminium foil. However, always check the manufacturer's instructions before putting aluminium foil into a microwave oven. The strips of foil must be secured, a wooden cocktail stick is useful for this. Foil must never touch the sides of the oven as this will cause sparking.

SHAPE AND POSITIONING OF FOOD

4 · Salmon Steaks in White Wine. See recipe on page 102

As in all other methods of cooking, the thinner parts of food will cook more quickly when microwaved. They can be protected, as in this recipe, by being folded and secured with a cocktail stick. Thicker or more dense pieces of food should always be placed towards the outside of any dish or turntable as this is where the microwave energy is strongest.

allowing the food to cook evenly. Leave a large gap at the top for the steam to escape, and secure with an elastic band, just as you would when using a roasting bag.

Slice vegetables thinly, or chop into evenly sized pieces; score or prick skins of those being cooked whole to prevent them bursting.

When cooking vegetables like asparagus or broccoli, place stems towards the outside of the container and florets or tender tips towards the centre. The stalks take longer to cook than the tops, and will receive more energy when arranged this way. It will be necessary to turn large vegetables over, and to reposition others during cooking, to make sure they are cooked through. Skins on baked potatoes don't crisp but can be placed under a preheated grill after cooking, if so desired. Skins of tomatoes and peppers never soften as completely as those cooked conventionally.

Roast potatoes are not possible in the microwave, but potatoes could be par-boiled in a boiling bag before roasting in an ordinary oven. Oven chips can be reheated successfully by microwave, but it is not possible to fry chips as there is no way of controlling the temperature of the oil.

Pound for pound no time is saved in cooking vegetables by micro-wave, although I have discovered that organically grown produce cooks much more quickly than chemically produced. Organically grown vegetables are becoming more widely available; if you are able to buy them you will probably find you develop a preference for them.

◆ 65

The browning dish can be used for stir-fried dishes, but if you are cooking a large quantity it is a lot easier and quicker to use a wok.

MANGE-TOUTS WITH MUSHROOMS

Serves 4

Use young, tender mange-touts for the best results. Top and tail them and remove any stringy bits before cooking. When fresh mange-touts are not available, frozen can be used. Cook from frozen, decreasing the cooking time slightly. No additional liquid is required as both mange-touts and mushrooms contain a lot of water. Drain after cooking, saving the liquid for soups or stocks. No fat is used as this dish is moist and well flavoured, although a little can be added after cooking, if you wish.

INGREDIENTS

8 oz/250 g fresh mange-touts, topped and tailed	**Container** Shallow oval plastic microware dish with lid. Increase timing by 30 seconds when using ovenproof glass or ceramic container.
4 oz/125 g button mushrooms, wiped	
a little lemon juice	
herb salt	

1 Place the mange-touts and mushrooms in the dish, spreading them out evenly.
2 Cover and microwave on high for approximately 6 minutes, or until the mushrooms are just tender and the mange-touts are still slightly crisp. Shake or stir once during cooking.
3 Stand for 3 minutes, drain and sprinkle with lemon juice and herb salt.
Reheat: covered on high for 2–2½ minutes. Stir once during this time. Take great care when reheating as the vegetables can easily start to cook again and the textures will be spoiled.

BAKED ONIONS WITH WHOLEWHEAT AND MUSHROOM STUFFING

Serves 4

Cooking whole onions by microwave is quick and easy;
they develop a delicious sweet flavour and hold their shape well.

INGREDIENTS

4 medium onions, each weighing approximately 5 oz/150 g, peeled	herb salt, black pepper
	½ small egg, beaten
1 tablespoon finely chopped parsley	1 oz/25 g cheese, grated
4 tablespoons fresh wholewheat breadcrumbs	**Container**
	Shallow oval plastic microware dish with lid.
1 oz/25 g mushrooms, finely chopped	Increase timing by 1 minute when using
1 teaspoon mixed herbs	ovenproof glass or ceramic container.

1 Slice a good ½ in/1 cm off the top of each onion, and a little off the bottom so that they stand upright.
2 Place the onions in the dish, cover and microwave on high for 6 minutes. Turn the dish once during cooking. Drain most of the liquid out of the dish and put to one side to cool.
3 Using a grapefruit knife or teaspoon, scoop out the centres of the onions, leaving a good firm shell at least ½ in/1 cm thick. Chop half the scooped out flesh finely and save the remainder for soups or other dishes.
4 Mix together the chopped onion flesh, half the parsley, the breadcrumbs, mushrooms, mixed herbs, a little salt and pepper, and bind together with the beaten egg.
5 Fill the onions with the stuffing, pressing it down well.
6 Cover and microwave on high for 4 minutes, turning the dish once during cooking.
7 Sprinkle the cheese over the onions and microwave uncovered on high for 1 minute, until just melted, or transfer to a flameproof dish and brown under a preheated grill. Sprinkle with the remaining parsley.
Reheat: omit step 7 if you are going to reheat this dish. Microwave for 1 minute on high, covered, sprinkle on the cheese and allow a further minute, uncovered. Sprinkle the parsley over the cheese.

STUFFED AUBERGINES

Serves 2 or 4 (see colour plate 2)

Aubergines cook extremely quickly in the microwave and if a recipe requires them to be cooked whole, the microwave certainly saves a lot of time.
It is essential to prick the skins all over, otherwise the aubergines may explode as pressure builds up inside during cooking. This quick and easy dish will serve 4 as an accompaniment to fish, meat or poultry dishes, or will make a vegetarian main course for 2.
Coriander leaves could be substituted for the parsley.

INGREDIENTS

2 medium aubergines, each weighing approximately 8 oz/250 g, stalks removed	black pepper
	good squeeze of lemon juice
	2–3 tablespoons finely chopped parsley
1 large red onion, finely sliced	herb salt
1 clove garlic, crushed	4 black olives
1 tablespoon olive oil	2 slices of lemon
3 medium tomatoes or 1 large beefsteak tomato (approximately 8 oz/250 g), roughly chopped	**Container** Medium plastic microware bowl. Increase timing by 2–3 minutes when using ovenproof glass or ceramic bowl.
1 medium green pepper, seeded, deveined and roughly chopped	

1 Line the oven floor or turntable with a piece of white kitchen paper. Prick the aubergines all over and arrange so that the thinner ends are pointing inwards and the fatter ends face the outside edges of the turntable or oven cavity.

2 Microwave uncovered on high for 3 minutes. Turn each aubergine over and cook for a further 3 minutes; they should be just tender. If not, cook for a further 2 minutes. Put to one side to cool slightly while preparing the filling.

3 Put the onion, garlic and olive oil into the bowl. Cover and microwave on high for 3 minutes. Shake or stir the ingredients halfway through the cooking time.

4 Stir in the tomatoes and green pepper and season well with black pepper. Three-quarters cover and microwave on high for 4 minutes. Stir once during cooking.

5 Meanwhile, slit the aubergines lengthways and, using a teaspoon or small knife, scoop out most of the flesh, leaving a thin shell. Transfer the shells to a shallow gratin dish and arrange them lengthways, side by side. Sprinkle with lemon juice.

6 Roughly chop the aubergine flesh and add to the bowl of almost cooked vegetables. Stir in 1 tablespoon parsley.

7 Three-quarters cover and microwave on high for 3 minutes until boiling and vegetables are just tender. Stir well and adjust seasoning to taste.

8 Pile the mixture into the shells, pressing well down, allowing any excess to spill over the sides.

◆ 67

9 Microwave uncovered on high for 2 minutes to reheat shells.
10 Sprinkle with the remaining parsley and garnish each with 1 olive and ½ slice of lemon.
Reheat: prepare to end of step 8. Cover and microwave on high for 4–5 minutes, turning the dish once. Garnish just before serving.

PARMESAN TOMATOES

Serves 4

Beefsteak tomatoes have a superb flavour when microwaved, and with this simple topping make a healthy, fresh tasting first course.
They reheat perfectly, so can be prepared well in advance, although they are just as delicious cold.

INGREDIENTS

2 beefsteak tomatoes, each weighing approximately 6 oz/175 g	black pepper
	1 teaspoon grated Parmesan cheese
1 small onion, finely chopped	chopped parsley
½ oz/15 g sunflower margarine or butter	**Containers**
1 teaspoon chopped fresh basil or ½ teaspoon dried	Small plastic microware bowl. 8 in/20.5 cm ovenproof glass flan dish.
4 tablespoons fresh wholewheat breadcrumbs	Reduce timing by 30 seconds when using a plastic microware flan dish.

1 Slice the tomatoes in half horizontally.
2 Place the onion, margarine and dried basil, if using, in the bowl. Cover and microwave on high for 2 minutes; shake or stir once during cooking.
3 Stir in the breadcrumbs and black pepper and fresh basil, if using. Microwave uncovered on high for 1 minute. Stir in the Parmesan cheese.
4 Place the tomatoes in the flan dish and spoon the filling over the tomato halves, pressing down slightly.
5 Microwave uncovered on high for 2½ minutes, or until just tender. Turn dish once during this time. To test if they are cooked, insert a skewer through the sides of the tomatoes. Sprinkle with parsley.
Reheat: uncovered, without parsley, on high for 1–1½ minutes. Take care as tomatoes will collapse if microwaved too long.

BRUSSELS SPROUTS WITH CHESTNUTS

Serves 4

Chestnuts are a lot easier to peel and their sweet flavour
is more pronounced when microwaved.

INGREDIENTS

4 oz/125 g fresh chestnuts, with a cross cut through the skin	½ oz/15 g butter or sunflower margarine (optional)
8 oz/250 g Brussels sprouts, trimmed, with a cross cut through the stalk end	**Containers** Serving dish.
2 tablespoons water	Microwave boiling bag.
herb salt	Round plastic microware container.

1 Place a piece of white kitchen paper on the oven floor or turntable and arrange the prepared chestnuts in a well spaced circle around the outside edges. If your oven does not have a turntable, place the paper on the floor of the oven and arrange the chestnuts in a circle, spacing them well apart.
2 Microwave uncovered on high for approximately 1½ minutes, until tender. Stand for 2 minutes.
3 Carefully remove the shells and inner skins and transfer the chestnuts to a serving dish.
4 Place the sprouts in the boiling bag with 2 tablespoons water. Secure top with an elastic band, leaving a gap for steam to escape. Place bag inside container and microwave on high for 6 minutes, turning the dish once during cooking.
5 Drain the sprouts and mix with the chestnuts. Season lightly before serving. Dot with butter or margarine if liked.
Reheat: covered on high for 2–2½ minutes. Stir once during this time.

◆ 69

PETITS POIS WITH YOUNG CARROTS

Serves 4

The delicate flavour of petits pois goes well with tender young carrots.
Slice the carrots thinly, or you may find that the peas overcook.

INGREDIENTS

8 oz/250 g young carrots, scrubbed, cut in half lengthways, then sliced into thin half-moon shapes	½ oz/15 g sunflower margarine (optional)
2 tablespoons water	**Container** Shallow oval microwave dish with lid.
8 oz/250 g petits pois, frozen	Increase timing by 1 minute when using
herb salt, black pepper	ovenproof glass or ceramic container.

1 Place the carrots in the dish with 2 tablespoons water, spreading out well to promote even cooking.
2 Cover and microwave on high for 6 minutes. Shake or stir once during cooking.
3 Add petits pois. Cover and microwave on high for 3 minutes, until cooked. Shake or stir once during cooking.
4 Drain, reserving any liquid for stock or soups, season lightly and dot with sunflower margarine, if you wish.
Reheat: covered on high for 2–2½ minutes. Stir once during this time.

CORN ON THE COB

Serves 1

Microwaved corn is moist and has a pronounced flavour. It can be eaten as it is, without adding extra fat. If the corn is bought with the husk intact, simply remove the silks and the husk will act as a cover. When cooking 4 or more cobs in a dish, reposition once during cooking, moving those outside to the centre of the dish, to promote even cooking. 2 corn cobs will take approximately 6–8 minutes, 4 will take 12–15 minutes. If you are planning to cook 4 or more cobs, you will find it quicker and more convenient to do this conventionally.

INGREDIENTS	
1 medium corn on the cob	**Container**
salt, black pepper	Corn on the cob with husk intact,
¼ oz/5 g sunflower margarine or butter (optional)	or wrap individual cobs in pierced cling film or greaseproof paper. Alternatively, use a shallow dish.

1 Wrap corn in chosen manner.
2 Microwave on high for 3½–4 minutes, until just tender.
3 Stand for 2 minutes, season and add margarine or butter.
Reheat: covered on high for 1 minute per cob.

VEGETABLE AND TOFU KEBABS WITH LIGHT ORIENTAL SAUCE

Serves 4

Naturally smoked tofu is a very nutritious food which can be obtained from health food shops. It is firm, and has a delicious smoky flavour which blends perfectly with the vegetables used here. Ordinary firm tofu can be used, but the flavour is rather bland.

INGREDIENTS

8 oz/250 g block of naturally smoked tofu, cut into 16 cubes	pinch of brown sugar
	black pepper
2 medium courgettes, sliced into ½ in/1 cm pieces	chopped parsley or toasted nori (optional)
8 medium mushrooms, wiped	**Container**
4 medium tomatoes, sliced in half	8 bamboo skewers.
¼ pt/150 ml hot stock or water	Shallow, oval microware dish with lid. Microware jug.
2 teaspoons cornflour dissolved in 1 tablespoon water	Increase timing by 30 seconds for each batch when using ovenproof glass or
2 teaspoons natural soy sauce (shoyu)	ceramic container.
1 teaspoon tomato purée	

◆ 71

1 Thread each bamboo skewer with tofu and vegetables in the following order: courgette, tofu, mushroom, tomato, tofu, courgette. They are placed in this order so that the vegetables that take the longest to cook receive more microwave energy.
2 Cook 4 skewers at a time; place them in the dish, cover and microwave on high for 2 minutes.
3 Move the outside skewers to the centre and continue to cook, covered, for a further 1½ minutes.
4 Repeat with the second batch.
5 Drain any juices from the dish into a microware jug, and make up with hot stock or water to ¼ pt/150 ml.
6 Microwave on high until boiling, then stir in the dissolved cornflour. Microwave for 30 seconds–1 minute until thickened.
7 Stir in the soy sauce, tomato purée, brown sugar and black pepper.
8 Microwave for a further 30 seconds until boiling and well blended.
9 To serve: 2 skewers per person, set on a bed of rice or noodles (rice thread, egg or soba noodles are all good) with the sauce poured over the kebabs. Sprinkle with a little chopped parsley or toasted nori, if you wish.
Reheat: these are much nicer served immediately, but can be assembled some time beforehand, except for the courgettes; these should be sliced and threaded on at the last moment.

CHICK PEAS WITH SPICY TOMATO SAUCE

Serves 2 or 4

Serve as a vegetarian main course for 2 people or as an accompanying dish for 4. Rice and one or two vegetable dishes would make a well balanced meal. Crush the cumin seeds with a pestle and mortar, or by placing the seeds on a chopping board and pressing down hard with the heel of a rolling pin.

INGREDIENTS

1 large onion, finely chopped	14 oz/425 g can tomatoes, crushed with their juice
1 clove garlic, crushed	
½ teaspoon finely grated fresh root ginger	1 tablespoon olive or sesame oil
	black pepper
1 teaspoon garam masala	salt
½ teaspoon ground coriander	2 tablespoons finely chopped coriander leaves or parsley
½ teaspoon turmeric	
1 teaspoon cumin seeds, crushed	**Container**
pinch of chilli powder	Medium plastic microware bowl. Increase timing by 1 minute when using ovenproof glass or ceramic container.
14 oz/425 g can chick peas, drained, or 8 oz/250 g cooked chick peas	

1 Place the onion, garlic and ginger in the bowl. Cover and microwave on high for 3 minutes, stirring once during cooking.

2 Add the garam masala, ground coriander, turmeric, crushed cumin seeds and chilli powder. Cover and microwave on high for a further minute.

3 Stir in chick peas, tomatoes, oil and black pepper.

4 Cover and microwave on high for approximately 7 minutes, until boiling and the flavours are well blended. Stir twice during cooking. Stand for 5 minutes.

5 Adjust seasoning to taste and stir in the finely chopped coriander leaves or parsley.

Reheat: covered on high for approximately 3 minutes. Stir once during this time.

WINTER VEGETABLE PUREE

Serves 4

This purée is sweet and rich tasting, so keep portions small.
It cooks best in a microwave boiling bag.

INGREDIENTS

6 oz/175 g carrots, thinly sliced	salt, black pepper
4 oz/125 g swede, thinly sliced into 1 in/2.5 cm pieces	1 tablespoon natural yoghurt
	snipped chives or parsley for garnish
4 oz/125 g parsnips, thinly sliced	**Containers**
1 medium leek, thinly sliced	Microwave boiling bag.
4 tablespoons water	Round plastic microware dish.
a little hot skimmed milk or stock	

1 Place the prepared vegetables in the boiling bag and add the water. Secure with an elastic band, leaving a gap at the top. Stand the bag inside the round container.
2 Microwave on high for 12–14 minutes until the vegetables in the centre of the bag are fork tender. Reposition the bag once during cooking.
3 Purée, adding a little hot skimmed milk or stock if necessary. Season lightly to taste.
4 Arrange in a serving dish and swirl the yoghurt over the top. Sprinkle with chives or parsley.
Reheat: covered on high for approximately 2½ minutes without the topping, then add the yoghurt and chives or parsley.

◆ 73

BOILED POTATOES

Serves 4

This is the easiest way of boiling potatoes in the microwave and gives the very best results. Old potatoes cook faster than new ones, so check these carefully during cooking, and remove when those in the centre are just tender.
When new potatoes vary in size and are required whole, position the larger ones towards the outside of the bag and the smaller ones in the centre.
Timing can only be approximate, as some types of potato will cook more quickly than others.

INGREDIENTS

1½ lb/750 g potatoes, peeled and sliced evenly	**Containers**
	Microwave boiling bag.
¼ pt/150 ml boiling water	Round plastic microware container.
salt	

1 Place the prepared potatoes in the boiling bag and add the boiling water. Secure the top loosely with an elastic band. Stand the bag in the container.
2 Microwave on high for approximately 12 minutes for new potatoes, and 10 minutes for old. Reposition the bag once during cooking.
3 Test by carefully inserting a fork through the gap in the bag. The potatoes in the centre should be tender.
4 Stand for 2–3 minutes, then drain and season.
Reheat: covered on high for approximately 2½ minutes.
For mashed potato, add a little hot stock or skimmed milk and butter.

RATATOUILLE

Serves 6

When conventionally cooked, this dish can take up to 2 hours, and needs approximately ¼ pt/150 ml oil. Microwaving saves enormously on cooking time as most of the vegetables used have a high water content and the microwaves are able to penetrate these very efficiently.
The quantity of oil required is small, and the colour, flavour and texture of the individual vegetables is more clearly defined when cooked this way. A very versatile dish, ratatouille can be served with meat, poultry, fish or dairy dishes, or cold as a salad.

INGREDIENTS	
1 large Spanish onion, finely chopped	8 oz/250 g can tomatoes, crushed with their juice or 2 large beefsteak tomatoes, peeled and chopped
1 clove garlic, crushed	
2 tablespoons olive oil	
1 medium aubergine, sliced thinly and immersed in cold, salted water for 30 minutes	4 teaspoons chopped fresh basil or 2 teaspoons dried
8 oz/250 g courgettes, sliced thinly on diagonal	2 tablespoons tomato purée
	black pepper
1 medium red pepper, stalk, seeds and membrane removed, sliced into rings or strips	herb salt
	Container Large plastic microware bowl. Increase cooking time by approximately 2 minutes when using ovenproof glass or ceramic bowl.
1 medium green pepper, prepared as above	
1 medium yellow pepper, prepared as above	

1 Place the onion, garlic and oil in the bowl. Cover and microwave on high for 3 minutes. Shake or stir once during cooking.
2 Place the aubergine slices in a colander and rinse under cold running water to remove excess salt.
3 Add all the other ingredients to the bowl, except fresh basil leaves, if using, and the salt. Mix together well. The bowl will be very full, but the contents

will reduce during cooking.

4 Cover and microwave on high for approximately 12 minutes, or until just tender. Stir 3 times during cooking. Add the fresh basil during the last 5 minutes of cooking time.

5 Adjust seasoning and stand, covered, for 5 minutes.

Reheat: covered on high for 4–5 minutes. Stir twice during this time.

MIXED VEGETABLES WITH GINGER AND SHOYU SAUCE

Serves 4–6

The combination of ginger and shoyu is used extensively in oriental cooking, and imparts a subtle flavour to the vegetables. If you wish, a few pieces of diced firm tofu can be added during the last 2 minutes of cooking.

INGREDIENTS

8 oz/250 g carrots, sliced thinly on diagonal	¼ pt/150 ml boiling water or stock
1 small onion, finely chopped	1 heaped teaspoon arrowroot, dissolved in a little cold water
1 teaspoon olive oil	1–2 teaspoons natural soy sauce (shoyu)
1 teaspoon finely grated fresh root ginger	finely chopped parsley for garnish
8 oz/250 g courgettes, sliced thinly on diagonal	**Container** 3 pt/1.8 litre deep plastic microware dish. Increase timing by 2 minutes when using ovenproof glass or ceramic casserole dish.
1 medium red pepper, stalk, seeds and white membrane removed, sliced into rings	

1 Place the carrots, onion, oil and ginger in the dish. Cover and microwave on high for 4 minutes, stirring halfway through cooking.

2 Add the courgettes and red pepper. Cover and microwave on high for a further 4 minutes, stirring once during cooking.

3 Put ¼ pt/150 ml boiling water or stock into a jug. Stir in the dissolved arrowroot and shoyu.

4 Microwave on high for 1 minute, stirring after 30 seconds, until clear and thickened.

5 Pour the sauce over the vegetables and sprinkle with parsley.

Reheat: covered on high for approximately 4 minutes. Stir once during this time.

BAKED POTATOES WITH RED BEAN STUFFING

Serves 4

Serve these with a mixed salad for a complete supper. If you wish, the tops can be browned and crisped under a preheated grill after cooking. Chick peas could be substituted for the red kidney beans.

INGREDIENTS

4 medium potatoes, scrubbed and pricked all over	1 teaspoon dried basil or oregano
	1 tablespoon finely chopped fresh parsley
1 small onion, finely chopped	salt, black pepper
1 small green pepper, stalk, seeds and white membrane removed, chopped	2 oz/50 g grated Red Leicester cheese
	Container
7 oz/200 g can red kidney beans, drained	Medium plastic microware bowl. Increase timing by 1 minute when using ovenproof glass or ceramic bowl.
7 oz/200 g can tomatoes	
2 tablespoon passata (p.209)	

1 Place the prepared potatoes well apart in a circle on a double layer of white kitchen paper on the turntable or oven floor.

2 Microwave uncovered on high for 15–20 minutes until tender. Turn over halfway through cooking time. Set to one side.

3 Place the onion and green pepper in the bowl. Cover and microwave on high for 4 minutes. Shake or stir once during cooking.

4 Add the red kidney beans, tomatoes, passata, basil or oregano, and most of the parsley. Mix well together.

5 Three-quarters cover the bowl with cling film and microwave for 4–5 minutes on high, until the mixture is boiling. Stir once or twice during cooking.

6 Slice the potatoes in half lengthways and remove most of the flesh. Mash the potato flesh, then stir into the bean and vegetable mixture. Season lightly to taste.

7 Spoon into the potato skins, allowing any extra mixture to spill over the sides. Sprinkle with the grated cheese.

8 Microwave on high until the cheese just melts. Sprinkle with the remaining parsley.

Reheat: use a medium setting as cheese can toughen and become stringy if microwaved on high. Stand in a serving dish, cover, and reheat for approximately 7 minutes.

SWEET PEPPERS WITH FRAGRANT RICE STUFFING

Serves 4

Basmati rice has a delicate flavour, and the tiny black seeds from cardamom pods give this dish its subtle fragrance. To release the seeds, stand the pods on a chopping board and place the flat blade of a knife across them. A little pressure on this will open the pods and release the seeds.
This makes a filling dish for 4 people, allowing 2 halves each, and is good served with chicken or fish, and salads.

INGREDIENTS

1 large onion, finely chopped	2 tablespoons water
4 cardamom pods, crushed, reserving the tiny black seeds	4 oz/125 g blanched whole almonds
1 tablespoon sunflower oil	3 tablespoons finely chopped parsley or coriander leaves
1 in/2.5 cm piece cinnamon stick	**Containers**
½ teaspoon turmeric	3½ pt/2 litre ovenproof glass casserole dish with lid.
½ teaspoon cumin seeds, crushed	11 in/28 cm round, shallow ovenproof glass dish.
½ teaspoon ground coriander	Decrease timing for rice by 2 minutes,
8 oz/250 g basmati rice, thoroughly washed and drained	and overall cooking time for stuffed peppers by 2 minutes, when using plastic microware containers.
¼ teaspoon salt	
1¼ pt/750 ml boiling water, vegetable or chicken stock	
4 medium red/green peppers, sliced in half lengthways, seeds and white membrane removed, stalk intact	

◆ 77

1 Place the onion, cardamom seeds, oil, cinnamon stick, turmeric, cumin seeds and ground coriander in the casserole dish. Cover and microwave on high for 2 minutes. Stir well to amalgamate all the spices with the onion.
2 Stir in the rice and add the salt. Pour over the boiling water or stock.
3 Cover and microwave on high for 15 minutes. At the end of this time all the liquid will have been absorbed. Stand for 5 minutes, then fork up.
4 Place the peppers in the shallow dish with the water. Cover and microwave on high for 3 minutes, repositioning halfway through cooking.
5 Stand for 5 minutes, then drain.
6 Spread the almonds over a dinner plate and microwave uncovered on high for 5 minutes, stirring once. Chop finely.
7 Mix the nuts and coriander leaves or parsley into the rice. Adjust seasoning to taste.
8 Fill the peppers with the rice mixture, pressing it down well and mounding it neatly. It is easier to do this with wet hands. Serve any leftover rice separately.

9 Cover and microwave on defrost, so that the peppers don't collapse, for approximately 10 minutes, until the rice is thoroughly reheated and the peppers are tender. Turn the dish twice during cooking.
Reheat: covered on defrost for 10–12 minutes until the top of the rice and the underside of the container feel very hot.

STUFFED CHINESE LEAVES AU GRATIN

Serves 4

These tender leaves with light bulgar wheat stuffing can be served as a main course. Salads, ratatouille (p.74) and bean dishes are perfect accompaniments. See p.60 for instructions on cooking bulgar wheat.

INGREDIENTS	
8 Chinese leaves, washed	1½ oz/40 g fresh wholewheat breadcrumbs
1 medium onion, finely chopped	
2 teaspoons sunflower oil	chopped parsley or coriander leaves for garnish
6 oz/175 g cooked bulgar wheat	
2 oz/50 g pine kernels	**Containers**
2 tablespoons finely chopped coriander leaves	Medium microware bowl. 11 in/28 cm round, shallow ovenproof glass dish.
herb salt, black pepper	Decrease timing by 2 minutes when using a plastic microware container.
2 tablespoons water	
1½ oz/40 g grated cheese	

1 Shave away a little of the thick stalk of each of the Chinese leaves, to make them easier to roll.
2 Place the onion and oil in the bowl. Cover and microwave on high for 4 minutes. Stir once during cooking.
3 Mix the cooked onion, bulgar wheat, pine kernels, coriander leaves, a little salt and black pepper together thoroughly.
4 Divide the mixture evenly between the 8 leaves, placing the mixture towards the centre of the leaves. Fold the long edges over a little, then roll from the top of the leaf to the stalk end. Secure with wooden cocktail sticks.
5 Arrange around the edges of the dish. Sprinkle the water over the leaves. Cover and microwave on high for 8 minutes until just tender.
6 Carefully transfer to a flameproof serving dish, using a fish slice. Remove the cocktail sticks.
7 Combine the cheese with the breadcrumbs and sprinkle over the rolled leaves. Place under a preheated grill until nicely browned. Garnish with parsley.
Reheat: covered on medium for 4–5 minutes.

CAULIFLOWER WITH CREAMY TOFU SAUCE

Serves 4

This is an unusual way of serving cauliflower and the tofu sauce is much healthier than a heavy roux-based sauce. Served cold, this dish goes well with rice salads, chicken and fish.

This recipe uses 'silken' tofu which is easily obtained from health food shops and is a softer version of the usual firm blocks.

Nori is used as the garnish; it is a mild-tasting Japanese seaweed, sold in thin sheets. To toast it, hold a single sheet a few inches above a gas flame for a few seconds. It will crisp, and the colour will change from black to green. Fold the toasted nori lengthways into 6 sections, and snip, with scissors, into thin strips. Nori can be obtained from some health food shops and oriental grocers.

INGREDIENTS

1 lb/500 g cauliflower florets	1 teaspoon natural soy sauce (shoyu)
4 tablespoons water	black pepper
1 medium onion, finely chopped	2 tablespoons toasted nori for garnish
1 teaspoon sunflower oil	**Containers**
10 oz/300 g packet tofu, whisked or liquidised until smooth	Microwave boiling bag. Small plastic microware bowl.
3 tablespoons finely chopped parsley	

1 Place the cauliflower and water in the boiling bag. Secure with an elastic band, leaving a gap for steam to escape. Stand the bag in a container for support during cooking.

2 Microwave on high for 10–12 minutes until the stalks are just tender. Reposition the bag once during cooking.

3 Place the onion and oil in the small bowl. Cover and microwave on high for 2½ minutes, or until the onion is softened. Stir or shake once during cooking.

4 Stir in the tofu and microwave on high, uncovered, for 1½ minutes. Whisk after 1 minute and at the end of cooking.

5 Stir in the parsley, soy sauce and a little black pepper.

6 Drain the cauliflower and arrange in a serving dish. Spoon the sauce over and garnish with toasted nori.

Reheat: covered on medium for 5–6 minutes. Turn the dish once during this time. Garnish.

BEETROOT WITH YOGHURT, CARAWAY AND CHIVES

Serves 4

Try to choose beetroot of a similar size to promote even cooking.
Baby beets cook the fastest and large beetroot will require turning once
during the cooking time. This dish is equally good served hot or cold.

INGREDIENTS	
1 lb/500 g raw beetroot, washed and pricked all over	2 teaspoons chopped chives or finely chopped spring onion tops
4 tablespoons water	**Container**
herb salt, black pepper	7 in/18 cm ovenproof glass soufflé dish.
3 fl oz/75 ml natural yoghurt	Decrease timing by 2 minutes when using a plastic microware container.
1 teaspoon caraway seeds	

1 Stand the beetroot in the dish and add the water. Cover and microwave on high for 10–12 minutes, until fork tender. Turn the dish twice during cooking.

2 Plunge the beetroot into cold water for a few seconds, then peel.

3 Slice thinly and arrange in a shallow serving dish. Sprinkle lightly with herb salt and black pepper.

4 Drizzle over the yoghurt and sprinkle with caraway seeds and chives.

Reheat: before garnishing, covered on high for approximately 2½ minutes.

RED BEAN AND COURGETTE CASSEROLE

Serves 2 as a main course, 4 as an accompaniment

This makes a high protein main course and goes well with rice or pasta
and a green salad.

INGREDIENTS	
1 teaspoon olive oil	1 teaspoon oregano
1 small onion, finely chopped	black pepper, salt
1 clove garlic, crushed	3 oz/75 g grated cheese
8 oz/250 g courgettes, thinly sliced	a little chopped parsley for garnish
8 oz/250 g can tomatoes, crushed with their juice	**Container**
6 oz/175 g can red kidney beans, drained	7 in/18 cm round plastic microware dish.
2 oz/50 g button mushrooms, thinly sliced	Increase timing by 2 minutes when using ovenproof glass or ceramic container.

1 Place the oil, onion and garlic in the dish. Cover and microwave on high for 2 minutes.
2 Add the courgettes, tomatoes, beans, mushrooms, oregano and pepper. Stir well.
3 Cover and microwave on high for 5–6 minutes, until boiling and the courgettes are just fork tender. Stir once during cooking. An extra minute or two may need to be added to this cooking time; larger, more mature courgettes will take longer than small, young ones.
4 Remove the cover, adjust seasoning to taste and sprinkle on the grated cheese.
5 Without covering, microwave on medium until the cheese melts. Garnish with parsley.
Reheat: covered on medium for 4–5 minutes. Turn dish once during this time.

BAKED PUMPKIN

Serves 4

Pumpkin looks tempting during the autumn months and this recipe is a quick and easy way of preparing the flesh. It can be served as an accompanying vegetable for fish, lamb and egg dishes, or placed (cooked) between pastry for a pie. No additional liquid is required as pumpkins contain a lot of water. Pumpkin also makes a delicious soup when cooked with tomatoes, onion and spices.

◆ 81

INGREDIENTS

1 lb/500 g pumpkin, peeled, seeded and cut into ½ in/1 cm pieces	**Container**
½ oz/15 g sunflower margarine	Shallow, oval plastic microware dish with lid. Increase timing by 1 minute when using ovenproof glass or ceramic container.
herb salt, black pepper	
finely chopped parsley for garnish	

1 Put the pumpkin into the dish and dot with margarine.
2 Cover and microwave on high for 5 minutes, stirring twice during cooking.
3 Season lightly and sprinkle with parsley to garnish.
Reheat: covered on high for 2 minutes. Stir once during this time.

CARROTS WITH ORANGE AND HERBS

Serves 4

Carrots and other root vegetables are denser than the more watery types and will take longer to cook as the microwaves are not able to penetrate them so efficiently. Always cook in a shallow container so that the vegetables can be well spread out, or cook in a boiling bag.
Salt at the end of cooking and only cook for the minimum time.
Overcooked root vegetables turn out dry and hard.
It is worth noting that it is virtually impossible to cook carrots to the 'almost disintegrating' stage; there is always a little bite remaining after microwaving. For those who prefer carrots very soft I would recommend that they continue to cook them in the conventional way.
To microwave carrots further in the hope that the distintegration stage can be reached will only result in tough, leathery carrots.
The herbs can be varied – fresh chopped tarragon or marjoram are also very good.

INGREDIENTS	
1 lb/500 g carrots, sliced thinly on diagonal or cut into matchsticks	1 tablespoon finely chopped fresh parsley
4 tablespoons pure orange juice	herb salt
½ oz/15 g sunflower margarine	**Container**
black pepper	Shallow, oval plastic microware dish with lid. Increase timing by 2 minutes when using ovenproof glass or ceramic container.
1 tablespoon snipped chives or 1 spring onion, sliced thinly on diagonal	

1 Place the carrots in the dish. Pour over the orange juice, and dot with margarine. Sprinkle on a little black pepper and the chives or spring onion.
2 Cover and microwave on high for 12 minutes, until just tender. Shake or stir twice during cooking.
3 Sprinkle with parsley and a little herb salt. Stand for 2 minutes before serving.
Reheat: covered on high for approximately 3 minutes. Stir once during this time.

WHOLEWHEAT AND WALNUT STUFFED MUSHROOMS WITH TOFU TOPPING

Serves 2 or 4

This makes a substantial vegetarian dish for 2 people, or a first course for 4. Cook the mushrooms until they are just tender as overcooking will toughen them.

INGREDIENTS

4 large open flat mushrooms, each weighing approximately 3 oz/75 g, wiped	1–2 teaspoons natural soy sauce (shoyu)
	black pepper
	2 oz/50 g firm tofu
1 medium onion, finely chopped	**Containers**
1 teaspoon oregano	Medium plastic microware bowl.
2 oz/50 g walnuts, chopped	Round, shallow 11 in/28 cm ovenproof glass dish.
1 egg, beaten	Decrease overall cooking time by 30 seconds when using plastic microware container.
1 tablespoon finely chopped coriander or parsley leaves	
3 oz/75 g fresh wholewheat breadcrumbs	

1 Remove the stalks from mushrooms and chop the stalks finely. Place the stalks in the bowl with the onion and oregano.
2 Cover and microwave on high for 3 minutes, or until the onion is tender. Stir once during cooking.
3 Mix the walnuts, egg, coriander or parsley leaves and breadcrumbs with the cooked onion. Add soy sauce and black pepper to taste. Mix together thoroughly.
4 Place the mushroom caps in the dish. Divide the stuffing equally beween the 4 mushrooms, pressing down slightly.
5 Microwave uncovered on high for 3½ minutes. Give each mushroom a half turn and turn the container. Continue to cook for a further 2½ minutes, until the mushrooms are just tender.
6 Place the tofu on a plate and brush with soy sauce. Microwave on high for 1 minute.
7 Slice the tofu into thin strips and place on top of the mushrooms.
8 If not using an ovenproof dish to this point transfer and place under a preheated grill to lightly toast the tops.
Reheat: these are best served soon after they are cooked, although the filling and tofu topping can be prepared well in advance.

◆ 83

GERMAN RED CABBAGE

Serves 6

This is traditionally cooked in a casserole in the conventional oven on a very low setting and requires 2–3 hours cooking. A great deal of time is saved by using the microwave, and the colours are much brighter and flavours more pronounced. It is excellent with pork and other meat dishes, and can be served hot or cold. I serve it cold as an hors-d'oeuvre with other salad dishes.

INGREDIENTS

1 lb/500 g red cabbage, finely shredded	½ teaspoon cinnamon
8 oz/250 g cooking apples, peeled cored and sliced thinly	½ teaspoon mixed spice
	black pepper, herb salt
1 medium onion, finely chopped	natural yoghurt for garnish
1 clove garlic, crushed	**Container**
2 tablespoons red wine vinegar	Large plastic microware bowl. Increase timing by approximately 2 minutes when using ovenproof glass or ceramic container.
2 tablespoons soft brown sugar	
2 level teaspoons wholegrain French mustard	
a little grated nutmeg	

84 ◆

1 Place all the ingredients, except the salt, in the bowl and mix together well.
2 Cover and microwave on high for approximately 15 minutes, until just tender. Stir 3 times during cooking.
3 Stand for 5 minutes, adjust seasoning to taste and garnish with a swirl of natural yoghurt.
Reheat: before garnishing, covered on high for 4–5 minutes. Stir once during this time.

LEMON TARRAGON SCORZONERA

Serves 4

Scorzonera is a mild flavoured, long, thin, black-skinned root;
use a vegetable peeler to peel thinly. Discard the dark skin and put the root
immediately in a bowl of water acidulated with lemon juice to prevent
discoloration. Salsify can be prepared in exactly the same way.
Extra cream can be added at the end of cooking if more sauce is required.
This dish is best served freshly cooked.

INGREDIENTS

1 lb/500 g scorzonera, peeled thinly and placed in acidulated water	½ oz/15 g unsalted butter
3 tablespoons unsalted vegetable or chicken stock or water	black pepper
	2 tablespoons single cream
juice of ½ lemon	salt
2 teaspoons finely chopped fresh tarragon, plus a few sprigs for garnish	**Container** Shallow plastic microware dish. Increase timing by 1½ minutes when using ovenproof glass or ceramic container.
2 sprigs lemon thyme (optional)	
1 teaspoon snipped chives	

◆ 85

1 Slice the scorzonera diagonally into ½ in/1 cm lengths and place in the
dish with the stock, lemon juice, herbs, butter and black pepper.
2 Cover and microwave on high for 12–13 minutes, or until just fork tender.
Stir twice during cooking.
3 Stir in the cream. Cover and microwave on high for 1 minute. Stir well and
adjust seasoning to taste. Stand, covered, for 2 minutes before serving.
Reheat: prepare to end of step 2. Cover and microwave on high for
4 minutes. Stir once during this time. Add the cream and microwave for a
further minute.

CHAYOTE SQUASH STUFFED WITH GRUYERE AND OYSTER MUSHROOMS

Serves 4

A pleasant light lunch or supper dish, best eaten immediately rather than cooled and reheated, which spoils the apperance of the dish. The turntable or oven floor must be lined with a double layer of white kitchen paper to absorb the large quantity of liquid from the vegetables during cooking. Chayote squash often requires 30 minutes to cook when boiled conventionally. Because of their high water content, cooking time is reduced considerably in the microwave. The flavour is also improved.

INGREDIENTS

2 chayote squash, each weighing approximately 10 oz/300 g	2 oz/50 g small or medium oyster mushrooms
4 oz/125 g fresh rye breadcrumbs (the type with caraway seeds)	**Container** Shallow flameproof glass or ceramic dish. Decrease timing by 1 minute when using plastic microware container.
2 medium spring onions, finely chopped	
4 oz/125 g grated Gruyère cheese,	
salt, black pepper	

86 ◆

1 Line the turntable or oven floor with a double layer of white kitchen paper. Wash the chayote, prick all over, and arrange on the paper with the thinner ends towards the centre and the fatter ends towards the outside edges of the turntable or oven cavity.

2 Microwave uncovered on high for 5 minutes. Turn over and continue to cook for a further 5 minutes on high, until fork tender. Wrap in kitchen paper and leave to cool.

3 Slit in half lengthways and carefully remove most of the flesh, leaving a ½ in/1 cm shell. Do this carefully so as not to damage the shells. (I find a small serrated palette knife the ideal tool for this, but you could use a teaspoon or a grapefruit knife.) Chop the flesh roughly, together with the seeds which add extra flavour. Stand the shells, cut side down, on absorbent paper to drain further.

4 Mix the chopped flesh with the breadcrumbs, spring onions and 3 oz/75 g of the cheese. Adjust seasoning to taste.

5 Divide this mixture between the shells, pressing down gently then rounding the top slightly.

6 Place the shells in a flameproof dish and microwave uncovered on medium for 5 minutes to reheat the mixture. Preheat the grill.

7 Sprinkle over the remaining cheese and arrange the oyster mushrooms attractively on top. Grill until golden and bubbling, and serve straight away.
Reheat: not recommended.

KOHLRABI WITH CHICK PEA AND OLIVE PATE

Serves 2 or 4

An excellent starter or vegetarian main course which can be served either warm or cold. The stuffed kohlrabi will keep in the refrigerator for up to 3 days but must be covered and chilled as soon as they have cooled. Cook the chick peas conventionally until they are quite tender. A 1 in/2.5 cm piece of washed kombu seaweed (available from some health food shops) added to the water helps to soften the chick peas and also imparts a sweet flavour. The resulting stock is very nutritious and has a good flavour. Light or dark tahini can be used, but I prefer the darker version which has a stronger flavour.

INGREDIENTS

2 medium kohlrabi, each weighing approximately 10 oz/300 g	1 tablespoon tahini
	1 tablespoon finely chopped fresh parsley
4 tablespoons water or light unsalted vegetable or chicken stock	juice of 1 lemon and a little zest
	salt, black pepper
1 medium onion, chopped	a few sprigs of parsley, oregano or marjoram for garnish
1 clove garlic, crushed	
1 tablespoon olive oil	**Containers**
1 tablespoon finely chopped fresh oregano or marjoram	Shallow plastic microware dish. Small plastic microware bowl. Increase timing for the kohlrabi by 2 minutes and for the onion and garlic by 1 minute when using ovenproof glass or ceramic containers.
8 oz/250 g cooked chick peas or 14 oz/425 g can chick peas, rinsed in cold water and drained	
about 20 calamata olives, stoned and chopped	

◆ 87

1 Remove any stalks and knobbly bits from the kohlrabi; cut a slice off the top, then cut each one in half horizontally.
2 Arrange the kohlrabi halves, cut side uppermost, in the dish. Spoon over the water or stock and microwave covered on high for 10 minutes, or until fork tender. Give each kohlrabi a half turn halfway through cooking time so that the parts positioned towards the outside of the dish are now at the centre.
3 Stand, covered, until almost cold. Drain off the liquid and use as stock in other dishes. Using a teaspoon or small serrated knife, remove most of the flesh, leaving a ½ in/1 cm shell.
4 Put the onion, garlic and olive oil into the bowl. Cover and microwave on high for 3 minutes until softened. Shake the bowl once during cooking. Stir in the oregano or marjoram.
5 Blend the kohlrabi flesh, chick peas and softened onion together in a processor until fairly smooth. Transfer to a bowl and stir in the olives, tahini

and parsley. Mix together thoroughly and add lemon juice, salt and black pepper to taste.

6 Pile the mixture into the shells, drawing the mixture into a dome with a fork.

7 Garnish with sprigs of herbs, olives and lemon zest. Serve warm or cover and chill.

CUSTARD MARROWS WITH RICE AND MACADAMIA NUTS

Serves 2 or 4

Serve as a starter or vegetarian main course. Custard marrows have a sweet flavour and look most attractive with a filling of rice and nuts. For a really special occasion use wild rice. Macadamia nuts can be obtained from some supermarkets. Their leguminous flavour and crunchy texture combine well with the other ingredients in this dish. Takuan pickle is pickled mooli (white radish or daikon); tan in colour, it can be sliced thinly and makes an attractive garnish. Alternatively, thin slices of pink sushi ginger could be used. Both of these specialist ingredients can be obtained from oriental stores or the Clearspring Grocer (p.209). This dish is best served freshly cooked.

INGREDIENTS

4 custard marrows, each weighing approximately 4 oz/125 g and about 4 in/10 cm across	black pepper
	1 in/2.5 cm piece pickled daikon radish (takuan pickle), sliced thinly for garnish
1 clove garlic, crushed	**Containers**
1 medium spring onion, finely chopped	Shallow plastic microware dish.
½ teaspoon finely grated fresh root ginger	Small plastic microware bowl. Plastic microware serving dish.
1 teaspoon toasted sesame oil (p.209)	Increase timing for the custard marrows by 2 minutes and for the garlic and spring onion
2 heaped tablespoons cooked rice	by 1 minute when using ovenproof glass or
3 oz/75 g macadamia nuts, chopped	ceramic containers.
soy sauce	

1 Slice a piece off the top of each custard marrow and prick the skins.
2 Put the marrows, cut side down, in the dish. Cover and microwave on high for 4 minutes. Turn over and give each a half turn.
3 Cover and microwave on high for a further 4 minutes, until fork tender. Stand, covered, for 5 minutes.
4 Using a teaspoon scoop out the flesh carefully, leaving a ½ in/1 cm shell. Chop the flesh finely.

5 Put the garlic, spring onion, ginger and sesame oil into the bowl. Cover and microwave on high for 1 minute.

6 Stir in the chopped flesh, rice and nuts, and season to taste with a little soy sauce and black pepper. Mix all the ingredients together thoroughly.

7 Fill each marrow carefully, pressing the mixture down into the shells and mounding the tops neatly.

8 Transfer to the serving dish. Cover and microwave on high for 3 minutes until heated through.

9 Sprinkle the tops with soy sauce and garnish with thin slices of pickled daikon radish.

Reheat: prepare to end of step 7. Cover and microwave on high for 3½ minutes. Give the dish a half turn once during this time.

MARINATED TOFU TRIANGLES

Serves 4

The completed dish is brightly coloured and makes an excellent light starter or accompaniment to a main course. It can be served chilled, in which case moisten the chard with leftover marinade or French dressing before serving. I was fortunate to get organically grown ruby chard when I first made this dish and the vibrant red veins and green leaves looked most attractive after microwaving. (Ruby chard can be obtained from some supermarkets and health food shops.) Dandelion, spinach or sorrel leaves, or a mixture of these, can be substituted for the chard.

INGREDIENTS	
8 oz/250 g block firm tofu (4 × 3½ × 1 in/ 10 ×8 ×2.5 cm) .	**Marinade** 1 tablespoon olive oil
4 oz/125 g carrots, grated	2 tablespoons brown rice vinegar or red wine vinegar
seeds from 4 green cardamom pods	1 clove garlic, crushed
2 tablespoons unsalted light vegetable or chicken stock	2 or 3 sprigs of fresh thyme
	1 teaspoon soy sauce
4 oz/125 g ruby chard leaves, washed, drained, piled one on top of the other and sliced diagonally into ½ in/1 cm strips	black pepper
	Containers Microwave boiling bags. Ceramic serving dish.
salt, black pepper	Decrease timing by 30 seconds when using plastic microware dish.
4 roasted salted almonds	

1 Mix the marinade ingredients together in a medium bowl.

2 Cut the tofu from corner to corner to make 4 triangles. Mark a ½ in/1 cm border around each triangle then, using a sharp teaspoon, scoop out some of the tofu until you are left with an attractive shell. Take care not to damage the base of each triangle as it will be stuffed with the carrot mixture. (Use the scooped out tofu in other dishes.)

3 Put the triangles into the marinade, spooning it into the hollows. Cover and refrigerate for 6 hours or overnight.

4 Put the carrots, cardamom seeds and stock into a boiling bag. Secure the top loosely with an elastic band.

5 Put the chard into a boiling bag and secure in the same way.

6 Position both bags on the turntable or oven floor. Microwave on high for 5 minutes. Rearrange bags halfway through cooking.

7 Stand for 2 minutes then drain the chard, season lightly and put to one side.

8 Blend the carrots and any liquid in a processor until fairly smooth. Add 2 teaspoons of the marinade to moisten further and season to taste.

9 Fill the hollows in the tofu with the carrot mixture, mounding it up neatly, then push 1 almond into the filling of each triangle. Arrange the tofu triangles like the spokes of a wheel on the serving dish and scatter the chard in between.

10 Drizzle a little of the remaining marinade over the top.

11 Cover and microwave on high for 3½ minutes, until heated through. Give the dish a half turn once during cooking.

Reheat: prepare to end of step 9. Drizzle over a little of the remaining marinade, cover and microwave on high for 4 minutes. Give the dish a half turn once during this time.

BROAD BEANS WITH LAVERBREAD AND GARLIC CROUTONS

Serves 4

The sweet, rich flavour of laverbread (Porphyra umbiliculis) (p.208) blends perfectly with broad beans, and the crunchiness of the croûtons completes this colourful dish. A perfect accompaniment for meat, poultry, fish and vegetarian main course meals, and equally good when served cold with a variety of salads.

INGREDIENTS	
garlic croûtons (p.35)	1 heaped tablespoon laverbread
8 oz/250 g shelled broad beans (1½ lb/750 g in shells will yield approximately 8 oz/250 g)	**Container** Shallow plastic microware dish. Increase timing by 2 minutes when using ovenproof glass or ceramic dish.
2 tablespoons unsalted vegetable or chicken stock or water	

1 Prepare and cook the croûtons as on page 35.

2 Put the beans in the dish with the stock or water. Cover and microwave on high for 3 minutes. Stir once during cooking.

3 Mix the laverbread with the beans. Cover and microwave on high for

1½ minutes. Stand for 2 minutes, then stir in the croûtons. If the croûtons have cooled down, reheat them by spreading on a plate and microwaving uncovered on high for 30 seconds.

Reheat: without the croûtons, cover and microwave on high for 3 minutes. Stir once during this time. Briefly reheat the croûtons separately then stir into the beans.

FRENCH BEANS AND BABY CORN

Serves 4

Toasted sesame oil imparts a nutty flavour to the French beans and baby corn cobs. It is quite strong and is used in small quantities or combined with other oils. This makes an excellent accompaniment for poultry, pork or vegetarian dishes. Runner beans or broad beans could replace the French beans in this recipe.

INGREDIENTS

4 tablespoons unsalted vegetable stock or water	6 oz/175 g baby corn
	soy sauce
1 teaspoon finely grated fresh root ginger	1 teaspoon sesame seeds
	Container
3 teaspoons toasted sesame oil	Shallow plastic microware dish.
6 oz/175 g French beans, topped and tailed	Increase timing by 2 minutes when using ovenproof glass or ceramic dish.

◆ 91

1 Mix the stock, ginger and oil together in the dish. Stir in the beans and corn.

2 Cover and microwave on high for 4 minutes. Stir well, cover and cook for a further 4 minutes.

3 Add soy sauce to taste and sprinkle with the sesame seeds. Cover and stand for 2 minutes.

Reheat: covered on high for 3 minutes. Shake the dish once during this time.

ASPARAGUS WITH UMEBOSHI DRESSING

Serves 3–4

Asparagus cooks beautifully in the microwave and this unusual dressing, based on the sweet/sour flavoured Japanese umeboshi plum, does not overpower the flavour.

Umeboshi plums are salty and, apart from black pepper, no additional seasoning is required. Although asparagus is best served freshly cooked, if the umeboshi dressing is poured over and the dish cooled and well chilled, the umeboshi 'pickles' the asparagus, which is very pleasant and most refreshing on a hot day. Umeboshi paste or plums can be bought from oriental stores or from the Clearspring Grocer (p.209).

INGREDIENTS

12 oz/375 g asparagus, woody ends trimmed and stems peeled thinly	**Containers**
	Shallow plastic microware dish.
1 rounded teaspoon umeboshi paste or 1 umeboshi plum, crushed	Small plastic microware jug or bowl. Increase timing by 1½ minutes for the asparagus and for the dressing by 15 seconds when using ovenproof glass or ceramic containers.
1 tablespoon olive oil	
3 tablespoons light unsalted vegetable stock or water	
black pepper	
a little finely grated orange zest	

1 Arrange the asparagus in a shallow dish so that half the tips are at either end. Cover the tips with the stalks.

2 Cover and microwave on high for 7 minutes. Rearrange halfway through cooking so that the asparagus at the edges of the dish are now in the centre and vice versa. Cook until the stems are just tender.

3 Mix the remaining ingredients together in the jug or bowl.

4 Microwave uncovered on high for 1 minute. Pour over the asparagus and sprinkle with the orange zest.

Reheat: not recommended. Asparagus should be served freshly cooked.

FRENCH BEANS, AUBERGINES AND HERBS

Serves 4

This succulent combination of vegetables has a prominent herb flavour and can be served hot or chilled. It makes a good accompaniment to pasta and fish, or a filling for pancakes and omelettes.

A larger proportion of herbs can be used; chervil, chives, marjoram or summer savory could replace the basil; add them with the oregano.

INGREDIENTS	
1 shallot, finely chopped	black pepper
2 tablespoons olive oil	1 tablespoon finely chopped fresh oregano
1 large aubergine (about 12 oz/375 g) sliced into 4 lengthways then cut into ¼ in/5 mm thick slices	about 6 fresh basil leaves, torn into shreds
8 oz/250 g French beans, topped and tailed, then cut diagonally into 1 in/2.5 cm pieces	salt
8 oz/250 g beefsteak tomatoes, peeled and roughly chopped	**Container** Shallow plastic microware dish. Increase timing by 2 minutes when using ovenproof glass or ceramic dish.
large sprig of fresh rosemary	

◆ 93

1 Put the shallot and olive oil into the dish. Cover and microwave on high for 1 minute.
2 Add the aubergine, beans, tomatoes, rosemary and some black pepper. Mix well.
3 Cover and microwave on high for 10 minutes. Stir twice during cooking.
4 Stir in the oregano. Cover and microwave on high for a further 3 minutes, until the vegetables are just fork tender. Stand, covered, for 2 minutes.
5 Stir in the torn basil leaves and adjust seasoning to taste.
Reheat: covered on high for 4 minutes. Stir once during this time.

RED RADISH WITH NATTO PICKLE

Serves 4

This pretty side dish can be served warm or chilled, with fish or poultry.
Alternatively serve cool as a relish.
Choose radishes that are all similar in size and spend time cutting them
into roses, as they open up during cooking.
Natto is a Japanese pickle made from miso, barley, seaweed and vegetables.
It has a delicious sweet flavour and can be obtained from oriental stores
or the Clearspring Grocer (p.209).

INGREDIENTS

3 shallots, finely chopped	2 heaped teaspoons natto pickle
2 teaspoons sunflower oil	black pepper
5 oz/150 g medium red radishes, each cut to form a rose	**Container**
juice of 1 lime	Shallow plastic microware dish. Increase the timing by 2 minutes when using ovenproof glass or ceramic dish.
3 in/7 cm piece cucumber, draw a fork to score through the skin all the way down, slice into four lengthways then cut into ¼ in/5 mm thick pieces	

94 ◆

1 Put the shallots and oil in the dish. Cover and microwave on high for 1 minute.
2 Stir in the radishes and lime juice. Cover and microwave on high for 2 minutes. Shake the dish once during cooking.
3 Stir in the cucumber. Cover and microwave on high for 1 minute.
4 Add the natto pickle and mix well. Cover and microwave on high for a further minute.
5 Stand, covered, for 2 minutes, then season with black pepper.
Reheat: covered on high for 2½ minutes. Shake the dish halfway through.

FISH

Fish is extremely nutritious, being high in protein, calcium, vitamins A and D, various minerals and especially low in fat. Even the oilier types of fish have less than 20% fat of which a healthy proportion is polyunsaturated. There are many advantages to microwaving fish. The fish doesn't shrink and shrivel or lose its shape; skin and bones are more easily removed; flavours and colours are enhanced and the result is a very appealing presentation. There are no lingering fishy odours in the kitchen and the cooking time is incredibly short – one medium-sized trout cooks in 2 minutes.

I would recommend that fresh fish is used in preference to frozen fish at all times. My experience has been that frozen white fish fillets microwave dismally compared to prime, fresh fillets. The texture of cooked frozen fish is rather watery, and, on close inspection after thawing, fillets can often be seen to be damaged or inferior. Fish should be purchased fresh, from a good reliable fishmonger and it is worth learning when different types of fish are in season to ensure that the fish you buy is at its best. If frozen fish is used then it should be cooked immediately after defrosting; thawed fish deteriorates rapidly. Fish can be microwaved in a number of different ways.

BAKING/STEAMING

Perhaps the best way of cooking fish. Simply arrange in the dish, cover, and cook for the appropriate time. No additional fat or liquid is required, so this method is ideal for weightwatchers and for healthier eating generally. Sprinkle the fish with a little lemon juice and black pepper before cooking but add salt at the end of cooking.

FRYING

With the use of a browning dish and very little oil, fish can be shallow fried after being lightly dusted with flour. Egg and breadcrumb coatings give you a fair result, but you may find that commercial coatings sometimes stick to the browning dish or fall off the fish during cooking. Fish fingers, however, can be successfully cooked from frozen. Preheat the browning dish for the recommended time, and add a teaspoonful of oil during the last 30 seconds. Cook uncovered and turn the fish fingers over halfway through cooking time. Ten fish fingers will take approximately 3½ minutes on a high setting.

Choose your fish fingers carefully; supermarkets are now introducing fish fingers made from first class ingredients, free from artificial additives, and my children enjoy these as an occasional treat.

Fish in breadcrumbs can be reheated successfully when placed on white kitchen paper. Fish in batter cannot be cooked or reheated by microwave without turning soggy.

Deep frying is not possible as the temperature of the fat cannot be controlled, and there would be a real risk of fire inside the oven cavity.

GRILLING

Grilling is a very popular way of cooking fish. The fish can first be cooked in the microwave without any additional fat or liquid, then lightly brushed with oil and placed under a preheated grill. Ensure that you cook the fish in a flameproof container. The fish will have a much better flavour than ordinary grilled fish when cooked this way.

POACHING

The microwave method of poaching requires much less liquid than conventional cooking; it should be reduced to 4 tablespoons whether it is wine, milk or stock. If too much liquid is added, the microwaves tend to concentrate in the liquid, rather than in the fish. The overall cooking time has to be increased, and there is a greater risk of fish being overcooked. Overcooked fish will be dry and tough.

A smoked fish containing a large quantity of salt is the only exception. Smoked fish takes longer to cook than white or oily fish; extra liquid is required to dilute the salt as it is drawn out of the fish during cooking. Smoked fish will need to be rearranged and turned over frequently. Lightly smoked fish, such as boil in the bag cutlets, are cooked without any additional liquid.

POSITIONING THE FISH IN THE MICROWAVE

Arrange fish fillets so that thicker parts are on the outside of the dish; overlap thinner bits and re-arrange, when necessary, during the cooking time. Fillets that are more than 1 in/2.5 cm thick must be turned over halfway through cooking. Fillets can also be rolled and positioned around the edges of the dish. Slash through the skins of whole fish two or three times before cooking; this prevents them from bursting as pressure builds up inside the fish during cooking.

SHIELDING

Small strips of foil can be wrapped around the heads and tails of whole fish to prevent these parts from overcooking and drying out. I find that when one or two medium sized fish are being cooked, shielding is not necessary as the overall cooking time is short. However, as the quantity of food increases, so does the cooking time, and three or more whole fish will require shielding.

Cook whole fish in an oval or oblong dish, arranging heads to tails. Halfway through cooking, turn over and reposition, by moving those on the outside of the dish to the centre. This can be tricky, as the fish are hot and fragile at this stage. Placing each fish on a strip of cling film or baking parchment before cooking will make this a lot easier. It will also prevent the fish skins from sticking together during cooking.

Apart from fried fish and whole salmon, fish is cooked covered, so that moisture is retained in the flesh. Salmon has a very thick skin, and this acts like a cover, protecting the flesh during cooking. Shellfish toughen very easily, and whenever possible should be cooked in shells for a minimum time.

Take great care when reheating fish dishes as they can easily dry out; some of the fish recipes in this chapter are best served straight away and this has been noted in their reheat instructions.

◆ 97

STEAMED FISH

Serves 4

This is a good way of cooking very fresh fish, particularly for those on fat-restricted diets and for slimmers. No water is required in this recipe.

INGREDIENTS

1 lb/500 g white fish fillets	**Container**
lemon juice	Shallow, oval plastic microware dish.
salt, pepper	Increase timing by 30 seconds when using ovenproof glass or ceramic dish.
Garnish	
parsley sprigs	
lemon wedges	

1 Wash the fish and pat dry on absorbent kitchen paper. Arrange the fish in the dish, positioning the thicker parts towards the outside edges and thinner parts towards the centre.
2 Cover and microwave on high for 4–4½ minutes or until the fish flakes. Overall time will depend on the thickness of the fillets. Reposition as necessary halfway through the cooking time. Very thick fillets will need turning over.

3 Stand, covered, for 2 minutes. Sprinkle on a little lemon juice, salt and pepper, and garnish with lemon wedges and parsley sprigs.

Smoked fish
Add 2 tablespoons cold water per 1 lb/500 g fish. The salt content in smoked fish affects the cooking time so allow up to 30 seconds longer per 1 lb/500 g fish.

Oily fish
Oily fish tends to cook faster, so decrease the cooking time by 30 seconds per 1 lb/500 g fish.

Reheat: not recommended.

KIPPERS

Serves 4

Kippers microwave well and always have a good flavour.
Boil in the bag kippers can be cooked in the plastic pouch, but slit it first to prevent it bursting during cooking. Stand the plastic pouch on a plate and always defrost the kippers before cooking because they do not cook evenly when cooked from frozen.

INGREDIENTS	
1 lb/500 g kippers	**Container**
butter or sunflower margarine	Shallow oval plastic microware dish.
lemon juice, parsley (optional)	Increase timing by 30 seconds when using ovenproof glass or ceramic dish.

1 Lay the kippers in the dish, skin side down. Arrange them so that the widest parts of the fish are at the outside edges and the thinner parts are towards the centre.
2 Cover and microwave on high for 4–4½ minutes. Check halfway through the cooking time and rearrange the fillets as necessary.
3 Stand, covered, for 2 minutes. The kippers can be dotted with a little butter or margarine and sprinkled with lemon juice and parsley after cooking.
Reheat: not recommended.

ORANGE STUFFED TROUT

Serves 2

Orange partners trout perfectly and makes a change from lemon which is so often served with this fish. This recipe is for two servings – for four, double up on all the ingredients and cook 2 at a time. When 4 trout are cooked together in the same dish shield heads and tails with foil. To prevent the skins sticking together place strips of cling film between each fish. Turn and reposition once during cooking. Cooking 2 at a time saves all this bother.

INGREDIENTS

½ oz/15 g sunflower margarine	2 medium trout (each weighing approximately 8 oz/250 g), gutted, washed and patted dry
1 small onion, finely chopped	
2 oz/50 g fresh wholewheat breadcrumbs or 1 oz/25 g fresh wholewheat breadcrumbs and 1 oz/25 g pine kernels	**Containers** Medium plastic bowl. Shallow oval plastic microware dish. Increase timing by 30 seconds when using ovenproof glass or ceramic dish.
1 tablespoon finely chopped fresh parsley	
grated zest of 1 orange	
3 tablespoons orange juice	
herb salt, black pepper	

◆ 99

1 Place the margarine in the bowl and microwave on high until just melted.
2 Stir in the onion, cover and microwave on high for 3 minutes or until the onion softens.
3 Stir in the breadcrumbs (and pine kernels if used), parsley, orange zest and juice. Season lightly with salt and black pepper. Mix thoroughly.
4 Slash the skin of each trout twice on either side. Lay the trout in the shallow dish.
5 Fill each fish with the stuffing, pressing it in firmly – don't worry if it spills out a little.
6 Cover and microwave on high for 3½–4 minutes until just tender. Take care not to overcook. Test by inserting a sharp knife into the thickest part of the flesh.
7 Stand for 2 minutes.
Reheat: not recommended as the fish can easily dry out and overcook. However, the stuffing can be made in advance.

SARDINES WITH WHOLEWHEAT TOPPING

Serves 1

Cheap, simple and delicious, this makes a light lunch or supper for 1 or, with salad or vegetables, for 2.

INGREDIENTS

1 small onion, finely chopped	1 small tomato, sliced thinly
½ level teaspoon sunflower margarine	good pinch of mixed dried herbs
4 tablespoons fresh wholewheat breadcrumbs	**Containers**
salt, black pepper	Small plastic microware bowl. Increase timing by 30 seconds when using ovenproof glass or ceramic bowl. Dinner plate.
squeeze of lemon juice	
4 sardines, fresh or frozen (4 oz/125 g total weight)	

1 Place the onion and margarine in the bowl. Cover and microwave on high for 2½ minutes. Stir once during cooking.

2 Stir in the breadcrumbs, a little salt and black pepper, and a squeeze of lemon juice. Put to one side while preparing the fish.

3 Remove the heads and tails and gut the sardines. Open out flat and remove the backbone if preferred. Arrange on a dinner plate, skin side down, with the widest parts of the fish towards the outside edges and the thinner parts towards the centre.

4 Spoon the filling over the fish, pressing down lightly, and top with the slices of tomato. Sprinkle the herbs over the tomatoes.

5 Microwave uncovered on high for 1½ minutes.

6 Stand for 2 minutes.

Reheat: not recommended.

100 ◆

CHINESE FISH WITH GINGER

Serves 4

This is one of my favourite ways of preparing fish, and I like to serve it with plenty of hot savoury rice or noodles and a mixed salad. Any type of white fish can be used in this recipe.

INGREDIENTS

1 lb/500 g cod fillets, washed and patted dry	2 teaspoons sunflower oil
	1 teaspoon sesame oil
6 tablespoons fish or vegetable stock or water	1 teaspoon arrowroot dissolved in a little cold water
2 spring onions, sliced thinly on diagonal	1–2 teaspoons natural soy sauce (shoyu)
1 in/2.5 cm piece of fresh root ginger, peeled and sliced into thin matchsticks	**Containers** Shallow oval flameproof dish. Large microware jug.
1 clove garlic, crushed	Increase cooking time by 1 minute when using ovenproof glass jug.
black pepper	

1 Place the fish in the shallow dish, arranging thicker parts towards the outside edges and thinner parts towards the centre. Add the stock or water, and sprinkle over 1 of the spring onions, the ginger, garlic and a little black pepper.

2 Cover and microwave on high for 4–5 minutes, until the fish is just done. Reposition the fish halfway through the cooking time if necessary.

3 Pour the juices from the dish into the jug. Add extra stock or water to make up to ¼ pt/150 ml. Put to one side.

4 Preheat a grill. Mix the sunflower and sesame oils and brush over the fish. Grill until the top is lightly browned.

5 Meanwhile, place the jug containing the fish stock in the microwave and cook on high until boiling.

6 Stir in the dissolved arrowroot and soy sauce.

7 Microwave uncovered on high for 1 minute, stirring after 30 seconds, until boiling. The sauce should thicken and clear. Do not allow the sauce to continue cooking once boiling point is reached.

8 Pour the sauce over the grilled fish and sprinkle with the remaining spring onion.

Reheat: not recommended.

◆ 101

SALMON STEAKS IN WHITE WINE

Serves 4 (see colour plate 4)

Salmon has a superb flavour when microwaved and can be finished under a preheated grill at the end of cooking if preferred.
Serve with Brown Rice Salad (p.55) and a mixed green salad of watercress, cucumber and lettuce.
The steaks used in this recipe are 1 in/2.5 cm thick; thicker steaks will need turning at least once during cooking, and the overall cooking time will need to be increased slightly. Take great care with the timing and cook until the thickest parts are just tender.

INGREDIENTS	
four 6 oz/175 g salmon steaks, washed and patted dry	herb salt, black pepper
	dill sprigs for garnish
½ oz/15 g sunflower margarine	**Container**
1 teaspoon finely chopped fresh dill	Shallow oval plastic microware dish.
4 slices lemon	Increase timing by 1½–2 minutes when using ovenproof glass or ceramic dish.
6 tablespoons dry white wine	

102 ◆

1 Fold the thinner ends of the fish steaks in towards the centre and secure with wooden cocktail sticks. Arrange in a shallow dish so that any wider parts are positioned towards the outside of the dish, and thinner parts are towards the centre.

2 Dot each fish steak with the margarine, and sprinkle with the chopped dill. Place a slice of lemon on each fish steak and spoon over the wine.

3 Cover and microwave on high for 3 minutes. Turn and reposition the fish steaks. Spoon the wine over and continue to cook for a further 2–2½ minutes until the fish flakes. Watch carefully; do not overcook. Season.

4 Stand for 2 minutes, or transfer the steaks to a flameproof plate and brown lightly under a preheated grill. Alternatively, heat a metal skewer over a gas flame and sear the top of each steak.

5 Garnish the top of each salmon steak with a sprig of fresh dill and a cooked lemon slice.

Reheat: not recommended.

MEDITERRANEAN FISH

Serves 4

This looks spectacular and yet is simple to make.
Keep the seasoning light – remember, olives are salty.

INGREDIENTS

1 small red pepper, finely diced	4 haddock fillets, approximately
1 small yellow pepper, finely diced	4 oz/125 g each
2 tablespoons finely chopped onion	salt (optional)
1 medium courgette, sliced thinly	2 tablespoons finely chopped
1 tablespoon olive oil	fresh parsley
1 teaspoon torn fresh basil leaves or	lemon slices
½ teaspoon dried basil	**Containers**
8 black olives, stones removed and	Medium plastic microware bowl.
roughly chopped	Shallow oval plastic microware dish.
6 tablespoons passata	Increase the timing by 1–2 minutes when
(sieved canned tomatoes)	using ovenproof glass or ceramic dish;
black pepper	2–2½ minutes for ovenproof glass or ceramic bowl.

♦ 103

1 Place the peppers, onion, courgette, olive oil and dried basil (add fresh basil later) in the bowl.
2 Cover and microwave on high for 4 minutes. Stir once during cooking.
3 Stir in the chopped olives, passata and black pepper. Microwave uncovered on high for 1 minute. Stir well.
4 Lay the fish in the shallow dish. Arrange thicker parts towards the outside of the dish and thinner parts towards the centre.
5 Cover and microwave on high for 2 minutes. Reposition the fish fillets and continue to cook for a further 2–2½ minutes, until the fish is almost cooked.
6 Spoon over the vegetable mixture – add the fresh basil at this stage. Adjust seasoning to taste.
7 Cover and microwave on high for 2 minutes, until heated through.
Garnish with parsley and lemon slices.
Reheat: not recommended, although the sauce can be prepared in advance.

POACHED FISH BALLS WITH DILL PICKLE SAUCE

Serves 4

Matzo meal produces very light and fine textured fish balls. The sauce is slightly piquant and I prefer to use dill pickles in brine, rather than those pickled in vinegar. Serve with saffron rice and lightly cooked vegetables.

INGREDIENTS

1 small egg	1 oz/25 g plain flour
¼ pt/150 ml cold water or fish stock	4 oz/125 g finely chopped dill pickles
2 oz/50 g fine matzo meal	2 tablespoons single cream or
½ teaspoon baking powder	natural yoghurt
1 lb/500 g haddock, skin and bones removed	1 teaspoon French mustard
	paprika
1 oz/25 g onion, finely chopped	**Containers**
1 tablespoon finely chopped fresh parsley or dill	Shallow plastic microware dish. Increase timing by 1–2 minutes when using ovenproof glass or ceramic container.
salt, pepper	Large plastic microware jug.
½ pt/300 ml skimmed milk, mixed with ¼ pt/150 ml cold water	Increase timing by 30 seconds when using ovenproof glass or ceramic jug.
1 oz/25 g sunflower margarine	

104 ◆

1 Beat the egg and cold water or fish stock together in a bowl. Stir in the matzo meal and baking powder and mix thoroughly together. Stand for 5 minutes.

2 The next part can be done in one of the following ways:

Food processor or blender method
Blend together the matzo mixture, fish, onion, parsley or dill, salt and pepper. Process until almost smooth.

Mincer method
Mince the fish and onion twice. Add to the matzo mixture together with the parsley or dill, salt and pepper. Mix thoroughly.

3 Next, form into 16 balls. It is easiest to do this with wet hands.

4 Pour ¼ pt/150 ml of the mixed milk and water into the dish. Microwave uncovered on high until boiling.

5 Carefully place the fish balls in the dish, arranging around the outside and leaving a space between each ball. Try to leave the centre empty.

6 Cover and microwave on high for 6 minutes. Halfway through the cooking time turn the fish balls over and reposition so that any towards the centre of the dish are now on the outside edges.

7 Stand, covered, for 5 minutes. Remove the balls from the dish and keep warm on a serving plate, covered with foil.

8 Place the margarine in the jug and microwave uncovered on high until melted. Stir in the flour and microwave uncovered on high for 1 minute or until the mixture puffs up.

9 Gradually whisk in the warmed cooking liquor and remaining milk and water.
10 Microwave uncovered on high for 1 minute. Whisk well. Continue to microwave on high, whisking every 30 seconds, until boiling point is reached.
11 Stir in the chopped pickles, single cream or yoghurt and mustard, and adjust seasoning to taste.
12 To serve, pour the sauce over the fish balls and sprinkle lightly with paprika.
Reheat: cover and microwave on medium for approximately 12 minutes, until heated through. Stir gently once or twice during this time. Do not allow the sauce to boil.

SEAFOOD PIE

Serves 4

A perfect dinner party dish, which could also be served in 4 scallop shells, accompanied by a salad of thinly sliced fennel and beefsteak tomatoes, torn fresh basil leaves and a light French dressing.

INGREDIENTS

1½ lb/750 g potatoes, peeled and cut into ½ in/1 cm slices	2 tablespoons finely chopped fresh parsley
¼ pt/150 ml boiling water	2 oz/50 g prawns, thawed if frozen
2 tablespoons natural yoghurt	2 oz/50 g mussels, thawed if frozen (optional)
salt, black pepper	
1 lb/500 g white fish (e.g. haddock, lemon sole, cod)	2 oz/50 g white button mushrooms, thinly sliced
1 lb/500 g naturally smoked haddock	paprika
1 oz/25 g sunflower margarine	**Containers**
1 oz/25 g plain flour	Microwave boiling bag. Large shallow microware dish.
½ pt/300 ml skimmed milk	Large microware jug.
2 oz/50 g fresh Parmesan or Cheddar cheese, grated	2½ pt/1.5 litre oval flameproof gratin dish.

1 Place the potatoes and boiling water in the microwave boiling bag, securing the top loosely with an elastic band. Stand the bag in a shallow dish.
2 Microwave on high for 12 minutes, or until the potatoes are fork tender. Reposition the bag once during cooking.
3 Drain, mash with the yoghurt and season to taste. Cover and put to one side.
4 Arrange the white and smoked fish in a single layer in a large shallow dish. Position thicker parts towards the outside of the dish, and thinner parts towards the centre.
5 Cover and microwave on high for approximately 8 minutes. Reposition

twice during cooking. Cook in 2 batches if the fillets are thin or the container is not large enough.

6 Reserve the juices. Skin, bone and flake the fish.

7 Place the margarine in the jug. Microwave uncovered on high until melted. Stir in the flour. Microwave uncovered on high for 1 minute, or until the mixture puffs up. Gradually whisk in the skimmed milk and the reserved fish juices.

8 Microwave uncovered on high for 1 minute. Whisk well. Continue to cook in this way, whisking every 30 seconds, until the sauce reaches boiling point.

9 Stir in 1 oz/25 g grated cheese and most of the parsley. Adjust seasoning to taste.

10 Mix the sauce with the prawns, mussels (if using), mushrooms and cooked flaked fish.

11 Transfer to the gratin dish. Microwave uncovered on high for approximately 4 minutes, stirring every 30 seconds, until the ingredients are heated through and the sauce is boiling.

12 Pipe the mashed potatoes around the edge of the dish. Microwave uncovered on high for 2–3 minutes, or until the potato is heated through.

13 Sprinkle the remaining cheese over the fish mixture and place under a preheated grill until the top is lightly browned.

14 Sprinkle with the remaining parsley and paprika.

Reheat: very carefully. Complete to the end of step 12, then stand the container on a trivet. Cover and reheat on medium for 12–14 minutes, turning the container 3 times during this time. Continue with steps 13–14.

KEDGEREE

Serves 4

Traditionally served for breakfast, kedgeree also makes a satisfying lunch or supper dish. When time is short, cook the rice conventionally while microwaving the fish.

A pair of Arbroath smokies could be substituted for the smoked haddock. These are young haddock and I consider that they have the finest flavour of all smoked fish; they are heat smoked in the traditional way so require no further cooking, simply reheating, which does save some time. While the rice is microwaving and the eggs are boiling remove the skin and bones from the smokies. This is not as irksome as it may sound; in fact it is easier than working with a hot, freshly microwaved fish. Leave some of the fish in large chunks then transfer to a shallow dish. Cover and, when the rice is cooked, microwave for 2–3 minutes on high, remembering to stir or shake the container halfway through cooking. Then combine all the ingredients together for a really splendid kedgeree.

1 oz/25 g of butter or margarine can be stirred into the hot kedgeree before serving for those who prefer this dish more moist.

INGREDIENTS

1 medium onion, finely chopped	good squeeze of lemon juice
1 tablespoon sunflower oil	black pepper
1 teaspoon curry powder	lemon wedges for garnish
8 oz/250 g basmati rice, rinsed and drained	**Containers**
1 pt/600 ml boiling water	3½ pt/2 litre deep ovenproof glass casserole dish.
¼ teaspoon salt	Reduce timing by 1–2 minutes when using a plastic microware container.
1 lb/500 g naturally smoked haddock	Shallow plastic microware dish.
2 eggs	Increase timing by 30 seconds when using ovenproof glass or ceramic dish.
3 tablespoons finely chopped fresh parsley	Microware serving dish.

1 Place the onion, oil and curry powder in the casserole dish. Cover and microwave on high for 2 minutes. Stir in the rice and microwave uncovered on high for 2 minutes. Stir in the boiling water and salt.

2 Cover and microwave on high for 15 minutes. Stand, covered, for 5 minutes. Fluff up with a fork and re-cover.

3 Place the fish, skin side down, in the shallow dish. Arrange so that the thicker parts are positioned towards the outside of the dish and the thinner parts towards the centre.

4 Cover and microwave on high for 4–5 minutes until the fish flakes. Turn and reposition once during cooking. Meanwhile, boil the eggs on the hob for 6–8 minutes.

5 Stand the fish covered for 2 minutes. Remove the skin and bones and flake the fish.

6 Combine the cooked rice and fish together with most of the parsley, a good squeeze of lemon juice and adjust the seasoning to taste. Transfer to a serving dish.

7 Cover and microwave on high for 2–3 minutes until all the ingredients are heated through. Turn the dish once during cooking.

8 Garnish with the quartered hard-boiled eggs, lemon wedges and remaining parsley.

Reheat: very carefully. Prepare the recipe to the end of step 6. Sprinkle over 2 tablespoons water, cover and microwave on high for approximately 4 minutes. Stir once during this time. Garnish to complete the dish.

HADDOCK AND RICE TIMBALE

Serves 4–6

A light but filling and flavoursome main course; serve with salads or lightly cooked vegetables. Cod could replace haddock, and plaice makes a good alternative when lighter flavour and texture is desired.

INGREDIENTS

1 lb/500 g haddock fillets, washed and patted dry	**Garnish** bunch of watercress
6 oz/175 g cooked basmati or other long grained rice	lemon twists
2 large eggs, beaten	**Containers** Shallow plastic microware dish. Increase timing by 20–30 seconds when using ovenproof glass or ceramic container. 3½ pt/2 litre plastic microware ring mould. Increase timing by 30 seconds when using ovenproof glass or ceramic container. Trivet.
4 oz/125 g Cheddar cheese, grated	
2 tablespoons finely chopped fresh parsley	
herb salt, black pepper	
grated zest of 1 lemon	

1 Lay the haddock in the shallow dish, skin side down. Arrange the thicker parts towards the outside of the dish and the thinner parts towards the centre.

2 Cover and microwave on high for 4–4½ minutes, until the fish is just cooked. Rearrange once during cooking.

3 Remove the skin and bones and transfer the fish to a mixing bowl. Mash with a fork and combine with the cooked rice, beaten eggs, grated cheese, parsley, herb salt, black pepper and lemon zest. Mix all the ingredients thoroughly.

4 Spoon the mixture into the lightly greased ring mould, pressing down firmly. Level the top. Cover.

5 Stand the container on a trivet and microwave on medium for 10 minutes, or until cooked. Turn once during cooking. To test: insert a skewer near the centre of the mould – it should feel firm and set.

6 Stand, covered, for 3 minutes. Loosen around the edges with a palette knife then invert on to a plate and fill the centre with watercress. Garnish with lemon twists.

Reheat: carefully – this dish can easily toughen when overcooked. Cover and stand ring mould on a trivet. Microwave on medium for 5 minutes until heated through.

COD WITH AROMATIC SPICES

Serves 4

Monkfish tails could be substituted for the cod. For those who like fiery food, add a deseeded chopped chilli in step 1. This dish looks beautiful and tastes good – serve with plenty of rice and green salad.

INGREDIENTS

1 medium apple, cored and sliced	black pepper
1 small onion, finely chopped	4 oz/125 g mushrooms, thinly sliced
1 clove garlic, crushed	1 lb/500 g cod, skin and bones removed, washed and patted dry, then cut into large chunks
2 tablespoons sesame oil	
1 teaspoon coriander seeds, crushed	
½ teaspoon cumin seeds, crushed	salt
1 teaspoon garam masala	4 tablespoons natural yoghurt
½ teaspoon turmeric	good squeeze of lemon juice
½ teaspoon chilli powder	2 tablespoons finely chopped coriander leaves
½ red pepper, diced	
½ yellow or green pepper, diced	**Container**
1 heaped tablespoon plain flour	Shallow plastic microware dish. Increase timing by 30 seconds–1 minute when using ovenproof glass or ceramic container.
1 teaspoon tomato purée	
½ pt/300 ml hot water, chicken or vegetable stock	

◆ 109

1 Place the apple, onion, garlic, sesame oil, crushed coriander seeds, crushed cumin seeds, garam masala, turmeric and chilli powder in the dish. Stir.
2 Cover and microwave on high for 4 minutes. Stir once during cooking.
3 Stir in the peppers. Cover and microwave on high for 2 minutes.
4 Stir in the flour and mix until completely absorbed into the oil and cooking juices. Stir the tomato purée and black pepper into the hot water or stock. Gradually stir into the vegetables. Blend all the ingredients together thoroughly.
5 Cover and microwave on high for 2 minutes. Stir well. Continue to cook for a further 1–2 minutes until boiling point is reached. Stir well.
6 Stir in the mushrooms, coating well with the sauce. Lay the pieces of cod on top – arranging thicker parts around the outside of the dish and thinner parts towards the centre.
7 Cover and microwave on high for 2½ minutes. Turn the pieces of fish over, reposition as necessary, and baste with the sauce.
8 Cover and microwave on high for a further 3 minutes until the fish is cooked.
9 Stir and adjust seasoning to taste. Cover and stand for 3 minutes.
10 To serve, beat the yoghurt and lemon juice together and swirl over the top. Garnish with the chopped coriander leaves.
Reheat: carefully, and without the topping. Cover and microwave on high for about 4 minutes. Stir once during this time. Garnish just before serving.

STUFFED PLAICE ROULADES WITH WHITE WINE AND CREAM

Serves 4

This is extremely easy to make and ideal for a special occasion.
Don't attempt to reheat this dish once fully assembled as it will spoil.
The plaice roulades can be prepared well in advance. Place in the cooking
container, cover and refrigerate until needed. Remember, chilled food needs
a little extra cooking time, so increase this by 30 seconds–1 minute. White
breadcrumbs are used to give a lighter stuffing and more attractive
appearance, but wholewheat breadcrumbs can be used if preferred.

INGREDIENTS

1 small onion, finely chopped	8 tablespoons dry white wine, plus a little more for the sauce
4 oz/125 g mushrooms, finely chopped	
1½ oz/40 g sunflower margarine	½ oz/15 g plain flour
3 oz/75 g fresh white breadcrumbs	½ pint/300 ml hot fish stock or water
3 tablespoons finely chopped fresh parsley	4 tablespoons single cream
	4 slices of lemon, cut in half, for garnish
finely grated zest of 1 lemon	**Containers**
lemon juice	Medium plastic microware bowl.
2 teaspoons finely chopped fresh marjoram plus 8 whole leaves for garnish	Increase timing by 30 seconds when using ovenproof glass or ceramic bowl. Shallow oval plastic microware dish.
herb salt, black pepper	Increase timing by 30 seconds when using ovenproof glass or ceramic dish.
8 plaice fillets (total weight 1 lb/500 g), washed, patted dry and skinned	

110 ◆

1 Place the onion, mushrooms and 1 oz/25 g sunflower margarine in the
bowl. Cover and microwave on high for 4 minutes. Stir once during cooking.
2 Stir in the breadcrumbs, 2 tablespoons parsley, lemon zest and juice,
marjoram, herb salt and black pepper. Mix all the ingredients together
thoroughly.
3 Lay the plaice fillets out, skinned side uppermost. Place about a tablespoon
of the filling at the widest end. (It will be easier if you squeeze the filling into
a sausage shape first.) Roll the fish fillets up firmly, finishing at the tail end.
Arrange the rolled fillets side by side, around the edges of the shallow dish.
The fillets should fit snugly together – if they don't they may unroll during
cooking. To prevent this secure each fillet with a wooden cocktail stick.
4 Spoon a tablespoon of wine over each roulade. Cover and microwave on
high for 4½–5 minutes. When the roulades are positioned around the
outside edges of the dish they should not require repositioning. Turn the dish
once during cooking. Transfer the roulades to a hot serving dish and cover
with foil, shiny side in to retain heat.
5 Place the remaining margarine in the cleaned bowl. Microwave uncovered
on high until melted. Stir in the flour. Microwave on high for approximately

1 minute, until the mixture puffs up.

6 Make the hot water or fish stock up to ¾ pt/450 ml with the strained cooking juices and extra white wine.

7 Gradually whisk this into the roux. Microwave uncovered on high for 2½–3 minutes, until boiling point is reached. Whisk well after every 30 seconds of cooking time.

8 Stir in the cream and adjust seasoning to taste. Pour the sauce over the roulades.

9 To serve, garnish each roulade with half a slice of lemon and 1 marjoram leaf. Scatter the remaining parsley over the dish.

Reheat: not recommended.

MONKFISH KEBABS

Serves 3

Monkfish has an excellent flavour and good firm texture which makes it an ideal fish for kebabs. Bamboo skewers are used for microwave kebabs and can be found in many large supermarkets, oriental stores and some hardware shops. Serve kebabs with rice or noodles, plus a mixture of salads. This dish should not be reheated, but most of the preparation can be done beforehand – the kebabs can be assembled, covered and chilled. Add a few seconds to the overall cooking time if cooking chilled kebabs.

INGREDIENTS

Kebabs	1 teaspoon peeled and finely grated fresh root ginger
½ medium red pepper, cut into 8 squares	
	2 teaspoons natural soy sauce (shoyu)
½ medium green pepper, cut into 8 squares	good squeeze of lemon juice
	black pepper
½ medium yellow pepper, cut into 8 squares	⅛–¼ pt/70–150 ml fish stock or water
	1 teaspoon cornflour dissolved in a little cold water
1 lb/500 g monkfish, skinned, boned and cut into 12 equal pieces	
12 small white mushrooms, wiped	**Containers**
6 baby onions, defrosted if frozen	6 bamboo skewers.
6 bay leaves	Oval plastic shallow microware dish.
Sauce	Increase timing by 20–30 seconds when using ovenproof glass or ceramic container.
2 tablespoons sesame oil	Ovenproof glass 1 pt/600 ml jug.

1 Prepare the sauce. Mix the sesame oil, ginger, soy sauce, lemon juice and black pepper together. Cover and stand at room temperature for 30 minutes.

2 Meanwhile prepare the kebab ingredients and leave in separate piles ready for assembling. You should have the following ingredients prepared: 24 pieces of assorted peppers, 6 baby onions, 12 pieces monkfish, 12 small mushrooms, 6 bay leaves. Proceed to thread these ingredients on to the

6 bamboo skewers as follows: pepper/fish/pepper/mushroom/bay leaf/baby onion/pepper/fish/pepper/mushroom. The order is important for even cooking.

3 Place 3 skewers in the dish and brush liberally with the sauce. Cover and microwave on high for 1½ minutes.

4 Turn each kebab over and reposition so that one of the outside kebabs is switched to the centre and vice versa. Brush liberally with the sauce. Cover and microwave on high for 30 seconds–1 minute, until the fish is just cooked.

5 Remove to a heated serving dish and cover with foil, shiny side down to retain heat.

6 Microwave the remaining batch in the same way.

7 Strain the cooking juices and any remaining sauce into the jug. Make up to ¼ pt/150 ml with fish stock or water. Stir in the dissolved cornflour.

8 Microwave on high for 2–3 minutes, until boiling. Stir well after every 30 seconds of cooking. Adjust seasoning to taste. To serve, pour the sauce over the kebabs.

Reheat: not recommended.

CUT MACKEREL

Serves 2

This dish has a fresh clean flavour and was named 'cut' mackerel by my husband. The citrus juice and grilling at the end of cooking cut through the oiliness which often puts people off this splendid fish. Mackerel should always be bought fresh and cooked on the day of purchase. You can replace the oregano with fresh marjoram or summer savory, or simply increase the quantities of dill and parsley.

INGREDIENTS

2 mackerel (total weight approximately 1 lb 4 oz/625 g)	2 tablespoons fresh orange juice
	2 oz/50 g fresh wholewheat breadcrumbs
Stuffing	**Garnish**
2 shallots or 1 small onion, finely chopped	orange slices
	sprigs of dill
1 tablespoon finely chopped fresh dill	**Container**
1 tablespoon finely chopped fresh oregano	3½ pt/2 litre shallow oval flameproof dish. Decrease timing by 30 seconds when using plastic microware container, but don't put this under the grill. Transfer the fish to a heatproof plate before browning.
grated zest of 1 lemon	
3 tablespoons fresh lemon juice	
grated zest of 1 orange	

1 First prepare the mackerel: gut, remove heads and tails, and cut off any fins with scissors. (Ask your fishmonger to do this if you don't want to.) Lay the fish out flat on a board, skin side uppermost, and press along the backbone.

Turn the fish over and with a sharp knife, remove the backbone. Pull out any remaining bones with tweezers. Wash the fish in cold water and pat dry with absorbent kitchen paper. Slash through the skins to prevent them bursting.
2 Mix all the stuffing ingredients together thoroughly. Divide the stuffing between the fish, placing it on one side. Press down firmly and fold the other half of the fish over. Arrange the fish in a shallow flameproof dish so that the fleshy back parts are positioned towards the outside edges, and the stuffing side of each fish is towards the centre.
3 Cover and microwave on high for 4½ minutes. Turn the dish once during cooking. Preheat the grill as soon as the fish starts cooking. Test by inserting a skewer into the thickest part of the fish – it should feel tender.
4 Place immediately under the preheated grill to brown and crisp the skin. Garnish with orange slices and sprigs of dill.
For 4
Double all the ingredients and cook the fish in two containers. Cover the first 2 with foil to retain heat as they are removed from the grill.

Reheat: not recommended. The stuffing can be made in advance and the fish can be cleaned, boned and stuffed. Chill until required.

SOUSED HERRINGS

Serves 4–6

Good as an hors d'oeuvre or with a selection of salads,
they are quick and easy to make by microwave.
They will keep, covered, in the refrigerator for up to 4 days.

INGREDIENTS

6 herrings (total weight 2 lb 4 oz/1.1 kg), filleted	1 teaspoon clear honey
¼ pt/150 ml white wine vinegar	8 tablespoons cold water
1 small onion, thinly sliced	herb salt
3 dill pickles, thinly sliced	**Containers**
½ teaspoon allspice berries	2½ pt/1.5 litre shallow plastic microware dish.
6 black peppercorns	Increase timing by 30 seconds when using ovenproof glass or ceramic dish.
2 teaspoons finely chopped fresh dill	3½ pt/2 litre plastic microware jug.
3 bay leaves	Increase timing by 30 seconds when using ovenproof glass or ceramic jug.
3 lemon slices, halved	
1 teaspoon wholegrain mustard	

1 Place the herring fillets skin side down. Firmly roll each fillet from the widest end to the tail end, and secure with a wooden cocktail stick. Arrange around the outside edges of the shallow dish.
2 Place all the remaining ingredients (except the salt) in the jug.
3 Microwave uncovered on high for approximately 4½ minutes, until boiling.

4 Pour the marinade over the fish. Cover and microwave on high for 4½ minutes. Turn the dish and rearrange the fish once during cooking. If an oblong dish is used, the fish in the centre will need moving to the ends of the dish and vice versa. Sprinkle herb salt over the fillets. Cover and cool. Refrigerate.

PRAWN PILAU

Serves 4

This looks very pretty and is delicately flavoured. For a special occasion, replace the turmeric with a few strands of saffron. Add the prawns just before serving as frozen fish deteriorates rapidly once thawed.

INGREDIENTS	
7 oz/200 g basmati rice, washed and drained	8 oz/250 g prawns, defrosted if frozen
1 pt/600 ml boiling chicken or vegetable stock	2 tablespoons finely chopped fresh parsley
½ teaspoon turmeric	herb salt, black pepper
½ teaspoon salt	**Containers**
1 medium onion, finely chopped	5 pt/2.8 litre plastic microware bowl. Increase timing by 2 minutes when using ovenproof glass or ceramic bowl.
1 medium red pepper, diced	Medium plastic microware bowl. Increase timing by 1 minute when using ovenproof glass or ceramic bowl.
1 tablespoon olive oil	
4 oz/125 g frozen peas	
4 oz/125 g mushrooms, thinly sliced	

1 Place the rice, boiling stock, turmeric and salt in the bowl. Stir well. Cover and microwave on high for 15 minutes. Stand while cooking the vegetables.
2 Place the onion, red pepper and oil into the medium bowl. Cover and microwave on high for 4 minutes. Stir once during cookng.
3 Stir in the frozen peas. Cover and microwave on high for 2 minutes.
4 Add the mushrooms. Cover and microwave on high for 3 minutes. Stir once during cooking.
5 Fork up the rice and stir in the vegetables, together with their cooking juices and the prawns. Adjust seasoning and stir in the parsley.
6 Cover and microwave on high for 2–3 minutes until heated through.
Reheat: prepare up to the end of step 4, then mix the rice and vegetables. Just before reheating, defrost the prawns and stir them into the rice. Cover and microwave on high for 6–8 minutes. Stir twice during this time.

TUNA AND PASTA SALAD

Serves 4

My children love this dish accompanied by a green salad and tomatoes.
The dressing is added to the pasta and beans while they are hot, which allows
the full flavours to permeate, though I have often mixed all the remaining
ingredients in and served this warm on a cold day.

INGREDIENTS

6 oz/175 g wholewheat macaroni	2 teaspoons finely chopped fresh oregano or marjoram
4 oz/125 g of fresh or frozen broad beans	
2 tablespoons olive oil	1 tablespoon finely chopped fresh parsley
1 clove garlic, crushed	**Garnish** black olives
1 teaspoon wholegrain mustard	
2 tablespoons lemon juice	lemon zest
herb salt, black pepper	**Containers**
7 oz/200 g can tuna in brine, drained and flaked	5 pt/2.8 litre plastic microware bowl. Don't use ovenproof glass for pasta as it takes too long to cook.
1 tablespoon capers	Small plastic microware bowl.
6 in/15 cm piece cucumber, diced	Increase timing by 30 seconds when using ovenproof glass or ceramic container.
2 sticks of celery, finely sliced on the diagonal	

◆ 115

1 First cook the macaroni (p.50).
2 While the macaroni is standing place the beans in a small bowl. If you are
using frozen beans cover and microwave on high for 3½ minutes; if they are
fresh they will need a minute longer and 2 tablespoons of water. Stir once
during cooking.
3 Place the olive oil, garlic, mustard, lemon juice, salt and pepper in a screw
topped jar. Shake vigorously until all the ingredients are well mixed.
4 Pour over the hot macaroni and beans, mix well. Cover with a clean
teatowel.
5 When the macaroni and beans have cooled, stir in the remaining
ingredients. Garnish with a few black olives and lemon zest.

FISH LASAGNE

Serves 4–6

This is a recipe to try when you have had a bit of experience with microwave cooking. Although there are a number of stages in the preparation, it is very easy to make. Prepare everything beforehand and then assemble and cook close to serving time for the very best results. Serve with a mixed green salad and fresh sliced tomatoes.

INGREDIENTS

12 oz/375 g cauliflower florets	¼ pt/150 ml natural yoghurt
4 tablespoons water	1 egg, beaten
1 lb/500 g haddock fillets	2 oz/50 g grated cheese
1 small onion, finely chopped	**Containers**
6 oz/175 g sweetcorn kernels	Microwave boiling bag.
4 oz/125 g mushrooms, sliced thinly	Oval ceramic flameproof 2½ pt/1.5 litre
1 oz/25 g sunflower margarine	2½ in/6 cm deep dish.
1 oz/25 g plain flour	Medium plastic microware bowl.
¾ pt/450 ml skimmed milk	Increase timing by 1 minute when using
2 tablespoons finely chopped fresh parsley	ovenproof glass or ceramic bowl. 3½ pt/2 litre plastic microware jug.
herb salt, black pepper	Increase timing by 1 minute when using ovenproof glass or ceramic jug.
7 oblong sheets 'pre-cooked' lasagne or 6 long strips raw lasagne	Trivet.

116 ◆

1 Place the cauliflower and water in the microwave boiling bag. Secure the top loosely with an elastic band. Stand the bag in the bowl.
2 Microwave on high for 7 minutes or until just fork tender. Drain, cover and set to one side.
3 Place the fish in the dish. Arrange the thicker parts towards the outside of the dish and the thinner parts towards the centre. Cover and microwave on high for 3½–4 minutes, until the fish flakes. Remove any skin and bones, flake the fish and set to one side.
4 Place the onion in the bowl. Cover and microwave on high for 2 minutes. Stir in the sweetcorn. Cover and microwave on high for 3 minutes. Stir once during cooking. Stir in the mushrooms. Cover and microwave on high for 2½ minutes. Drain, reserving the juices for the sauce.
5 Place the margarine in the jug and microwave uncovered on high until melted. Stir in the flour and microwave uncovered on high for 1 minute or until the mixture puffs up. Gradually whisk in the milk and reserved cooking juices. Microwave on high for 1 minute, then whisk well. Continue to cook in this way, whisking every 30 seconds, until the sauce reaches boiling point. Stir in the parsley and season to taste.
6 'Pre-cooked' or 'no cook' lasagne
Plunge the lasagne into a large bowl of boiling water. Stand for 5 minutes. Drain and place on absorbent kitchen paper.

Raw lasagne
Cook conventionally and drain on absorbent kitchen paper.
7 Finally, assemble the lasagne. Check that you have all the following in front of you: cauliflower; bowl of mushrooms, onion and sweetcorn; cooked fish; jug with cooked sauce; drained lasagne; and flameproof dish at least 2½ in/6 cm deep. Divide the sauce equally beween the cauliflower, sweetcorn mixture and fish. Mix well, taste each bowl and adjust seasoning if necessary.

Next, spoon the sweetcorn mixture into the dish. Lay 2½ sheets lasagne on top. Spoon the fish over and cover with another 2 sheets of lasagne. Spoon the cauliflower over and cover with 2–2½ sheets lasagne.

Beat the yoghurt until smooth, add the beaten egg and mix thoroughly. Spread over the top of the lasagne, taking care to cover every bit of pasta.
8 Stand the container on a trivet. Microwave covered on medium for 20 minutes. Turn the dish 3 times during cooking.
9 Sprinkle with the grated cheese and place under a preheated grill until golden and bubbling.
Reheat: stand the container on a trivet, cover and microwave on medium for 12–15 minutes. Turn the dish 3 times during reheating.

KIPPER PATE

Serves 6

High in protein and low in fat, this well flavoured pâté is ideal for slimmers and those on fat-restricted diets.

INGREDIENTS

12 oz/375 g kipper fillets, defrosted first if frozen	**Garnish** paprika, parsley and lemon twists
1 small onion, finely chopped	**Containers**
1 oz/25 g sunflower margarine	Shallow oval plastic microware dish.
8 oz/250 g fromage frais or other low fat soft cheese	Increase timing by 30 seconds–1 minute when using ovenproof glass or ceramic container.
2 tablespoons lemon juice	Small plastic microware bowl.
black pepper	Increase timing by 30 seconds when using
a little grated nutmeg	ovenproof glass or ceramic bowl.

1 Arrange the kippers with the widest parts towards the outside of the shallow dish. Cover and microwave on high for 2 minutes. Reposition and continue to cook for 1–1½ minutes, until done. Remove the skin.
2 Put the onion and margarine in the bowl. Cover and microwave on high for 3 minutes, stirring once during cooking.
3 Using a processor or blender, combine all the ingredients until smooth.
4 Spoon into a bowl or 6 ramekin dishes. Garnish with paprika, parsley and lemon twists.
5 Cover and chill before serving.

TERRINE OF MONKFISH, HADDOCK, SCALLOPS AND PRAWNS WITH A FRESH HERB SAUCE

Serves 6

The flavour of this is superb, the texture is light and the delicate salmon colour is offset by the green sauce. The dill sprigs retain their colour after microwaving and a few whole prawns add a final garnish.

A ring mould is used in preference to a loaf shaped container because it shortens the cooking time and removes the need to shield the corners with foil part way through cooking.

The microwave oven is perfect for dishes such as this, which would normally require longer cooking in a bain marie.

INGREDIENTS

12 oz/375 g haddock, skinned	salt, black pepper
6 oz/175 g prepared large scallops, black beards removed	¼ pt/150 ml sunflower oil
	juice of ½ lemon
4 oz/125 g cooked, peeled prawns	2 heaped tablespoons thick Greek yoghurt (preferably sheep's milk)
¼ pt/150 ml double cream	
1 large egg, beaten	3 teaspoons of each of the following: chopped fresh basil, dill, chives, parsley and chervil
1 tablespoon melted slightly salted butter	
salt, pepper	**Containers**
sprigs of fresh dill	1½ pt/900 ml plastic microware ring mould. Increase timing by 2 minutes when using ovenproof glass or ceramic mould. Less time will be required when a larger plastic ring mould is used as mixture will not be quite so deep. Trivet.
8 oz/250 g monkfish, membrane removed, then sliced into ½ in/1 cm medallions	
Sauce	
1 egg yolk	
½ teaspoon Dijon mustard	

1 In a processor blend the haddock, the scallops and most of the prawns (reserving a few for garnish) until almost smooth.

2 In a large mixing bowl beat the cream and egg together, then add the processed fish and melted butter. Mix thoroughly and season with salt and pepper.

3 Lay a few sprigs of dill in the base of the lightly greased ring mould. Spoon half the mixture into the mould, smooth the top, then lay the slices of monkfish over. Spoon in the remainder of the mixture and level the top.

4 Stand the container on a trivet, cover and microwave on medium for 12 minutes. Give the container a half turn twice during cooking.

5 Test to see if it is cooked by inserting a skewer through the centre of the mixture – it should feel set on the inside and outside edges, and the skewer should pass easily through the monkfish.

6 Stand, covered, for 5 minutes, then carefully invert on to a serving dish.

There may be a little liquid which can be left in the dish or removed and used as stock in other dishes. Cover, cool and chill well before serving.

7 To make the sauce: In a medium mixing bowl beat the egg yolk, mustard, salt and pepper together thoroughly. Add the sunflower oil, drop at a time at first, beating all the time. When a good half has been incorporated, the rest can be added in a slow stream. Finally add the lemon juice, still beating constantly. Whisk the yoghurt until smooth in a separate bowl, then gradually add the mayonnaise.

8 Pound the herbs together in a mortar or chop finely in a food processor and mix into the sauce. Adjust seasoning to taste. Cover and chill well before serving.

SUSHI

Serves 4

An unusual starter which will always be well received by guests.
The sushi can be cut into quarters and served as finger food at buffets.
Once cut into, colourful layers of saffron rice, prawn paste and white sole are revealed, encased in the jet black nori; a garnish of sushi ginger adds a final authentic touch.
The rice could be conventionally cooked while the fish is being microwaved if that is more convenient.
It is best to chill sushi for at least 6 hours before serving so that the sushi is firm and cuts more easily. Triangular or oval moulds could be used instead of round ramekin dishes.
See page 208 for instructions for toasting nori seaweed.

♦ 119

INGREDIENTS

8 oz/250 g lemon sole fillet, skinned, washed and patted dry	a few pieces sushi ginger or sushi cucumber for garnish (available from oriental stores and Clearspring Grocer (p.209)
1 tablespoon sake or dry white wine	
4 oz/125 g cooked, peeled prawns	
2 teaspoons olive oil	**Containers**
herb salt, black pepper	Shallow plastic microware dish. Increase timing by 1½–2 minutes when using ovenproof glass or ceramic container. 4 plastic microware ramekins.
a little lemon or lime juice	
4 sheets nori, toasted	
4–6 heaped tablespoons saffron rice (p.54)	

1 Put the lemon sole in the shallow dish and spoon over the sake or wine. Cover and microwave on high for 2 minutes or until the fish flakes. Cover and cool.

2 Put the prawns and olive oil into a processor and blend until fairly smooth. Add salt, pepper and lemon or lime juice to taste.

3 Fold each toasted nori sheet in 4 lengthways and cut along the folds with scissors. Each sheeet should now be in 4 long strips.

4 Line each ramekin dish with 4 strips, laying the strips criss-cross fashion and pressing them gently into the base so that the ramekin is completely lined. The strips will protrude above the rim. Don't worry if any of the strips tear slightly. Check that you have the following in front of you before assembling the sushi: the prawn paste divided into 4; the sole divided into 4; saffron rice.

5 Put 2 heaped teaspoons of rice into each mould and press down with the back of a teaspoon. Next add a layer of prawn paste, pressing down lightly and smoothing the top. Add a layer of sole and finally 2 more teaspoons of rice. Press down gently.

6 Fold over the strips of nori so that they overlap. The strips may lift up a little at first but the nori soon absorbs moisture from the filling and the strips will then stick together to form a smooth casing. I usually stand 1 ramekin on top of the other (but don't do this when heavy glass or ceramic ramekins are used), then switch them round.

7 After about 5 minutes very carefully invert each mould on to your hand – the sushi should fall out gently. If there are any parts that are not covered with nori, then tear a little off from the overlap at the top and press it over lightly so it sticks to the exposed filling.

8 Return the sushi to the ramekins and cover with cling film. Stand them one on top of the other in the refrigerator for a few hours to set. Switch them round once.

9 Remove the sushi from the ramekins and garnish the tops with paper-thin slices of sushi ginger or sushi cucumber.

EXCELLENT FISH CAKES

Serves 4   Makes 12 fish cakes

The flavour of these substantial cakes is truly delicious.
The combination of bloaters, lightly smoked whiting and sweet flavoured laverbread raises the fish cake into a different class.
I serve these simply with fried field mushrooms and onions.
The bloaters must be cleaned before cooking and any soft roe chopped and then added to the fish during the last 30 seconds of cooking time.
The laverbread binds the mixture together perfectly and can be obtained from some fishmongers, health food shops and delicatessens. The potatoes can be conventionally cooked while the fish is microwaving, though they will not be quite so well flavoured. Taste the mixture before forming into cakes; do not automatically season with salt and pepper as the laverbread and fish have plenty of flavour.
Once the cakes are formed they must be cooked on a microwave browning dish and not an ordinary dish, otherwise they will not crisp or brown but will end up soft and soggy. If you have no browning dish, complete the cooking by frying for a couple of minutes on each side in hot oil and then grilling for about 5 minutes until they are crisp, browned and heated through.

INGREDIENTS

1 lb/500 g bloaters, cleaned, heads and tails removed	fine oatmeal
	2 tablespoons sunflower oil
8 oz/250 g smoked whiting fillets	**Containers**
1 lb/500 g cooked potatoes, mashed	Shallow plastic microware dish.
1 heaped tablespoon laverbread	Microwave browning dish.
good squeeze of lemon juice	Increase timing by 1½ minutes when using
1 large egg, beaten	ovenproof glass or ceramic container.

1 Wash and pat dry the bloaters and whiting and slash the skin of the bloaters twice on either side.

2 Put the fish in the shallow dish, arranging the thickest part of the bloaters towards the outside of the dish and the whiting fillets in the centre.

3 Cover and microwave on high for 5–6 minutes. Rearrange halfway through cooking so that the bloaters are in the centre of the dish.

4 Test by inserting a skewer into the thickest part of the fish – it should just flake. Cover and stand for 5 minutes or until cool enough to handle.

5 Remove all the skin and bones from the fish and mash with a fork.

6 Mix thoroughly with the mashed potato, laverbread and lemon juice. Taste and add other seasonings if you feel it necessary. (At this stage I generally cover and chill the mixture before forming into cakes but this can be done as soon as the mixture has cooled a little.)

7 Form the mixture into 12 oval cakes about 1 in/2.5 cm thick. Dip into the beaten egg and coat lightly with fine oatmeal.

8 Preheat a browning dish according to the manufacturer's instructions. During the last 30 seconds of preheating time add 1 tablespoon sunflower oil.

9 Once the dish has preheated work quickly – the dish loses heat as soon as it is removed from the oven. Press half the fish cakes on the dish and microwave uncovered on high for 3 minutes. Quickly turn the fish cakes over and microwave uncovered on high for a further 2½ minutes.

10 Transfer to a plate lined with absorbent kitchen paper and cover with foil so that the heat is retained while cooking the second batch.

11 Wipe over the browning dish with kitchen paper and preheat for 2 minutes, adding 1 tablespoon sunflower oil for the last 30 seconds. (This is essential, otherwise the second batch of cakes won't crisp and brown properly.)

12 Cook the second batch in the same way as the first.

Reheat: not recommended as they would lose their crispness. The mixture can be formed into cakes, but don't dip them in the egg and oatmeal. Before preheating the browning dish microwave the cakes on a plate, 6 at a time, for 30 seconds uncovered on high to remove the chill. (When chilled food is placed directly on a browning dish it cools the dish down and will not crisp and brown properly.) Dip the cakes in the egg and oatmeal and proceed with steps 7–10.

◆ 121

SEA BASS, SAKE AND SHIITAKE

Serves 2 (see colour plate 3)

The combination of sake, shiitake and kombu, together with the dipping sauce and daikon relish, is a popular Japanese way of cooking fish. The traditional dipping sauce and relish are said to aid the digestion and are commonly served with fish and with fried food such as tempura. Any white fish can be cooked in this way and when fillets are used, the shiitake mushrooms can be spread over the top. Lemon and Dover sole both make excellent substitutes for sea bass although the beautiful flavour and texture of sea bass is particularly complementary to all the other ingredients. Kombu is a seaweed which imparts a delicate sweetness to the fish. It is used principally to flavour stocks and is not meant to be eaten in this recipe. It must be washed and soaked prior to cooking. Kombu and sake are both easily obtainable from oriental stores and the Clearspring Grocer (p.209).

INGREDIENTS

sea bass weighing 1 lb/500 g, cleaned, scaled and fins removed	1 teaspoon finely grated fresh root ginger
2 in/5 cm strip kombu, washed under cold running water then soaked in cold water for 5 minutes and drained	**Daikon relish** 4 in/10 cm piece mooli (daikon radish), peeled and finely grated
4 medium fresh shiitake mushrooms, thinly sliced (p. 209)	2 medium spring onions, finely chopped
4 tablespoons sake or dry white wine	a few drops of natural soy sauce (shoyu)
1 lemon, thinly sliced	a few slices of sushi ginger for garnish
salt, black pepper	**Container**
Dipping sauce	Shallow plastic microware dish. Increase timing by 2 minutes when using ovenproof glass or ceramic container.
2 tablespoons natural soy sauce (shoyu)	
2 tablespoons cold water	

1 Mix together the ingredients for the dipping sauce, cover and stand at room temperature for 2 hours or more before serving. Stir together the mooli, spring onions and soy sauce for the daikon relish. Cover and refrigerate for 2 hours before serving.
2 Wash the sea bass and pat dry, then slash through the skin twice on either side.
3 Lay the prepared fish on top of the kombu in the shallow dish. Wrap a small piece of foil around the tail end and another piece around the head to prevent them from overcooking; make sure that the foil does not touch the oven lining.
4 Stuff the belly of the fish with the mushrooms, packing them well in. Spoon over the sake. Lay a few lemon slices on the fish. Cover and stand at room temperature for 30 minutes before cooking.
5 Microwave covered on high for approximately 5 minutes. Give the dish a half turn once during cooking. Test by inserting the tip of a sharp knife into

the thickest part of the fish – the flesh should just flake. Stand, covered, for 2 minutes.
6 Remove the foil, season with salt and black pepper. Replace the cooked lemon slices with fresh ones and garnish with sushi ginger slices.
7 Serve the dipping sauce and daikon relish in individual dipping bowls.
Reheat: not recommended.

RED EMPEROR BREAM WITH PESTO

Serves 1

This simple method of preparing a small whole fish is quick and delicious.
Other non-oily fish can be substituted for the Red Emperor.
Rosemary, oregano or marjoram can be used if chervil or thyme are not available.
Purchase a good quality pesto from a delicatessen or supermarket, or, if the ingredients are available, prepare a home-made one, which is always superior in flavour.

INGREDIENTS

small red emperor bream weighing 8 oz/250 g, cleaned and scaled	salt
	2 slices of lemon or lime
a few sprigs of fresh chervil and thyme	**Container**
2 tablespoons dry white wine	Shallow plastic microware dish.
freshly ground black pepper	Increase timing by 1½ minutes when using
1 teaspoon pesto	ovenproof glass or ceramic dish.

◆ 123

1 Remove the fins from the fish – take care as they can be sharp. Wash the fish and pat dry, then slash the skin twice on either side.
2 Put the prepared fish in the shallow dish. Stuff the belly with chervil and thyme sprigs. Spoon over the wine and add a few turns of the pepper mill.
3 Cover and microwave on high for 2½–3 minutes or until the thickest part of the fish flakes. Take great care not to overcook.
4 Transfer fish to a warm serving plate and stir the pesto into the fish juices.
5 Microwave uncovered on high for 1½ minutes until boiling.
6 Season the fish lightly and pour the sauce over. Garnish with lemon or lime slices.
Reheat: not recommended.

RED MULLET ON A BED OF WARM LEAVES

Serves 3–4

Red mullet is sometimes cooked without cleaning which adds extra flavour to the flesh, but the fish must be cleaned before microwaving otherwise the insides could explode. However, microwaved red mullet has a splendid flavour and looks beautiful shining pink on a bed of warm, green leaves.
I use small fish, although a couple of larger fish could be used.
Use a red onion when available; its strong red colour and distinctive flavour add extra appeal to this dish.

INGREDIENTS	
1 medium onion (preferably red), finely chopped	about 10 lollo rosso lettuce leaves, in shreds
1 clove garlic, crushed	1 heaped tablespoon grated mooli (white radish)
1 tablespoon olive oil	
1 tablespoon finely chopped fresh chervil, plus a few sprigs for garnish	1 tablespoon vinaigrette
	Garnish
grated zest and juice of 1 lemon	a few black olives
salt, black pepper	lemon slices
6 red mullet, each weighing around 4 oz/125 g	**Containers** Small plastic microware bowl. Shallow plastic microware dish. Increase timing by 1 minute for the onion mixture and by 2 minutes for the fish when using ovenproof glass or ceramic container.
Salad a few radicchio leaves, torn in half	

1 Put the onion, garlic and olive oil in the bowl. Cover and microwave on high for 4 minutes. Shake the bowl once during cooking. Stir in the chervil, lemon zest and salt and pepper.

2 Clean the red mullet, wash and pat dry, then slash through the skin twice on each side of the fish.

3 Arrange the fish, heads to tails, across the shallow dish. Press the onion mixture into each fish and sprinkle with a little lemon juice.

4 Cover and microwave on high for 4 minutes. Rearrange the fish so that those at the ends of the dish are now in the centre and vice versa.

5 Cover and microwave on high for a further 2–2½ minutes until the fish is just tender. Stand, covered, for 2 minutes.

6 Meanwhile, put the salad ingredients in the cleaned bowl and pour over the vinaigrette.

7 Microwave uncovered on high for 1 minute. Toss and put on a serving dish. Lay the fish on top of the leaves and garnish with olives, lemon slices and chervil sprigs.

Reheat: not recommended, although the recipe can be completed to step 3 ahead of time.

TURBOT WITH RICARD, SAFFRON AND CREAM SAUCE

Serves 4

This is one of my favourite ways of serving turbot. The creamy saffron sauce with a hint of Ricard (more can be added if a stronger flavour is desired) is most complementary to the turbot's taste and texture. The cooked fish must be covered with foil so that heat is retained while the sauce is being reduced conventionally. A dish such as this should not be reheated.

INGREDIENTS

generous pinch of saffron strands	2 tablespoons single cream
6 tablespoons hot light, unsalted vegetable stock	1 oz/25 g butter, diced
	salt
1½ lb/750 g turbot fillets, washed and patted dry	**Container**
2 tablespoons Ricard	Shallow flameproof ceramic dish. Decrease timing by 1½–2 minutes when
pepper	using a plastic microware container.

1 Infuse the saffron in 2 tablespoons of hot vegetable stock for about 30 minutes.
2 Arrange the fish in the shallow dish, positioning thicker parts towards the outside and thinner parts towards the centre.
3 Mix the Ricard with the remaining stock and spoon over the fish. Sprinkle with pepper.
4 Cover and microwave on high for approximately 6½ minutes. Rearrange fish halfway through cooking time. The fish is cooked when it flakes, even though it may still look slightly opaque in parts. Strain off the cooking juices and cover with foil, shiny side down, to retain the heat.
5 Put the strained juices, saffron strands and infused stock into a pan.
6 Boil hard until reduced by about half. Stir in the cream and return to the boil, stirring all the time. Remove from the heat, whisk in the butter and adjust seasoning to taste.
Reheat: not recommended.

◆ 125

MEAT AND POULTRY

MEAT

Health education guidelines recommend that for an improvement in general health the consumption of red meat should be reduced in favour of white meat and fish. The saturated fats that are contained in red meat are directly linked to heart and circulatory disorders.

Meat that is to be microwaved must be lean; fatty meat will not cook evenly. Steaks, topside, silverside, braising steak, minced beef, veal and lamb, low fat sausages, ham and bacon joints or slices, fillets of pork, beef, veal and lamb, offal and chops are suitable for microwaving, but trim off all excess fat.

Microwaves are attracted to fats and any food that has a high proportion will heat up rapidly. Microwaves draw fats away from food and unless fat is removed before cooking, the microwaves will concentrate in the fat, rather than in the food itself, and slow down the overall cooking time. A bulb baster is the best tool for removing fat from the container during cooking.

When using cuts like braising steak it helps to marinate the meat prior to cooking. Other ways to tenderize are by beating with a meat mallet or using a natural meat tenderizing powder (sold in spice racks in supermarkets).

Tougher cuts of meat don't microwave successfully and are best cooked in a pressure cooker or by long, slow cooking methods, such as pot roasting. Even when tougher cuts are cooked for a long period on a low power setting, the connective tissue does not break down and the meat remains tough. I would not recommend using cuts such as stewing beef or scrag end of lamb in the microwave. Instead, buy the best cuts you can afford and pay particular attention to the special notes in the recipes regarding slicing the meat to the required thickness.

The shape and density of the meat affect the overall cooking time. A boned joint with a diameter of no more than 5–6 in/12–15 cm and a fairly even shape is the easiest to cook. Care must be taken when microwaving unevenly shaped joints; shield the thinner parts with foil for half the cooking time to prevent them from overcooking and drying out. Large joints are best half cooked by microwave, then finished by conventional methods. The joint will be cooked evenly throughout without being either too dry on the outside or uncooked in the centre,

126 ◆

and a crisp crust will form from the dry heat of the conventional oven. The overall cooking time will be greatly reduced, the meat will be more moist and will carve well. Do not transfer a container from the conventional oven to the microwave because the container is much too hot and will crack the turntable or damage the oven floor.

It is best to use a microwave roasting rack or trivet when microwaving joints so that they do not stew in their own juices, although a small joint (weighing 2 lb/1 kg or less) will microwave well on a browning dish for the whole of the cooking time. If you don't have a browning dish and want the meat to have a darker crust there are 3 ways of achieving this:

1. Brush on a light coating of soy sauce, yeast or beef extract, prior to cooking.
2. Fry the meat in a frying pan before microwaving.
3. Brown under a preheated grill after microwaving.

Chops, small joints, gammon slices, sausages and burgers benefit from being browned under the grill after microwaving because they do not crisp or brown when cooked in an ordinary dish. It is worth considering the time needed to preheat a browning dish (approximately 7 minutes); if, for example, 1 pork chop is to be cooked then it is much quicker to microwave the chop on a plate and brown under the grill. All this can be done in the time it takes to preheat the browning dish.

◆ 127

There are different views about covering joints, and some people feel that if a complete covering is used the meat is 'steamed' rather than 'roasted'. Try both ways to discover which one suits you best. If the meat is enclosed in a roasting bag it will be very moist throughout and the bag encourages some natural browning. Some people recommend a cover for the first part of cooking, which is removed during the latter half. I feel it is better to cover, even if simply with greaseproof paper held down with cocktail sticks. This helps to keep the oven interior clean as meat splatters a lot during cooking.

Do not salt joints before microwaving as this toughens the meat. When gammon or bacon joints are to be cooked, soak for a few hours in cold water to remove excess salt before cooking. Care must be taken when pork chops or joints are being microwaved; pork contains a fair proportion of water which is drawn out during microwaving. Timing of such cuts is critical; overcooking can result in tough, dry meat.

Standing times can be up to 30 minutes for large joints and 15–20 minutes for smaller ones. During this time, the internal temperature of the meat will rise as the cooking process is completed by conduction. The meat must be enclosed in a tent of foil, shiny side facing the meat, as soon as it is removed from the oven.

A microwave thermometer helps to determine the exact cooking time of joints of meat, and some ovens are fitted with a temperature probe which is inserted into the thickest part of the meat while it is cooking. The probe should not touch any bones or rest in a mass of fat. Fat can sometimes splatter up the probe and this may result in an incorrect reading, which could result in the oven automatically switching off before the cooking is completed. It is therefore safer to calculate the exact cooking time by using the charts at the end of this book rather than relying on a probe reading. Ordinary meat thermometers must not be left in the meat during cooking as they contain mercury and this reacts with the microwaves. A little time must be allowed to pass after inserting an ordinary thermometer into food after microwaving so that the correct temperature can register.

Dishes using lean minced meat adapt well to microwave cooking and will brown naturally. Mincing breaks down the fibres in the meat and tender results are always obtained. Adding salt to dishes such as meatballs, meat loaves, pâtés and beefburgers before cooking is fine; these items will only toughen if they are overcooked. Minced meat tends to lump together during cooking, and for dishes like bolognese sauce and chilli con carne it will be necessary to break up the lumps with a fork, moving browned bits to the centre of the dish and red bits to the outside. This will ensure good even cooking.

Liver and kidneys microwave well. Cut them into slices and take care to remove any inedible parts. Cover while cooking so that moisture is retained and the oven stays clean.

There are three different ways of cooking bacon in the microwave. The easiest and quickest method is to lay the rashers over a trivet on a plate and cover with greaseproof paper. A browning dish gives a good crisp result but requires preheating and is probably not worthwhile if only 1 or 2 rashers are required. The bacon may be put on a plate or in a baking dish but this method does not allow the fat to drain away and the cooked bacon will not be so crisp. Don't cover with cling film or a browning dish lid otherwise the steam will be trapped inside the container and the bacon will be very soft. Never layer bacon between sheets of kitchen paper as it sticks to the bacon and is almost impossible to remove after cooking.

Take care not to overcook; bacon will crisp further during a short standing time. Low fat sausages always give good results and simply need pricking all over to prevent them from bursting. They can be cooked on a trivet so that any fat can drain away, or on a preheated browning dish for a crisper result.

PORK CHOPS IN SPICED ORANGE SAUCE

Serves 4

Choose chops no more than 1 in/2.5 cm thick, and trim off as much fat as possible before cooking. Take great care with the overall timing as pork chops toughen when overcooked. I have used arrowroot in preference to cornflour as it adds an attractive glaze to the finished dish.

INGREDIENTS

4 boneless pork chops (total weight 1 lb/500 g)	2 teaspoons arrowroot dissolved in a little cold water
1 small onion, thinly sliced	herb salt
6 tablespoons red wine	8 slices of orange
2 heaped teaspoons brown sugar	parsley for garnish
pinch of ground cloves	**Container**
good pinch of ground coriander	Shallow oval plastic microware dish. Increase overall timing by 1 minute when using ovenproof glass or ceramic container.
juice of 1 orange	
black pepper	
1 teaspoon soy sauce	

◆ 129

1 Trim the chops of excess fat and arrange in a single layer in the dish. Position the widest parts towards the outside of the dish, and the thinner parts towards the centre. Scatter the sliced onion over.
2 Cover and microwave on high for 5 minutes.
3 Mix together the wine, brown sugar, ground cloves, ground coriander, orange juice and black pepper.
4 Turn and reposition the chops then spoon the wine mixture over. Top each chop with a slice of orange.
5 Cover and microwave on high for 5–6 minutes until the chops are just tender.
6 Transfer the chops to a serving dish and cover with foil.
7 Stir the soy sauce and dissolved arrowroot into the cooking juices.
8 Microwave uncovered on high for approximately 3 minutes, or until the sauce reaches boiling point. Stir after every minute of cooking.
9 Adjust seasoning to taste and pour a little sauce over each chop, topping with fresh orange slices. Garnish with parsley and serve the remaining sauce separately.
Reheat: covered on high for 5 minutes. Turn the dish once during this time.

ROAST LEG OF LAMB

Serves 4 (see colour plate 6)

I have used a lean, boned fillet end leg of lamb for this recipe as it microwaves splendidly. Much of the fat is drawn out of the meat during cooking and the finished joint is succulent, moist and carves easily. The joint browns naturally, but can be crisped under a preheated grill before or after standing time if preferred.

INGREDIENTS

1 small onion, finely chopped	herb salt, black pepper
1 oz/25 g butter or sunflower margarine	2 lb/1 kg fillet end leg of lamb, boned
3 oz/75 g fresh wholewheat breadcrumbs	**Containers**
1 teaspoon finely chopped fresh parsley	Trivet.
1 teaspoon chopped fresh rosemary, or ½ teaspoon dried	Shallow dish. Medium plastic microware bowl. Increase timing by 30 seconds when using
½ teaspoon paprika	ovenproof glass or ceramic bowl.

1 First prepare the stuffing. Put the onion and butter in the bowl. Cover and microwave on high for 3 minutes. Stir once during cooking.

2 Stir in the breadcrumbs, herbs, paprika, salt and pepper.

3 Open out the meat and press the stuffing in firmly. Reshape, and tie with string (not plastic) or secure with wooden skewers.

4 Stand the joint on a trivet in a shallow dish and cover with a split roasting bag, tucking the ends in loosely under the trivet.

5 Microwave on high for 10 minutes. Remove the juices from the dish and turn the joint over. Sometimes the breadcrumbs swell up during cooking and may need pressing back into the meat.

6 Re-cover and microwave on medium for 18 minutes. Remove the juices from the dish once during cooking.

7 Wrap in foil immediately (unless browning under the grill), shiny side in, and stand for 20 minutes.

Reheat: don't attempt to reheat the whole joint. Meat should be sliced then layered with gravy so that moisture is retained. One portion will take approximately 2 minutes to reheat, covered on high.

CHILLI BEEF AND BEANS

Serves 4

The flavour of this is very good indeed but improves even more when made a few hours, or even a day ahead. Either process some good quality lean braising or rump steak or buy ready ground, not minced, beef for a good texture dish.
Cool rapidly after standing time by placing the container in cold water, then cover and refrigerate until required. The reheating time will need to be increased by as much as 3 minutes when the dish is well chilled.
Lean lamb could be used as an alternative to beef.

INGREDIENTS

1 medium onion, finely chopped	2 tablespoons finely chopped fresh parsley
1 clove garlic, crushed	
1 large green pepper, finely diced	salt
1 lb/500 g lean beef, ground	**Container**
12 oz/375 g ripe tomatoes, peeled and roughly chopped	3½ pt/2 litre ovenproof glass bowl or casserole dish.
1 teaspoon chilli powder, or 2 teaspoons Mexican chilli seasoning	Decrease timing by 3 minutes when using a plastic microware container.
black pepper	(A plastic microware dish will absorb colour and flavour from this recipe and will need to be sterilized after use.)
15 oz/475 g can red kidney beans, rinsed under cold running water and drained well	

◆ 131

1 Put the onion, garlic and green pepper in the casserole dish. Cover and microwave on high for 3 minutes. Stir once during cooking.
2 Using a fork, mix thoroughly with the meat.
3 Three-quarters cover with cling film and microwave on high for 6 minutes. Break up with a fork halfway through cooking.
4 Add the tomatoes, chilli powder or Mexican seasoning and black pepper.
5 Three-quarters cover and microwave on high for 6 minutes. Stir once during cooking.
6 Stir in the red kidney beans. Three-quarters cover and microwave on high for 5 minutes.
7 Stir in the parsley and microwave uncovered on high for 2 minutes. Stir well.
8 Cover and stand for 5 minutes. Adjust seasoning to taste.
Reheat: covered on high for 6–8 minutes. Stir twice during this time.

VEAL MEATBALLS WITH EGG AND LEMON SAUCE

Serves 4

These cook remarkably quickly and have a delicate fresh flavour and light texture. The veal mixture should be quite smooth before forming into balls and if a mincer is used then it is best to mince the meat twice. Hands are the best tool for mixing all the ingredients together; beat and squeeze the mixture until smooth.

I used chunks of veal in preference to ready minced veal, which must be very lean. Beware also of dried mint as much of this has a rather musty taste and would spoil the delicate flavour of this dish.

Take care with the sauce; it must be cooked on either medium or low setting to prevent the eggs from curdling. Less lemon juice can be used if preferred as the sauce is quite tangy.

This is another dish that I feel is best served straight away.

INGREDIENTS

2 heaped teaspoons finely chopped fresh mint	2 egg yolks
1 teaspoon finely choppped fresh parsley	juice of 1 lemon
	salt, black pepper
	parsley or coriander leaves for garnish
1 small onion, finely chopped	**Container**
1 lb/500 g lean veal	Shallow plastic microware dish.
2 slices of white bread, crusts removed, soaked in cold water and squeezed out	Large plastic microware jug.
salt, black pepper	Increase timing by 2–2½ minutes when using ovenproof glass or ceramic containers.
Sauce	
¼ pt/150 ml unsalted light chicken stock or water	

1 Process the mint, parsley, onion and veal together in that order. Make sure that the onion is very finely chopped before adding the veal.

2 Transfer to a mixing bowl, add the bread and season to taste. Mix thoroughly together with your hands until a smooth paste is formed.

3 Form into 20 small balls then arrange these in the shallow dish. Position as many towards the outside edges as possible, leaving a small space between each ball.

4 Cover and microwave on high for 6 minutes. Turn each ball over and reposition halfway through cooking.

5 Stand, covered, for 2 minutes then drain off the cooking juices. Make up to ¼ pt/150 ml with cold water. Cover the meatballs with foil so that heat is retained.

6 Beat the egg yolks and lemon juice together in the jug. Beat in the stock and season with salt and pepper.

7 Microwave uncovered on medium for 2–2½ minutes, whisking after every

30 seconds of cooking time until the sauce thickens. Do not allow this sauce to boil otherwise the eggs will curdle.

8 Pour the sauce over the meatballs and microwave covered on medium for 2 minutes, until heated through.

9 Garnish with parsley or coriander leaves.

Reheat: not recommended. The mixture can be formed into balls, covered and refrigerated until close to serving time. An extra 2 minutes will need to be added to the cooking time as the starting temperature affects the overall cooking time.

ESCALOPES OF LAMB WITH AUBERGINE AND TOMATOES

Serves 4

The absence of fat and connective tissue makes lean escalopes of lamb a perfect choice for microwaving. The lamb takes on an attractive colour from the marinade and looks most appetizing when the dish is completed. The cooking juices are reduced conventionally after microwaving; this saves time and is much more practical. I would recommend serving this immediately after cooking. If the dish is reheated, make sure that the vegetables are covering the meat to prevent it from drying out.

◆ 133

INGREDIENTS

12 oz/375 g lamb escalopes	**Marinade**
8 oz/250 g aubergine, slit in 4 lengthways, then sliced into ½ in/1 cm thick pieces	6 allspice berries, crushed
	¼ teaspoon ground cinnamon
	¼ teaspoon ground cumin
1 small onion, chopped	4 tablespoons dry red wine
8 oz/250 g beefsteak tomato, thinly sliced	1 clove garlic, crushed
	black pepper
salt, black pepper	**Container**
good squeeze of fresh lemon juice	Shallow plastic microware dish.
fresh parsley or coriander leaves for garnish	Increase timing by 3 minutes when using ovenproof glass or ceramic container.

1 Mix all the marinade ingredients together and pour over the lamb escalopes. Cover and marinate at room temperature for a minimum of 2 hours.

2 Immerse the prepared aubergine in a bowl of salted water for 30 minutes. Drain and rinse thoroughly under cold running water.

3 Put the onion and aubergine slices into the dish. Cover and microwave on high for 5 minutes. Shake once during cooking.

4 Put the tomato slices over the top, cover and microwave on high for 2 minutes.

5 Spread the escalopes over the vegetables and pour over the marinade.

Cover and microwave on high for 3½ minutes. Rearrange the lamb, re-cover and microwave for a further 3 minutes or until cooked to your liking.

6 Carefully drain off the cooking juices, pressing the meat and vegetables down firmly with a spatula. Transfer the juices to a pan. Cover the lamb and vegetables immediately with foil so that heat is retained while the sauce is being reduced.

7 Boil the sauce hard until reduced by half. Season and add lemon juice to taste.

8 Put the vegetables in a shallow serving dish and arrange the lamb escalopes down the centre. Pour over the reduced sauce and garnish.

Reheat: not recommended, although the meat can be marinated well ahead and the recipe completed up to the end of step 5.

IRISH STEW

Serves 4

A delicious stew with a good full flavour. The power setting is reduced to medium so that the meat becomes tender and the flavours develop.
It is important to use best end neck of lamb and not a tougher joint, otherwise the connective tissue will not have sufficient cooking time to break down before the vegetables are cooked.

INGREDIENTS	
1½ lb/750 g best end neck of lamb, trimmed of excess fat	black pepper
1 medium onion, sliced thinly	1 lb/500 g potatoes, sliced into ½ in/1 cm pieces
4 oz/125 g carrots, sliced thinly	salt
3 tablespoons pearl barley	**Container**
½ pt/300 ml boiling chicken or vegetable stock	Large ovenproof glass casserole dish. Reduce the timing by 5 minutes when using a plastic microware dish.
2–3 bay leaves	
1 medium tomato, peeled and chopped	

1 Fry the meat in a frying pan until browned on all sides.

2 Put the onion and carrots into the casserole dish. Cover and microwave on high for 5 minutes. Stir once during cooking.

3 Add the lamb, barley, boiling stock, bay leaves, tomato and black pepper.

4 Cover and microwave on high for 10 minutes. Give the dish a half turn once during cooking.

5 Turn and reposition the meat as necessary then scatter the potatoes over.

6 Cover and microwave on high for 5 minutes. Turn the dish and reduce the power setting to medium. Cook for a further 20 minutes or until the meat and potatoes are quite tender. Turn the dish twice during cooking. Season to taste. Stand, covered, for 10 minutes.

Reheat: covered on high for 12 minutes. Stir or turn the dish 3 times during this time.

LAMB'S KIDNEYS IN SPICY SAUCE

Serves 4

This dish is good served over rice or pasta. To balance the meal, make a mixed green salad or lightly cook some green vegetables. The sauce is spiced and tastes quite rich – extra chilli powder or Mexican chilli seasoning can be added for those who like their food really hot. Remember though, microwaving enhances the flavour of spices. Prepare the kidneys properly before cooking – the flavour of the finished dish will be greatly improved.

INGREDIENTS

1 lb/500 g lamb's kidneys	black pepper
1 teaspoon bicarbonate of soda	parsley
1 tablespoon wine or cider vinegar	2 teaspoons potato flour dissolved in a little cold water
1 medium onion, finely chopped	
1 clove garlic, crushed	1–2 teaspoons natural soy sauce (shoyu)
½ teaspoon turmeric	**Container**
½ teaspoon chilli powder or 1 teaspoon Mexican chilli seasoning	3½ pt/2 litre deep ovenproof glass casserole dish.
1 tablespoon sunflower oil	Decrease timing by 1 minute when using a plastic microware dish.
14 oz/425 g can chopped tomatoes	

◆ 135

1 First prepare the kidneys. Skin, slice in half horizontally and remove the core and tubes with scissors or a small sharp knife. Wash thoroughly in cold water then pat dry on absorbent kitchen paper. Place the kidneys in a colander. Sprinkle over the bicarbonate of soda, stir and stand for 15 minutes. Rinse quickly in the vinegar, then drain for 30 minutes. This procedure removes any bitter flavour, firms and tenderizes the kidneys. Pat the kidneys dry with absorbent kitchen paper before cooking. Slice each half in 2.
2 Place the onion, garlic, turmeric, chilli powder or seasoning and oil in the casserole dish. Cover and microwave on high for 3 minutes. Stir once during cooking.
3 Stir in the tomatoes and black pepper. Cover and microwave on high for 5 minutes. Stir once during cooking.
4 Stir in the prepared kidneys. Cover and microwave on high for 5 minutes. Stir once during cooking.
5 Stir in the parsley and dissolved potato flour. Cover and microwave on high for 2–2½ minutes, until the kidneys are just tender and the sauce has thickened. Stir once during cooking.
6 Stir in the soy sauce, cover and stand for 5 minutes. Adjust seasoning to taste if necessary before serving.
Reheat: with great care; if microwaved too long the kidneys will continue to cook and end up tough and leathery. Cover and microwave on high for 4–5 minutes. Stir once during this time.

HOT MARINATED BEEF SALAD

Serves 4 (see colour plate 7)

A salad with an interesting variety of textures. Choose 2 or 3 types of lettuce.
I suggest cos or iceberg and either radicchio leaves, curly endive or oak leaf
lettuce. A light dressing can be drizzled over the leaves just before the meat
is added.
Chicken breast and white wine can be substituted for the beef and red wine
if preferred.

INGREDIENTS

12 oz/375 g rump steak or topside, cut into thin strips	2 tablespoons lemon juice
	1 clove garlic, crushed
1 tablespoon olive oil	**Salad**
1 small onion, sliced thinly	1 small lettuce
4 oz/125 g mushrooms, sliced thinly	few radicchio, curly endive leaves
1 teaspoon arrowroot dissolved in a little cold water	1 quantity of croûtons (p.34)
1 teaspoon soy sauce	**Container**
black pepper	Browning dish or shallow dish.
Marinade	When an ordinary shallow dish is used
2 teaspoons olive oil	instead of a microwave browning dish, start cooking by mixing the oil and meat
¼ teaspoon finely grated fresh root ginger	together and microwave uncovered on high for 3 minutes. Stir once during cooking. Add the other ingredients when the beef is a
4 tablespoons dry red wine	light brown colour.

136 ◆

1 Mix the marinade ingredients together and add the meat. Stir well. Cover
and refrigerate overnight. Remove from refrigerator 30 minutes before
cooking.
2 Prepare the salad ingredients and mix with the croûtons in a large bowl.
3 Preheat the browning dish to maximum, adding the oil during the last
30 seconds.
4 Drain the meat from the marinade. As soon as the dish has preheated, add
the meat, turning over to brown and sear on all sides.
5 Microwave uncovered on high for 2 minutes. Stir in the onion and
mushrooms.
6 Microwave uncovered on high for 3 minutes. Stir once during cooking.
7 Mix the arrowroot with the remaining marinade, stir in the soy sauce and
black pepper. Stir into the meat.
8 Microwave on high for 3–4 minutes until thickened and the meat is just
cooked. Stir once during cooking.
9 Combine the meat and vegetables with the salad ingredients and serve
straight away.
Reheat: not recommended.

CASSEROLED BEEF

Serves 4

A rich casserole in which flavours are well combined. Meat tenderizing powder is used to break down the fibres of the meat before cooking. Without this, the casserole would take much longer, and the vegetables would have to be added later to prevent them overcooking.
Slice the meat fairly thinly, and use a large container so that ingredients are well spread out to promote quick, even cooking.

INGREDIENTS

1½ lb/750 g lean braising steak, cut into slices approximately 1½ in/4 cm square and no more than ½ in/1 cm thick	½ pt/300 ml hot unsalted beef stock
	sprigs of fresh parsley and thyme
1 teaspoon meat tenderizing powder	black pepper
1 small onion, thinly sliced	salt
1 clove garlic, crushed	2 oz/50 g chestnut mushrooms, wiped and thinly sliced
1 tablespoon sunflower oil	1 tablespoon potato flour dissolved in 2 tablespoons cold water
1 stick celery, thinly sliced	
2 medium carrots, peeled and thinly sliced	**Container** Large ovenproof glass casserole dish. Reduce timing by 3 minutes when using a plastic microware casserole.
2 bay leaves	
8 oz/250 g beefsteak tomato, liquidized and sieved	

◆ 137

1 Put the meat into a medium bowl and sprinkle over the tenderizing powder. Stir, cover, and stand for 30 minutes.
2 Put the onion, garlic and oil into the casserole dish. Cover and microwave on high for 3 minutes.
3 Stir in meat. Cover and microwave on high for 6 minutes. Stir twice during cooking, moving the browned pieces of meat to the centre of the dish and red pieces to the outside. The meat should be browned after 6 minutes – if not, microwave 1 minute more.
4 Stir in the celery, carrots, bay leaves, sieved tomato, hot stock, parsley and thyme sprigs, and black pepper. Mix all the ingredients together thoroughly.
5 Cover and microwave on high for 10 minutes. Stir once during cooking.
6 Reduce the power setting to medium and cook for 15 minutes. Stir 3 times during cooking.
7 Stir in the mushrooms and dissolved potato flour. Mix well.
8 Cover and microwave on medium for 5 minutes. Stand for 5 minutes. Remove the bay leaves and parsley sprigs and adjust seasoning to taste.
Reheat: covered on high for 6–8 minutes. Stir once during this time.

CASSOULET

Serves 4

This is not identical in flavour to a traditional slow cooked cassoulet,
in which the ingredients blend together gradually and the breadcrumb crust
breaks and forms crisp layers between ingredients from the dry heat
of the oven.
However, if all the stages in this recipe are followed precisely the dish
will be very well flavoured indeed.
It is essential to use lean cuts of meat, unlike a conventionally cooked
cassoulet, which contains belly pork and goose fat. If these were used in the
microwave method the appearance would be quite distasteful as it would be
swimming with fat.
The meat is marinated to tenderize it and add extra flavour before browning
in a frying pan. It is more practical to cook the beans on top of the stove.
The cooking time is the same as in the microwave and the beans absorb more
flavours from the aromatic stock during cooking; the resulting stock adds
a more robust character to this dish.
An important point to note is that salt is omitted completely from the beans,
marinade and completed cassoulet until close to the end of cooking, and
added only after the meat is fork tender. If it is added at an earlier stage
the contracting quality it possesses would prevent the flavours from
expanding and blending well together. It would also toughen the beans
and meat during cooking.
The breadcrumbs are crisped in the microwave while the cassoulet is
standing halfway through cooking.
Altogether this makes an excellent main course; the overall cooking time
is considerably less and the resulting cassoulet is lighter than the
conventionally cooked dish.
Haricot beans could be replaced by flageolet beans which take a similar
length of time to cook and look most attractive.

138 ◆

INGREDIENTS

8 oz/250 g pork fillet, fat and membrane removed, sliced diagonally into 1 in/2.5 cm thick pieces	bouquet garni
	black pepper
	2 oz/50 g butter
1 lb/500 g neck of lamb fillet, fat and membrane removed, sliced into 1 in/2.5 cm pieces	3 shallots, chopped
	2–3 bayleaves
	sprigs of fresh thyme
6 oz/175 g haricot beans (dry weight), picked over and soaked for 6 hours or overnight	sprigs of fresh parsley
	8 oz/250 g beefsteak tomatoes, skinned and roughly chopped
1 medium carrot, sliced into 4 lengthways	3 oz/75 g fresh breadcrumbs
4 in/10 cm stick celery	4 oz/125 g garlic sausage, thickly sliced
1 small onion, chopped	salt

Marinade	Containers
4 tablespoons dry red wine	Large ovenproof glass casserole dish.
1 clove garlic, crushed	Medium plastic microware bowl.
sprig of thyme	Decrease overall cooking time by 5 minutes
black pepper	when using plastic microware container.

1 Mix all the marinade ingredients together. Stir in the prepared pork and lamb. Cover and leave for 2 hours or longer.

2 Cook the haricot beans conventionally. Discard the soaking water as this will now have a bitter flavour. Put the beans in a medium pan with the carrot, celery, onion, bouquet garni and black pepper. Add cold water to cover the beans by 2 in/5 cm. Cover and bring to the boil, then simmer for about 1 hour, or until the beans are tender. Discard the bouquet garni and strain the beans, reserving the stock. (The beans can be cooked well in advance of microwaving.) You are now ready to assemble your cassoulet.

3 Drain the meat, pat dry and reserve the marinade. Melt 1 oz/25 g butter (or goose fat if you have some) in a frying pan. Raise the heat and add the meat. Stir quickly until well browned on all sides, then pour in the marinade. Allow to boil, stirring all the time so that the juices are well mixed. Transfer to the casserole dish.

4 Scatter over the shallots, bay leaves, thyme and parsley sprigs, tomatoes and ¼ pt/150 ml hot stock from the beans.

5 Cover and microwave on high for 10 minutes. Stir once during cooking.

6 Add the cooked beans. Stir well.

7 Cover and microwave on high for 5 minutes. Stir, re-cover, reduce setting to medium and cook for a further 5 minutes.

8 Stand, covered, for 15 minutes to allow full flavours to develop and blend.

9 While the casserole is standing prepare the breadcrumbs. Melt the remaining butter in the bowl. Stir in the breadcrumbs, coating evenly in the butter.

10 Microwave uncovered on high for 4 minutes until crisp. Stir once during cooking.

11 Return the casserole to the microwave after standing time. Microwave covered on medium for 5 minutes. Stir well. Discard the bay leaves and sprigs of herbs. Test the meat – it should be quite tender at this stage. If not, microwave on medium for a further 2 minutes.

12 Season well and add the sausage. Sprinkle over the breadcrumbs so that they completely cover the top.

13 Microwave uncovered on medium for 7 minutes. Cover and stand for 10 minutes before serving.

Reheat: covered on high for 8 minutes. Give the container a half turn, reduce power to medium and cook for a further 8 minutes until heated through.

◆ 139

POULTRY

6–8 minutes per 1 lb/500 g is the speed at which the microwave cooks chicken, and the results are always moist, tender, succulent and easy to carve. Free-range birds are far superior in flavour, less fatty and therefore microwave better than those raised in batteries. Spring chickens, capons, roasting chickens (look out for corn fed and poulet noir breeds – both have a good distinctive flavour) and small turkeys all microwave successfully. Poultry should be stuffed from the neck end only and weighed afterwards to calculate the exact cooking time. Boiling fowl are unsuitable as they require long, slow cooking to tenderize the flesh. Turkeys over 10 lb/5 kg are best cooked for half the time by microwave and the remaining time conventionally. It is better to cook extremely large birds in a conventional oven; it is far too much trouble to be constantly shielding different areas, turning and basting to prevent uneven cooking. Use the microwave to cook other dishes for the meal.

If poultry is cooked on a medium setting it is not always necessary to shield the wing tips and breast, but if it is cooked on high throughout, it must be shielded to prevent these parts from overcooking and drying out. Large birds are turned 4 times; ¼ of cooking time breast down, next ¼ of cooking time left side down, then right side down and last ¼ of cooking time on their back.

To improve the colour of the skin while the bird cooks, melt a little sunflower margarine or butter and mix with some soy sauce or paprika. Wipe the bird with kitchen paper and brush on your own additive-free browning agent.

Raise birds out of their juices by standing on a trivet during cooking; place the trivet and bird inside a roasting bag. Fatty birds like ducks and geese are best covered with a split roasting bag or greaseproof paper, and the fat will need to be removed from the dish frequently during cooking.

As soon as the bird is removed from the oven, test by inserting a thermometer into the thickest part of the thigh, or by inserting a knife between the thigh and body. Cooking is complete when the juices run clear. Tent with foil, shiny side in, during standing time so that cooking by conduction can proceed with maximum effect. The internal temperature of the bird will rise during this time.

Whole ducks require cooking completely on defrost to tenderize the flesh, which is tougher than chicken. Individual duck portions cook well on high and the appearance is improved by grilling after cooking.

Poultry can be browned in a frying pan before microwaving, or under a grill afterwards, but unless a browning dish or coating is used, no natural browning occurs when chicken pieces are microwaved as the cooking time is so short. Boneless portions will cook even more quickly. Always place thicker parts towards the outside of the dish and thinner parts towards the centre, and turn and reposition as necessary. Fat is always found underneath the skin, so remove the skin for low-fat cooking. When skinned pieces are cooked with other ingredients the overall flavour is improved. If you prefer the chicken to be browned, use one of the deeper browning dishes with a lid. Preheat the dish and sear the poultry on all sides, add the remaining ingredients, cover and cook, repositioning and turning during cooking and stirring from time to time. This is an excellent way to make paella.

I have discovered that leaving the casserole to stand for 10 or 15 minutes halfway through the cooking time allows the meat to relax and flavours to blend. All casseroles improve in flavour when they are cooled rapidly after cooking, and then reheated later.

Always reheat poultry thoroughly to kill salmonella.

◆ 141

CHICKEN BREAST PARCELS

Serves 4 (see colour plate 5)

A perfect main course for weightwatchers and those on restricted fat diets.

INGREDIENTS	
4 boneless chicken breasts (total weight 1 lb/500 g) skinned and trimmed of fat	3 tablespoons dry white wine
	herb salt
lemon juice	natural yoghurt
black pepper	1 spring onion, sliced thinly on diagonal, for garnish
1 small red pepper, sliced into thin strips	**Containers**
1 small yellow pepper, sliced into thin strips	4 microwave boiling bags or silicone paper or cling film

1 Squeeze a little lemon juice over the chicken breasts and sprinkle with black pepper. Place in the bags or wrap loosely in silicone paper or cling film.
2 Arrange the red and yellow peppers on top of the chicken and spoon over the wine.
3 Secure the top of the bags loosely with elastic bands. Arrange on the turntable or oven floor so that the widest part of each chicken breast faces outwards.
4 Microwave on medium for 6 minutes. Half turn each bag, then cook on

medium for a further 6 minutes. Stand in the bags for 2 minutes.
5 Transfer the chicken breasts to warmed serving plates and spoon over the juices. Season with herb salt, swirl a little yoghurt over each one and garnish with the spring onion.
Reheat: not recommended, but the recipe can be prepared in advance up to the end of step 2, then chilled until required.

CHICKEN LIVER AND MUSHROOM PATE

Serves 4–6

Serve this delicious pâté with triangles of wholewheat toast and
a little fresh green salad.
When frozen chicken livers are used, transfer from their plastic container
to a shallow dish. Microwave on defrost for 2 minutes and allow to thaw
completely at room temperature.

INGREDIENTS	
8 oz/250 g chicken livers	½ teaspoon French mustard
3 oz/75 g unsalted butter	herb salt, black pepper
1 small onion, chopped	bay leaves, black peppercorns and paprika for garnish
1 clove garlic, crushed	
½ teaspoon mixed dried herbs	**Containers**
4 oz/125 g mushrooms, roughly chopped	Medium plastic microware bowl. Increase timing by 1–2 minutes when using ovenproof glass or ceramic container. Small ovenproof glass bowl.
2 tablespoons brandy	
2 tablespoons dry white wine	

1 Remove any inedible parts from the chicken livers. Wash, pat dry and slice.
2 Mix 1 oz/25 g butter, onion, garlic and mixed herbs together in the bowl.
3 Cover and microwave on high for 2 minutes. Stir in the chicken livers and mushrooms.
4 Cover and microwave on high for 5 minutes. Stir once during cooking.
5 Transfer the chicken livers and vegetables to a processor or blender.
6 Stir the brandy, wine and mustard into the remaining juices.
7 Microwave uncovered on high for 1 minute, or until the mixture boils.
8 Melt the remaining butter in a small bowl on high.
9 Add the cooking juices, melted butter, salt and pepper to the processor or blender. Blend until smooth.
10 Spoon into a small terrine or 6 individual ramekin dishes. Garnish with bay leaves, peppercorns and paprika. Chill well until set.

DUCKLING WITH FRUIT SAUCE

Serves 2–3

A duckling breast joint can be found in many supermarkets or obtained from an obliging butcher. A joint of this size cooks perfectly by microwave. It is essential to prick the skin thoroughly before cooking, and to stand the joint on a trivet so that much of the fat is drawn away from the flesh. Remove the juices and fat frequently during cooking, otherwise the microwaves will concentrate in these and overall cooking time will be affected.

INGREDIENTS

1 duckling breast joint, weighing 1 lb 6 oz/675 g	**Garnish** orange and lemon slices
salt, black pepper	parsley or watercress
4 tablespoons red wine	**Containers** Plastic trivet.
2 heaped tablespoons plum jam	Shallow dish. Roasting bag.
2 tablespoons pure orange juice	Shallow flameproof dish.
1 tablespoon lemon juice	1 pt/600 ml ovenproof glass jug.
1 teaspoon arrowroot dissolved in a little cold water	

◆ 143

1 Prick the duckling skin to allow as much fat as possible to escape during cooking.
2 Arrange the joint breast side down on the trivet, and place in the shallow dish. Cover with a split roasting bag, tucking the ends in loosely.
3 Microwave on high for 5 minutes. Turn the duckling over and remove juices and fat from the dish. Re-cover with the bag and microwave on defrost for 20 minutes, until the juices run clear and the flesh is just tender. Remove cooking juices twice during cooking.
4 Transfer the duckling joint to a flameproof container and season the skin well with salt and pepper.
5 Brown and crisp the skin under a preheated grill. Cover with foil.
6 Place the wine, jam, orange and lemon juice in the jug.
7 Microwave uncovered on high for 2 minutes until boiling, stir after 1 minute.
8 Stir in the dissolved arrowroot and microwave uncovered on high for 30 seconds, until the sauce thickens and clears.
9 Pour a little sauce over the duckling and serve the remaining sauce separately. Garnish with orange and lemon slices and sprigs of parsley or watercress.
Reheat: covered on high for 4 minutes. Turn the dish once during this time.

POULET CHASSEUR

Serves 4–6

This microwaves beautifully and is a perfect dish for entertaining.
It is more practical to reduce the sauce conventionally at the end of cooking.

INGREDIENTS

3½ lb/1.75 kg chicken, skinned and jointed into 8 pieces	black pepper
	2 tablespoons brandy
1 small onion, thinly sliced, or 3–4 shallots, peeled and quartered	4 oz/125 g mushrooms, thinly sliced
	herb salt
1 clove garlic, crushed	a little extra parsley for garnish
12 oz/375 g fresh ripe tomatoes, liquidized then sieved	**Containers**
	Large ovenproof glass casserole dish.
¼ pt/150 ml dry white wine	Decrease timing by 5 minutes when using
¼ pt/150 ml boiling chicken stock (make this from the giblets)	a plastic microware container.
	3½ pt/2 litre plastic microware jug.
sprigs of parsley and thyme	Increase timing by 1 minute when using
2 bay leaves	ovenproof glass or ceramic jug.

144 ◆

1 Put the chicken in the dish. Arrange the thicker parts towards the outside and the thinner parts towards the centre.

2 Cover and microwave on high for 12 minutes. Reposition once during cooking time.

3 Put the onion and garlic in the jug. Cover and microwave on high for 2 minutes.

4 Add the tomatoes, wine, boiling stock, parsley, thyme, bay leaves and black pepper. Stir well.

5 Microwave uncovered on high for 3 minutes. Stir twice during cooking.

6 Stir in the brandy. Pour the sauce over the chicken.

7 Cover and microwave on high for 8 minutes. Stir once during cooking.

8 Add the mushrooms. Stir well. Microwave covered on medium for 10 minutes.

9 Test the chicken. If it is cooked, remove to a serving dish and cover with foil. If a larger chicken was used than that specified, continue to cook on a medium setting until tender.

10 Strain the sauce into a pan and scatter the vegetables over the chicken, discarding the bay leaves, parsley and thyme sprigs. Re-cover with foil.

11 Reduce the stock conventionally by boiling over a high heat until reduced by one third, stirring frequently.

12 Adjust seasoning to taste and pour the sauce over the chicken and vegetables. Garnish with extra parsley.

Reheat: covered on high for 10–15 minutes. Turn the dish and spoon the sauce over the chicken twice; test after 12 minutes.

CREAMY CHICKEN CASSEROLE

Serves 4

If you have never cooked a casserole in the microwave then this is the one I would recommend you to try first. Microwaved casseroles can be disappointing if the flavours have not blended together completely. When all the ingredients are cooked together from the beginning, flavours will not have had the opportunity to blend together during the short cooking time, even though the finished dish resembles a casserole.
It is essential that the onion and garlic are cooked first; this draws out the acids which in turn encourage flavours from other ingredients to be transferred and also helps to tenderize the chicken.
Here is a succulent casserole, full of flavour and good for those who need to discover the very best way of casseroling by microwave. The stock is thickened using a roux to make a creamy sauce.
Standing time is allowed halfway through cooking to enable the meat to relax and full flavours to develop.
A large deep casserole dish is necessary, or the milk could boil over during cooking.

INGREDIENTS

1 medium onion, finely chopped	1 oz/25 g sunflower margarine or butter
1 clove garlic, crushed	1 oz/25 g plain flour
2 medium carrots, thinly sliced	1 tablespoon chopped fresh parsley
2 sticks celery, finely sliced	salt
3 lb/1.5 kg roasting chicken, skinned and jointed into 4	paprika
1 bay leaf	**Containers**
¼ pt/150 ml boiling water or chicken stock	Large ovenproof glass casserole dish. Reduce the timing by 4–5 minutes when using a plastic microware dish.
¼ pt/150 ml milk	3½ pt/2 litre plastic microware jug.
black pepper	

1 Put the onion and garlic in the casserole dish. Cover and microwave on high for 2 minutes.
2 Add a layer of carrots and one of celery. Cover and microwave on high for 3 minutes.
3 Arrange the chicken over the vegetables and add the bay leaf, hot water or stock, milk and black pepper.
4 Cover and microwave on high for 10 minutes. Rearrange halfway through cooking.
5 Stand for 10 minutes. Rearrange the chicken joints if necessary.
6 Microwave 8 more minutes or until the chicken and vegetables are tender. Give the dish a half turn once during cooking.
7 Strain off the liquid and put to one side. Cover the casserole dish with foil.
8 Put the margarine or butter in the jug. Microwave uncovered on high until

melted. Stir in the flour and microwave uncovered on high for 1 minute, or until the mixture puffs up.

9 Make up the stock from the casserole to ¾ pt/450 ml with extra milk or water. Gradually whisk this into the roux.

10 Microwave uncovered on high for 1 minute. Whisk well. Continue to microwave uncovered on high, whisking after every minute of cooking until the sauce reaches boiling point – approximately 3 minutes. Adjust seasoning to taste.

11 Pour the sauce over the chicken and vegetables. Sprinkle with parsley and paprika.

Reheat: covered on medium for 12–15 minutes. Turn the dish 3 times during this time.

TURKEY WITH LOTUS ROOT AND HIZIKI

Serves 4

This dish of turkey escalopes with a mixture of aromatic vegetables, lotus root and hiziki should be served with soba (buckwheat) or udon (flat Japanese wheat) noodles for a truly Japanese flavoured meal. The resulting stock is richly flavoured and is transformed into a clear sauce with kuzu root powder. Save the stock from the soba noodles (which are easiest to cook conventionally) as this will serve as an excellent base for soups.

Dried lotus root needs reconstituting before cooking and would usually require soaking and then simmering for about 45 minutes. The microwave method does save some time.

Hiziki (*Hizikia fusiforme*) (p. 207) is a mild, sweet flavoured seaweed with a black, stringy appearance. It requires soaking before cooking.

Kuzu (sometimes called kudzu) is a white starch obtained from the root of a prolific leguminous vine of the genus Pueraria, native to the Far East. Kuzu is used extensively in Japanese cooking to thicken sweet and savoury dishes and also as a base for confectionery. It thickens in a similar way to arrowroot (which could be substituted if kuzu is not available), is bland in flavour, yet seems to impart a silkiness to sauces. It is most commonly bought in chunks which need crushing to a fine powder in a mortar or coffee grinder before use. In times of famine, bowls of kuzu mixed with water and cooked to a thick consistency were the only form of sustenance that kept many people from starvation. Kuzu is also said to have numerous medicinal properties, the main one being its alkalinity which is beneficial to digestion.

All these specialist ingredients can be obtained from most oriental stores or from the Clearspring Grocer (p.209).

INGREDIENTS

1 oz/25 g dried lotus root	black pepper
¾ pt/450 ml cold water	½ pt/300 ml hot unsalted chicken or
small handful of dried hiziki	vegetable stock
2 sticks celery, cut into julienne strips, then into tiny dice	4 turkey escalopes, weighing about 1 lb/500 g in total
8 oz/250 g carrots, prepared as above	2 heaped teaspoons ground kuzu
1 small onion, finely chopped	soy sauce
1 clove garlic, crushed	**Containers**
1 teaspoon finely grated fresh root ginger	Medium plastic microware bowl. Shallow plastic microware dish.
4 tablespoons sake or dry white wine	Large plastic microware jug. Increase timing by 4 minutes when using
2 bay leaves	ovenproof glass or ceramic containers.

1 First reconstitute the lotus root: place in the bowl with the water. Cover and microwave on high for 10 minutes. Stand, covered, until cooled, then drain and discard the water.

2 Cover the hiziki with plenty of cold water and allow to soak for at least 20 minutes. Drain, discard the water and chop into ½ in/1 cm lengths.

3 Put the celery, carrots, onion, garlic, lotus root, ginger, wine, bay leaves, black pepper and ¼ pt/150 ml hot stock into the shallow dish. Mix the ingredients together well.

4 Cover and microwave on high for 8 minutes. Stir once during cooking.

5 Stir in the hiziki. Cover and microwave on high for 3 minutes.

6 Lay the turkey escalopes over the vegetables. Microwave covered on high for 10 minutes. Rearrange the turkey once during cooking, positioning cooked parts towards the centre of the dish and pinker parts nearer the outside. At the end of this time the turkey should be cooked and the vegetables will have retained some crispness.

7 Strain off the juices into the jug, discard the bay leaves and cover the dish with foil to retain the heat.

8 Make the cooking juices up to ½ pt/300 ml with the remaining stock. Mix the kuzu powder with a little cold water and pour the hot stock over, whisking all the time. Add a generous amount of soy sauce to taste.

9 Microwave uncovered on high for 2–2½ minutes, until boiling, thickened and clear. Whisk after every 30 seconds of cooking time.

10 Arrange the turkey escalopes down one side of a shallow serving dish and decorate with a few pieces of cooked lotus root. Pour some of the sauce over so that all the turkey is covered, then mix the remainder into the vegetables. Arrange the vegetables on the other half of the serving dish. Serve with tagliatelle, soba or udon noodles.

Reheat: much nicer when served straight away, but if you wish to reheat, make sure that the turkey is covered with sauce otherwise it could dry out. Cover and microwave on high for 5 minutes. Turn the dish once during this time.

CHICKEN CURRY

Serves 4

One of the greatest advantages of microwaving curry is the absence of lingering cooking smells; chicken curry is also remarkably quick and easy to make. All curries improve when they are made a day, or at least a few hours, in advance – the flavours then have a chance to develop further. Cumin and coriander seeds can be ground in a mortar or placed on a chopping board and crushed with the end of a rolling pin.

INGREDIENTS

2 tablespoons groundnut oil or sesame oil	2 bay leaves
2 teaspoons coriander seeds, crushed	½ pt/300 ml hot chicken stock
2 teaspoons cumin seeds, crushed	8 oz/250 g beefsteak tomato, peeled, liquidized and sieved
3 lb/1.5 kg chicken, jointed into 4, skinned, washed and patted dry	black pepper
1 medium onion, chopped	2 tablespoons sultanas
1 medium apple, cored and sliced	whole coriander leaves for garnish
1 teaspoon finely grated fresh root ginger	salt
1 clove garlic, crushed	**Containers**
seeds from 3 green cardamom pods	Large ovenproof glass casserole dish. Decrease timing by 3 minutes when using a plastic microware container.
1–2 teaspoons curry powder	3½ pt/2 litre plastic microware jug.
1 teaspoon turmeric	Increase timing by 30 seconds when using an ovenproof glass jug.
1 in/2.5 cm piece cinnamon stick	

1 Make a paste from 1 tablespoon oil, the crushed coriander and cumin seeds.

2 Arrange the chicken in the casserole dish, positioning the thicker parts towards the outside of the dish and the thinner parts towards the centre.

3 Insert the tip of a sharp knife through the chicken pieces in several places. Spread or rub the prepared paste over the chicken.

4 Cover and microwave on high for 10 minutes. Reposition halfway through cooking. Stand, covered, while preparing the sauce.

5 Place the remaining oil, onion, apple, ginger, garlic, cardamom seeds, curry powder and turmeric in the jug. Mix the ingredients together well.

6 Cover and microwave on high for 4 minutes. Stir once during cooking. Stir in the cinnamon stick, bay leaves, hot chicken stock, sieved tomato and black pepper.

7 Microwave uncovered on high for 2 minutes or until boiling. Stir in the sultanas.

8 Spoon the sauce over the chicken. Cover and microwave on medium for 12 minutes or until the chicken is cooked. Halfway through the cooking time check the chicken, reposition if necessary and spoon the sauce over.

9 Stand, covered, for 5 minutes. Discard the bay leaves and cinnamon stick

and adjust seasoning to taste before serving. Garnish with coriander leaves.
Reheat: covered on medium for approximately 15 minutes. Spoon the sauce
over the chicken halfway through this time. The sauce can be diluted with
extra hot stock at the end of cooking if preferred.

POULET NOIR WITH SPICES

Serves 2

Many of the larger supermarkets now sell poulet noir, a chicken with a good
distinctive taste, which is not overpowered by the spiced yoghurt marinade.
I used part boned chicken breasts and left the skin intact as this crisps under
the grill after microwaving and the marinade forms a beautiful golden crust.
Serve immediately; if allowed to cool and then reheated, the crisp coating
will turn soggy.

INGREDIENTS

1 teaspoon turmeric	3 tablespoons thick yoghurt
1 teaspoon paprika	black pepper
1 teaspoon ground coriander	lemon juice
1 teaspoon ground cumin	1 lb/500 g poulet noir chicken breasts, part boned with skin intact
1 teaspoon sambal oelek (hot pepper condiment) or a dash of Tabasco	
	salt
1 teaspoon finely grated fresh ginger root	**Container** Shallow flameproof container.
2 teaspoons toasted sesame oil	

1 Mix all the spices, sambal oelek, ginger, sesame oil, yoghurt, black pepper
and a squeeze of lemon juice together thoroughly.
2 With the tip of a sharp knife, prick the chicken in several places. Spoon
over the marinade.
3 Cover and stand at room temperature for 30 minutes, or up to 3 hours.
4 Cover and microwave on high for 3½ minutes. Reposition the chicken and
spoon over the sauce.
5 Cover and microwave on high for a further 3½ minutes until just tender.
6 Season well, then brown and crisp under a preheated grill.
Reheat: not recommended.

SPRING CHICKENS WITH OKRA AND CHERRY TOMATOES

Serves 4

Spring chickens are greatly improved when the microwave is used in preference to conventional cooking methods. Quite often these little birds do not have much flavour, and I would recommend that they are purchased fresh from a good butcher. The chickens are grilled until browned and crisp for an attractive finish, the whole cherry tomatoes add flavour and colour, and the sprigs of herbs pushed under the chicken skin prior to cooking impart a pleasant flavour to the flesh.

INGREDIENTS

two 1 lb/500 g spring chickens, cut in half lengthways	1 heaped teaspoon chopped fresh marjoram
a few sprigs of lemon thyme or thyme	8 oz/250 g tiny cherry tomatoes, pierced with the tip of a sharp knife
lemon juice	
black pepper, salt	20 small black olives, stoned
1 tablespoon olive oil plus a little extra	2 tablespoons finely chopped fresh parsley
1 clove garlic, crushed	
2 shallots, chopped	lemon slices for garnish
4 oz/125 g okra, tips and stalks removed	**Containers**
8 oz/250 g beefsteak tomatoes, peeled and roughly chopped	Large shallow ovenproof glass dish. 3½ pt/2 litre ovenproof glass casserole dish. Decrease timing by 3 minutes when using plastic microware containers.
1 bay leaf	
1 heaped teaspoon chopped fresh basil	

150 ◆

1 Push the sprigs of lemon thyme or thyme underneath the skin of the chicken. Sprinkle with lemon juice and season well with black pepper.
2 Arrange in the shallow dish, cover and microwave on high for 12 minutes. Rearrange twice during cooking. They are cooked when the juices run clear.
3 Reserve the cooking juices for the sauce. Brush a little olive oil over the chicken and season with salt and extra black pepper. Finish under a preheated grill until the skins are nicely browned and crisp.
4 Put the remaining 1 tablespoon olive oil, garlic and shallots into the casserole dish. Cover and microwave on high for 2 minutes.
5 Stir in the okra, beefsteak tomatoes, herbs and reserved cooking juices.
6 Cover and microwave on high for 8 minutes or until the okra is tender. Stir once during cooking.
7 Stir in the cherry tomatoes, olives and 1 tablespoon parsley. Cover and microwave on high for 2½–3 minutes or until the tomatoes are just tender. Season well and arrange the spring chickens on top. Garnish with the remaining parsley and lemon slices.
Reheat: the chicken should have some of the vegetables and sauce spooned over. Cover and microwave on high for 8 minutes. Give the container a half turn once during this time.

CHICKEN ARTICHOKE MOUSSES

Serves 6

These light mousses can be made well in advance. They are pale green in colour and look pretty in their pool of golden sauce. For an even lighter version, replace the double cream with thick Greek yoghurt and reduce or eliminate the mayonnaise. Asparagus makes a good substitute for the artichoke hearts.
I used round ramekin dishes, but if you have some small heart-shaped or oval dishes then the presentation will look delightful.

INGREDIENTS

8 oz/250 g chicken breasts, skinned and boned	salt
black pepper	**Sauce**
½ oz/15 g butter	3 tablespoons thick Greek yoghurt
4 medium artichoke bottoms, cooked or an 11 oz/350 g can, drained and rinsed	½ teaspoon turmeric
	1 heaped tablespoon good mayonnaise
1 large egg, beaten	2 tablespoons pure orange juice
3 good tablespoons double cream	salt, black pepper
2 heaped teaspoons chopped fresh lemon thyme	**Containers**
	Shallow plastic microware dish.
2 heaped teaspoons chopped fresh tarragon, plus a few small sprigs	6 plastic microware ramekin dishes. Increase overall cooking time by 2–2½ minutes when using ovenproof glass
lemon juice	or ceramic containers.

◆ 151

1 First prepare the sauce. Beat the yoghurt until smooth then add the turmeric, mayonnaise and orange juice. Beat together until all the ingredients are well blended. Season to taste. Cover and chill until ready to serve.
2 Arrange the chicken breasts in the shallow dish. Sprinkle with black pepper and dot with the butter.
3 Cover and microwave on medium for 6 minutes. Stand, covered, until cooled.
4 Process the chicken together with its cooking juices and the artichoke hearts until almost smooth. Beat in the egg, cream and chopped herbs. Mix thoroughly, then add lemon juice, salt and black pepper to taste.
5 Put a small sprig of tarragon or a few tarragon leaves in the base of each ramekin. Divide the chicken mixture evenly between the 6 moulds, pressing down firmly with the back of a spoon. Smooth the tops.
6 Cover and arrange in a circle around the edges of the turntable or on the oven floor.
7 Microwave on medium for 10 minutes. Give each ramekin a half turn once during cooking.
8 Stand, covered, for 5 minutes. Carefully loosen around the edges with a small palette knife and invert on to a serving dish. Cover, cool and chill well before serving.

CHICKEN BREASTS WITH TARRAGON

Serves 4–6

The chicken breasts and sauce have an excellent fresh flavour and the completed dish looks most attractive. Serve as a starter or light main course in the summer.

It is essential to arrange the chicken in a single layer otherwise the cooking will need to be interrupted more frequently. When a large container is not available cook in two batches instead; allow approximately 8 minutes of cooking time per batch and rearrange the chicken once.

It's quicker and more practical to reduce the sauce conventionally after cooking; the reduced sauce should then be cooled completely before mixing with the other ingredients.

INGREDIENTS	
2 lb/1 kg chicken breasts, skinned and boned	1½ heaped tablespoons mayonnaise
black pepper	lemon juice
few sprigs of fresh tarragon	salt
6–8 tablespoons dry white wine	lemon slices and tarragon sprigs for garnish
¼ pt/150 ml chicken stock	**Container**
1 tablespoon double cream	Large shallow ovenproof glass flan dish.

152 ◆

1 Open out the chicken breasts and season well with pepper (not salt at this stage). Put a sprig of tarragon on each one, allowing the stalk to protrude for easy removal after cooking. Fold the fillet over so that the tarragon is enclosed and arrange, fold side down, in the shallow dish. Spoon over the wine.

2 Cover and microwave on medium for approximately 14–16 minutes. Rearrange the chicken breasts twice during cooking, positioning any cooked parts towards the centre of the dish and raw pieces close to the outside.

3 Allow to stand, covered, until completely cool. Put the cooking juices in a pan and make up to ¼ pt/150 ml with more white wine. Add the chicken stock. Boil hard until reduced to 4 tablespoons. Cool.

4 Whisk the double cream and mayonnaise together, then gradually whisk in the reduced stock. Add a good squeeze of lemon juice and season to taste with salt and pepper.

5 Remove the tarragon sprigs from the chicken breasts and arrange on a serving dish. Carefully spoon over the sauce, making sure that every bit of chicken is covered. Cover and chill well before serving.

6 Just before serving put a fresh tarragon sprig and half a slice of lemon on each chicken breast.

Reheat: not recommended.

BAKING, PUDDINGS AND DESSERTS

The speed at which the microwave cooks cakes is quite remarkable – a light sponge cake bakes in 4 minutes, but it will rapidly degenerate into a trifle sponge if overcooked by as little as 30 seconds. Gone are the days when Christmas puddings were steamed for 6–8 hours. The microwave will cook a 1½ pt/900 ml pudding to perfection in 5 minutes. The oven does not need to be preheated and will not heat up the kitchen. There is less condensation from cooking, the mixture does not get 'burned on' to containers so washing up becomes less of a chore and the oven door can be opened as often as is necessary without spoiling food.

When a light sponge cake or pudding is required the microwave can produce these in a few minutes. The cook is limited to a few simple recipes when baking by microwave, and the puddings and cakes I have included in this chapter all microwave well.

CAKES

Only cakes made with a batter of soft dropping consistency microwave successfully. The correct consistency is crucial; if it is too stiff the cake will bake hard or rubbery and if it is too watery it will not set in the centre.

Cakes conventionally cooked form a crust and remain moist inside, whereas microwaves can only bake crisp throughout (e.g. flapjacks) or soft throughout (e.g. light steamed puddings). Gingerbread and light sponge mixtures are the most successful.

Traditional heavy fruit cakes do not microwave well and cakes containing more than 4 oz/125 g of dried fruit should not be attempted. The fruit will sink to the base of the container and can 'burn' from the inside – quite different from the way it would scorch in a conventional oven.

It is often necessary to add a little extra raising agent to prevent a cake from shrinking after cooking. This, surprisingly, does not affect the taste although I hold it partly responsible for the short keeping qualities of microwaved cakes. Don't overbeat the mixture especially if using a processor or electric beater, otherwise the cake will sink after cooking and the texture will be uneven.

Baked items don't brown in the microwave so use ingredients such as mixed spices, honey, black treacle or molasses, malt extract, brown sugar and wholemeal flour to give the finished dish more colour. Dark cakes such as chocolate or parkin present no problems.

After many experiments I prefer to use a mixture of flours. All wholemeal flour can produce a hard textured cake which quickly turns stale. All white flour can be used so long as brown sugar or spices are included. My preference is for Allinson's Farmhouse flour (p.207) or half Farmhouse and half white flour. Half wholemeal and half white are acceptable but not as successful as the Farmhouse flour.

PUDDINGS

Most moist puddings such as rice, tapioca, semolina, ground rice, baked egg custards and steamed puddings, microwave well. Rice pudding has an excellent flavour and the rice swells up beautifully although it can take almost as long to cook in the microwave as it does in the conventional oven. A low setting is required for most of the cooking time to prevent the milk from boiling over and to allow time for the grains to swell and tenderize. The cooking time for egg custards can be reduced by using ramekin dishes; one cooked in a large container requires microwaving on a low setting to enable the centre to set and prevent the outside edges from forming a rubbery casing.

Light sponge puddings are easily cooked and have a good high rise and light texture. These are usually cooked on a high setting but I would recommend a medium or low setting when a jam or syrup capped pudding is being microwaved. The syrup can caramelize in the base and the jam, which heats up rapidly, can work its way up the sides of the container during cooking. It is more practical to microwave the sponge on high and reheat the jam or syrup separately.

Crumble mixtures are successful although the topping can become unsettled during cooking if the crumble has been sprinkled over raw fruit. Microwave the fruit until almost tender then drain off excessive juices before covering with the crumble.

There are limitations when microwaving meringues; a cooked fruit base with meringue is acceptable, although the meringue will be softer than one that has been conventionally cooked. It will be necessary to brown the top under the grill after microwaving or sprinkle with chopped nuts or toasted coconut. For pavlova, or when any crisp meringues are required, use the conventional oven.

154 ◆

PASTRY

Pastry does not microwave well from its raw state and I would only attempt a shortcrust base for a quiche or fruit flan. I recommend using the same combination of flours as for cakes. Double crust fruit pies are disastrous as the filling heats up rapidly due to the high sugar content and spills out of the sides and over the top crust. Rough puff and flaky pastries contain a larger proportion of fat and the microwaves concentrate in these, leaving the pastry extremely soggy and uncooked. With the speed of microwave cooking pastry has a tendency to shrink and toughen so extra care must be taken when preparing it. Be very light handed when mixing and use the blade of a knife. Chilling after mixing makes it easier to roll out lightly without any undue stretching. The more you stretch the more it will shrink. It is easier to roll out thinly if the dough is placed on greaseproof paper; use the paper to turn the dough around instead of handling it. Very little flour will be needed if you follow this method. Surplus flour is best brushed off before you line the dish as it will only leave a crust on the pastry after cooking. If there is time, chill again before microwaving and the pastry will shrink less during cooking. You will need to add an extra 30 seconds to the cooking time to allow for the cold temperature of the dish and ingredients.

◆ 155

BISCUITS

Traditional thin crispy biscuits don't microwave well and are better conventionally cooked; thicker 'cookies' are more successful. I find it much easier to cook a whole batch of biscuits in the conventional oven; the same quantity of biscuit dough would need to be microwaved in several batches, and as the biscuits crisp on cooling, quite a few plates or shallow containers would be needed.

Flapjack type recipes microwave well but care must be taken when microwaving as they can overcook and become brittle. They can be left in the cooking container until cold.

Shortbread microwaves splendidly and the lovely buttery taste is enhanced. Shortbread is fragile and should be handled carefully after microwaving and transferred to a lined cooling rack immediately after standing time.

BREAD

Yeast breads do not microwave well. White bread looks pallid and there is no crispy crust so the flavour is not comparable with conventionally baked bread. The microwave can be used for proving mixes. Soda breads can be microwaved successfully but require browning under the grill afterwards. A yeasted pizza dough cooked on a browning dish is superior to one that is cooked in an ordinary container.

TESTING

As microwave cooking times are only approximate it is confusing for the beginner to know just when to remove the food from the oven. Cakes must be cooked for a minimum time and be removed from the oven whilst still slightly moist on top. When a skewer is inserted into the centre of the cake it should come out clean and the mixture should be shrinking away from the sides of the container.

When in doubt, always allow the full standing time and then test again. It does not spoil the food if a further minute of baking is required after the standing time. The golden rule is always remove baked items from the oven when they look as though they could do with a little longer.

TO FINISH

Cakes usually require some form of decoration after cooking as the tops are soft and often have a pitted appearance. Scones look rather raw but simply need brushing with a little beaten egg or milk after microwaving, then grilling briefly to toast the tops. Other baked goods can also be quickly flashed under a preheated grill to brown and crisp the tops.

Baked items must be stored in airtight containers as soon as they are cooled. They do not keep as long as conventionally baked ones and can dry out after 3–4 days.

COOKING TECHNIQUES

Stand the container on a trivet whilst cooking to allow air to circulate underneath the food and the microwaves to penetrate more efficiently. The centre will always be set if this method is adopted.

Both the shape and the thickness of the container will affect the overall cooking time. A cake cooked in a light plastic microware dish will take approximately 30 seconds less than one cooked in ovenproof glass.

Never fill containers more than half full or the mixture may rise up and spill over the top.

It is necessary to give the container a half turn once or twice during cooking to encourage an even rise and texture even if the oven has a turntable.

CONTAINERS

A ring mould is perfect for cakes as the microwaves are able to penetrate the mixture from all angles. The absence of a centre means that the mixture cooks evenly and the overall cooking time is reduced.

Food cooks more evenly in round containers but these should have straight sides and be no more than 9 in/23 cm diameter. If a wider container is used the outside of the cake will be overcooked by the time the centre has set.

Loaf shaped containers can create problems as the ends tend to cook first and it is often necessary to shield these parts with foil halfway through the cooking time. Overwrap the foil with cling film and ensure that the foil never touches the sides of the oven.

Square containers should have rounded corners otherwise microwaves can become concentrated in these areas and the ingredients will be overcooked.

For fairy cakes a double thickness of paper cake cases works well. Special microwave bun trays can be used but cakes need to be removed fairly quickly from these after standing time or the bases will become soggy.

◆ 157

PREPARING CONTAINERS

Light plastic microware does not usually require greasing although it is advisable to line the base with greased greaseproof paper or baking parchment. Ovenproof glass and ceramic containers need lightly greasing and base lining so that the mixture can rise freely up the sides. Don't overgrease though, or you may find the fat melts and rises up the container which can have the effect of preventing the cake from rising properly and the fat can settle on top of the cake.

Never grease and then flour containers as this simply bakes into a rather nasty crust.

COVERINGS

Cakes, crumbles, meringues, scones, biscuits, flan cases, bread and pizzas are cooked uncovered. Rice puddings, egg custards and sponge puddings are cooked covered. Cover pudding basins loosely with a pierced cling film, pulling it up a little in the centre to allow extra space for rising.

YORKSHIRE MOGGY CAKE

Serves 6–8

A sticky moist cake which improves if kept for a few days in an airtight container. Molasses has a slightly stronger taste than black treacle. It is a natural unprocessed product very rich in iron, calcium and essential minerals, and is easily obtained from health food shops.

INGREDIENTS

Ingredients	Containers
4 oz/125 g sunflower margarine	**Containers**
2 level tablespoons clear honey	Medium microware bowl.
1 level tablespoon molasses or black treacle	7 in/18 cm round, light plastic microware dish, base lined with baking parchment. Increase timing by 30 seconds – 1 minute when using ovenproof glass or ceramic containers. These will need lightly greasing. Trivet.
2 size 1 eggs, beaten	
4 oz/125 g Farmhouse self-raising flour (p.207)	
1 level teaspoon baking powder	
2 level teaspoons ground ginger	

158 ◆

1 Place the margarine, honey and molasses or black treacle in a medium bowl.

2 Microwave uncovered on high for 1½–2 minutes, until melted. Cool slightly.

3 Beat in the eggs and sift in the flour, baking powder and ginger. Beat until smooth.

4 Pour into the prepared container and stand on a trivet.

5 Microwave on high for 3½–4 minutes turning the dish once during cooking.

6 Stand for 10 minutes.

7 Carefully loosen around the edges with a palette knife then invert on to a cooking rack that has been lined with greaseproof or absorbent paper. Once cold store in an airtight container.

PEARS WITH BLACKCURRANT AND APPLE SAUCE

Serves 4

A simple yet elegant dessert that can be served either warm or chilled, topped with a swirl of yoghurt and a sprinkling of chopped nuts.

INGREDIENTS

4 medium pears, peeled, leaving stalks intact	**Containers**
½ pt/300 ml pure apple and blackcurrant juice	3 pt/1.8 litre deep round ovenproof glass casserole. Decrease timing by 1 minute when using a plastic microware container. Microware jug.
2 rounded teaspoons arrowroot	
pinch of ground cinnamon	
1 tablespoon crème de cassis (optional)	

1 Slice a little off the bottom of the pears so that they stand upright in the dish.
2 Place ¼ pt/150 ml juice in the dish with the pears. Cover and microwave on high for 4½–5 minutes until the pears are just tender. Turn the dish once during cooking.
3 In the jug, mix the arrowroot with the remaining juice until well blended. Pour off the hot juice from the pears and add to the jug. Stir in the cinnamon.
4 Microwave uncovered on high for 1 minute, then stir well. Repeat until the mixture boils. Stir in the crème de cassis if using. Pour over the pears. Serve warm or chilled.

◆ 159

PEAR MERINGUE

Serves 4

A light pudding that can be served either warm or chilled.
Meringue is softer when microwaved, so chopped nuts are used to add interest to the texture.

INGREDIENTS

1½ lb/750 g fresh pears, peeled if preferred, cored and quartered	**Containers**
zest of 1 lemon	7 in/18 cm ovenproof glass soufflé dish. Do not use a light microware dish for this recipe. Trivet.
2 egg whites	
3 oz/75 g demerara sugar, ground in a coffee grinder until it resembles icing sugar, or 3 oz/75 g icing sugar, sifted	
1 tablespoon mixed chopped nuts	

1 Place the pears in the soufflé dish and sprinkle on the lemon zest.
2 Cover and microwave on high for 4 minutes until the pears are almost tender. Shake the dish once during cooking. Drain off excess juice.
3 Whisk the egg whites until stiff, fold in the sugar and spread over the pears, ensuring that the meringue is touching the edges of the dish.
4 Stand on a trivet and microwave uncovered on high for 2½–3 minutes until just set in centre.
5 Sprinkle the nuts over the top and stand for 5 minutes.
Reheat: not recommended.

BLACKBERRY BAKED APPLES

Serves 4

Baked apples have a lovely fresh flavour when microwaved. Take care not to overcook them and remove them from the oven when just tender otherwise they will rapidly turn to apple purée. Test by inserting a skewer through the side of the apples. If in doubt, remove from the oven and allow to stand for a few minutes. Test again. If necessary cook for a further minute or two. If cooking apples are used increase the amount of sweetening and cooking time, remembering that the time can vary quite a lot with different types of apples.

INGREDIENTS	
4 medium eating apples, cored	**Container**
juice of ½ lemon	7 in/18 cm ovenproof glass soufflé dish.
4 oz/125 g blackberries, defrosted if frozen	Decrease timing by 30 seconds when using a plastic microware container.
½ teaspoon ground cinnamon	
3–4 tablespoons clear honey or soft brown sugar	

1 Remove ⅓ of the apple skin with a peeler, working from the top of the apple to just above the centre. Brush with lemon juice to prevent discoloration. Place in the soufflé dish.
2 Sprinkle the blackberries with cinnamon, and use to fill the apple cavities. Drizzle honey over the stuffing, or sprinkle with sugar.
3 Cover with pierced cling film or a casserole lid and microwave on high for 6 minutes until the apples are just tender. Turn the dish once during cooking. Stand for 5 minutes.
Reheat: covered on high for 2–3 minutes.

BOILING BAGS

5·Chicken Breast Parcels. See recipe on page 141

Boiling bags are ideal for cooking most vegetables and allow quick and even cooking. Secure the top of the bag loosely with an elastic band or non-metallic tie leaving a gap at the top of the bag to allow steam to escape. Stand the bag in a microware container so that it remains upright and is easy to remove from the oven.

TENTING

6·Roast Leg of Lamb. See recipe on page 130

Standing time is an essential part of microwave cooking. Food that requires a long standing time should be tented with foil, this will maintain the temperature of the food and allow cooking to continue. Arrange the foil so the shiny side is facing inwards.

BROWNING DISH

7·Hot Marinated Beef Salad. See recipe on page 136

A browing dish is the only container that can be put
into a microwave oven empty. They have a specially
impregnated base which absorbs microwave energy and
becomes very hot. They are ideal for cooking bacon,
fish cakes and any meat you wish to seer, they can also
be used, as in this recipe, for stir-frying.

CONTAINERS

8·Almond Sponge with Strawberries and Cointreau Cream. See recipe on page 165

The shape and thickness of containers has a marked affect on the cooking times of food. Food cooks more quickly in plastic microware containers as they absorb little of the microwave energy. The ring mould used in this recipe is ideal for cooking any dense food such as cakes or patés. The hollow centre solves the problem of food being overcooked at the edges but remaining uncooked in the centre.

CRUNCHY MUESLI

Serves 3–4

Microwaving cereals is very successful as they brown and crisp very quickly.
Serve with yoghurt or milk and fresh sliced fruit, or use as
a topping for desserts. Children love to eat this as a dry snack, which makes a
healthy alternative to crisps and sweets.

INGREDIENTS

2 tablespoons clear honey	1 tablespoon wheatgerm
2 tablespoons sunflower oil	1 tablespoon bran
6 oz/175 g rolled oats	**Container**
2 oz/50 g almonds or other nuts, chopped	Medium ovenproof glass bowl. 10 in/25 cm round shallow ovenproof glass dish. Do not use plastic microware for this recipe.
1 oz/25 g sunflower seeds	
3 oz/75 g raisins or sultanas	

1 Place the honey and oil in the bowl and microwave uncovered on high for
45 seconds. Stir.
2 Stir in the oats, nuts and sunflower seeds.
3 Spread around the outside of the shallow dish, leaving the centre of the
dish empty.
4 Microwave uncovered on high for 5–6 minutes. Stir twice during cooking.
5 Mix in the dried fruit, wheatgerm and bran.
6 Cover and stand for 10 minutes.
7 Remove the cover and stir, then leave to cool in the dish. Once cold store in
an airtight container.

◆ 161

FRUIT SCONES

Makes 8

INGREDIENTS

8 oz/250 g Farmhouse (p.207) self-raising flour	1 large egg, beaten
	2–4 tablespoons milk
1 teaspoon baking powder	**Container**
2 oz/50 g sunflower margarine	Greaseproof paper or baking parchment to fit turntable or oven floor.
2 oz/50 g sultanas	
1½ oz/40 g soft brown sugar	

1 Sift the flour and baking powder into a mixing bowl.
2 Fork in the margarine. Stir in the sultanas and sugar.
3 Add the beaten egg, reserving a little for the tops, and enough milk to mix
to a stiff dough. Knead lightly for a few seconds.
4 Pat out lightly to an 8 in/20 cm thick round and cut out 8 scones, using a
2½ in/6 cm cutter.

5 Line the turntable or oven floor with greaseproof paper. Arrange the scones in a wide circle, well spaced out.
6 Microwave uncovered on high for 3½ minutes. Test by inserting a cocktail stick into the centre of the scones. When removed it should be clean.
7 Brush the tops with the remaining egg and place under a preheated grill until lightly browned.

HONEY NUT FLAPJACKS

Makes 10

Flapjack mixtures microwave well but take care to cook until just set otherwise they will be much too hard to chew. They crisp on cooling and need storing in an airtight container otherwise they will soften.
For an alternative flavour try using malt extract (obtainable from health food shops) instead of honey.

INGREDIENTS

2 oz/50 g sunflower margarine	**Containers**
2 oz/50 g honey	Medium ovenproof glass bowl.
5 oz/150 g porridge oats	8 in/20 cm round ovenproof glass flan dish, lightly greased. Decrease timing by
2 oz/50 g mixed chopped nuts	30 seconds when using plastic microware.
½ teaspoon vanilla essence	Trivet.

1 Place the margarine and honey in the bowl and microwave uncovered on high for 1½ minutes or until melted.
2 Stir in all the remaining ingredients and mix thoroughly together.
3 Press down firmly into the prepared dish.
4 Stand the container on a trivet and microwave uncovered on high for 1 minute, then on medium for 6 minutes, until the mixture is just set. Turn the container twice during cooking.
5 Mark into 10 sections and allow the flapjacks to cool in the container.
6 Once cold cut into sections and store in an airtight container.

ORANGE AND SULTANA PUDDING

Serves 4–6

This pudding has a good fresh orange flavour and the sultanas plump up nicely. Serve with custard or heat 4 tablespoons marmalade in a small ovenproof glass bowl for 1 minute and pour over the pudding.

INGREDIENTS

4 oz/125 g sunflower margarine	½ teaspoon baking powder
3 oz/75 g soft brown sugar	2–4 tablespoons orange juice
grated zest of 1 orange	**Container**
1 teaspoon vanilla essence	1½ pt/900 ml plastic microware pudding basin, lightly greased. Increase timing by 30 seconds when using ovenproof glass or ceramic basin.
4 oz/125 g Farmhouse self-raising flour (p.207)	
2 eggs, beaten	
2 oz/50 g sultanas	

1 Cream together the margarine and sugar until light and fluffy.
2 Mix in the orange zest and vanilla essence.
3 Sift in a little flour and gradually beat in the eggs.
4 Stir in the sultanas and sift in the remaining flour and baking powder.
5 Mix together thoroughly, adding enough orange juice to produce a soft dropping consistency.
6 Place in the prepared pudding basin and cover loosely with pierced cling film, tenting up a little in the centre.
7 Microwave on high for 3½–4 minutes, or until cooked. Stand for 5 minutes.
Reheat: covered on high for 2 minutes.

◆ 163

MARBLED PUDDING

Serves 4–6

The marbled effect is achieved by darkening half the mixture with carob or cocoa powder. It looks attractive and tastes delicious when served with a carob sauce (p.178).

INGREDIENTS

4 oz/125 g sunflower margarine	2–4 tablespoons milk
4 oz/125 g soft brown sugar	grated zest of 1 lemon
2 large eggs, beaten	**Container**
4 oz/125 g Farmhouse (p.207) self-raising flour, sifted	1½ pt/900 ml plastic microware pudding basin, lightly greased. Increase timing by 30 seconds when using ovenproof glass or ceramic container.
½ oz/15 g carob or cocoa powder, sifted	
½ teaspoon vanilla essence	

1 Cream together the margarine and sugar until light and fluffy.
2 Gradually beat in the eggs, adding a little sifted flour to prevent curdling.
3 Sift in the remaining flour and fold into the mixture.
4 Put half the mixture into another bowl.
5 Into 1 bowl add the carob or cocoa powder and stir in the vanilla essence. Add enough milk to obtain a soft dropping consistency.
6 In the other bowl, stir in the lemon zest and milk as above.
7 Place alternate spoonfuls of light and dark mixtures into the pudding basin and smooth the top.
8 Cover loosely with pierced cling film, pulling up a little at the centre to allow for a good rise.
9 Microwave on high for approximately 3½–4 minutes, or until cooked. Stand for 5 minutes.
Reheat: covered on high for approximately 2 minutes.

BAKED EGG CUSTARDS

Serves 4

Egg custards microwave perfectly but great care must be taken to prevent overcooking. Keep a close eye on the custards during the last 30 seconds of cooking time. Remove from the oven while the centres are still a bit wobbly, as they continue to set during standing time.
Use very fresh eggs for the best flavour. A medium setting is used to prevent the outside edges turning rubbery before the centres are cooked.
Custards made from whole milk cook faster than those made from skimmed or soya milk, because of the higher fat content. Decrease timing by 1–2 minutes and watch very carefully when a richer milk is used.
I was once caught out when I only had Jersey milk to use for a demonstration. I was alarmed when after just 5 minutes the custards shot up and out of the containers; the reason, of course, was the high fat content of that extra rich milk.
Standing the containers on a trivet speeds up cooking and allows the air and microwaves to circulate freely underneath.

INGREDIENTS	
¾ pt/450 ml skimmed milk	**Containers**
3 large eggs	Large plastic microware jug.
4 teaspoons caster sugar	4 microware plastic ramekin dishes. Increase the timing by 1 minute when
½ teaspoon pure vanilla essence	ovenproof glass or ceramic ramekins
good grating of nutmeg	are used.

1 Put the milk into the jug and microwave uncovered on high for 1½ minutes, until hot but not boiling.
2 Beat the eggs, sugar and vanilla essence together. Gradually add the warmed milk, whisking constantly.

3 Stand 4 ramekin dishes on a plastic trivet. Strain the custard into the ramekins. Top with a good grating of nutmeg.
4 Microwave uncovered on medium for approximately 9 minutes. Give the trivet a half turn halfway through cooking and give each ramekin a half turn also.
5 Remove from the oven while the centres are still a bit wobbly. Stand for 5 minutes. Serve warm or chilled.
Reheat: Not recommended.

ALMOND SPONGE WITH STRAWBERRY AND COINTREAU CREAM

Serves 6 (see colour plate 8)

A light sponge ring generously filled with strawberries and Cointreau cream and a stunning garnish of blue borage flowers with a light sprinkling of orange zest. It is important to line the mould to enable
the cake to be easily removed. If using a fluted ring mould, line with cling film.
Make sure that the sponge has completely cooled before scooping out the crumbs otherwise it could break. The cake crumbs can be used in other dishes and keep well stored in an airtight container.
Raspberries, loganberries and tayberries can be used in place of the strawberries. An alternative liqueur which is complementary to the chosen fruit could be used.

◆ 165

INGREDIENTS

5 oz/150 g sunflower margarine	1 lb/500 g strawberries, sliced
4 oz/125 g caster sugar	**Garnish**
3 large eggs, beaten	borage flowers
5 oz/150 g Farmhouse (p.207) self-raising flour	grated orange zest
2 oz/50 g ground almonds	**Container**
1 level teaspoon baking powder	3½ pt/2 litre plastic microware ring mould.
Filling	Increase timing by 1–1½ minutes when using ovenproof glass or ceramic mould.
¾ pt/450 ml double cream	Grease lightly, and line the base with
1–2 tablespoons caster sugar	4 strips of greased greaseproof paper or bakewell paper.
3 tablespoons Cointreau	Trivet.

1 Cream the margarine and sugar together. Gradually beat in the eggs. Sift in the flour, ground almonds and baking powder. Mix to a soft dropping consistency.
2 Transfer to the prepared ring mould and level the top. Stand the container on a trivet and microwave uncovered on high for 6½ minutes. Give the container a half turn once during cooking. At the end of cooking the cake

should be shrinking away from the sides of the dish. It may still look slightly moist on top. Insert a skewer into the centre; if the cake is cooked it should come out clean.

3 Stand for 5 minutes. Using a palette knife, carefully loosen around the edges. Tap the underside of the container to loosen the cake further. Line a cooling rack with greaseproof paper and carefully turn out. Leave to cool completely.

4 Whip the double cream with the caster sugar and 2 tablespoons of Cointreau. Stir the remaining Cointreau into half of the strawberries, cover and stand for 2 hours before serving.

5 When the cake is completely cool, cut around the top neatly to a depth of ½ in/1 cm, leaving a ½ in/1 cm border on both edges. Carefully hollow out the cake crumbs. You should now have a ½ in/1 cm cake shell. Use the crumbs in other dishes.

6 Stand the cake shell on a serving plate and, using a spatula, spread a thin layer of cream inside the shell.

7 Stir the remaining half of the strawberries into the remaining cream and fill the cake shell. Press down lightly – all the fruit and cream will fit in – and finish by mounding up neatly. Chill well.

8 Just before serving, fill the centre with the strawberries which have been macerating in Cointreau. Garnish with borage flowers and a light sprinkling of orange zest.

166 ◆

ALMOND SHORTBREAD

Makes 12 pieces

This is melt-in-the-mouth shortbread, with an excellent flavour and a most acceptable appearance.

It is essential to use unsalted or slightly salted butter rather than salted butter – some brands are much too salty and can spoil the flavour. The semolina and hazelnuts add additional flavour and contrast to the texture. This is one recipe where I would never substitute sunflower margarine for the butter – it can be done if preferred, but the delicious aftertaste will be missing.

The shortbread is fragile and should not be removed from the container before standing time is complete. Shortbread crisps further on cooling.

INGREDIENTS	
4 oz/125 g plain flour	2 teaspoons brandy
1 heaped tablespoon semolina	1 egg yolk
2 oz/50 g ground almonds	**Container**
2 oz/50 g caster sugar	10½ in/26 cm ovenproof glass flan dish,
4 oz/125 g unsalted butter	lined with greaseproof paper or baking
1 oz/25 g hazelnuts, toasted and finely chopped	parchment. Do not grease the paper or the dish. Reduce timing by 1 minute when using plastic microware container.

1 Sieve the flour, semolina, ground almonds and caster sugar into a bowl.
2 Rub in the butter then stir in the hazelnuts, brandy and egg yolk. Press and squeeze the mixture together until a soft dough is formed.
3 Turn out onto a lightly floured surface and pat out to an 8 in/20 cm round. Flute the edges and, using a large knife, cut into 4 equal sections. Cut each section into 3, making 12 altogether. Prick all over with a fork or the end of a chopstick (I find the chopstick gives a more attractive finish).
4 Carefully transfer to the shallow dish, arranging the widest parts towards the outside edges. There should be a small space beween each piece.
5 Microwave uncovered on high for 5 minutes. Give the dish a half turn once during cooking.
6 Dust over with extra caster sugar. Stand for 10 minutes. Using a palette knife, transfer carefully to a cooling rack which has been lined with absorbent kitchen paper.

BLUEBERRY FLAN

Serves 6

For grown-ups only – I did allow the youngest of my brood a mouthful, but the slight tartness of the blueberries and wine was rejected.
The blueberries will each need pricking with the tip of a sharp knife to prevent them from bursting during the brief cooking time.
After many microwave experiments with pastry, I have to say that generally results have been disappointing but this pastry, which resembles a biscuit crust, is really good. The Farmhouse flour contributes to the attractive colour; pastry made from white flour does not look or taste so good after microwaving.
Agar agar is a vegetarian alternative to gelatine and can be obtained from health food shops. It sets rapidly so keep an eye on the fruit jelly as it cools slightly.

INGREDIENTS

Pastry	1–2 tablespoons blueberry or blackcurrant conserve
2 oz/50 g plain Farmhouse flour (p.207)	
1 oz/25 g plain white flour	1 teaspoon agar agar powder
1 oz/25 g ground almonds	**To decorate**
½ teaspoon ground cinnamon	whipped cream or thick Greek yoghurt
1½ oz/40 g sunflower margarine	**Containers**
1 egg yolk	Large plastic microware jug.
a little cold water to mix	8 in/20 cm plastic microware flan dish. Trivet.
Filling	Small ovenproof glass bowl.
8 oz/250 g blueberries, pricked with the tip of a sharp knife	Increase timing by 30 seconds when using ovenproof glass or ceramic flan dish, and by 2 minutes for ovenproof glass jug.
½ pt/300 ml dry red wine	
1 heaped tablespoon caster sugar	

1 Put the blueberries, wine and caster sugar in the jug. Cover and stand for 2 hours.

2 Prepare the pastry. Sift the flour, ground almonds and cinnamon into a mixing bowl. Using a fork, blend in the margarine, then the egg yolk and enough cold water to bind. Mix to a soft dough. Cover with cling film and chill for 15 minutes.

3 Roll the pastry out lightly (it is easiest to roll out on greaseproof paper that has had a light dusting of flour). The paper can be swivelled round to avoid overhandling the pastry. Line the flan dish, taking care not to stretch the pastry; the more you stretch at this stage the more it will shrink during cooking. Press the pastry well down into the base and sides, trim the top and prick all over with a fork.

4 Stand the container on a trivet and microwave uncovered on high for 4½ minutes until the base is just dry. Give the container a half turn once during cooking. If the pastry starts to rise up during cooking, open the door and prod back down with a fork.

5 Put the jam in the small bowl and microwave on high for 20 seconds until bubbling. Brush over the pastry shell, making sure that every bit of pastry is covered, especially where the sides meet the base. Leave to cool.

6 Once cooled, stir the blueberries and microwave uncovered on high for 2½ minutes. Using a slotted spoon, remove the blueberries, put to one side and continue to microwave the wine until boiling point is reached (about 1½ minutes). Stir in the agar agar until fully dissolved, then add the blueberries and any juices that have drained from them.

7 Leave the filling to cool slightly but keep a close eye on it as jellies made from agar agar set rapidly.

8 Spoon into the flan case and chill well before serving. Decorate with piped whipped cream or thick Greek yoghurt.

BUTTERNUT SQUASH PUDDING

Serves 4

Butternut squash has an excellent sweet flavour and bright orange colour, both of which are intensified after microwaving. This unusual dessert is extremely light, yet has a rich taste with a pleasant creamy texture.

INGREDIENTS	
1½ lb/750 g butternut squash	**To decorate**
¼ pt/150 ml pure orange juice plus 2 extra tablespoons	whipped cream or thick Greek yoghurt
	2 tablespoons pecan nuts
½ teaspoon ground cinnamon	**Containers**
2 teaspoons brandy (optional)	Microwave boiling bag.
1 tablespoon caster sugar	Small plastic microware jug.
½ teaspoon agar agar powder	

1 Peel away the thickish skin of the squash and the paler flesh beneath until you can see the bright orange flesh. Slice the squash in half lengthways, then scrape out and discard the seeds and slice the flesh fairly thinly. You should be left with approximately 1 lb/500 g flesh.

2 Put the prepared squash and 2 tablespoons of orange juice into a microwave boiling bag. Secure the top loosely with an elastic band.

3 Microwave on high for 6 minutes until fork tender. Give the container a half turn once during cooking.

4 Transfer to a food processor together with the cinnamon and the brandy (if using). Blend until smooth.

5 Put the remaining orange juice in the jug. Microwave uncovered on high for 2½ minutes or until boiling.

6 Stir in the caster sugar and the agar agar until dissolved.

7 Beat all the ingredients together thoroughly. Spoon into 4 individual bowls. Smooth the tops and chill well before serving. Decorate with whipped cream or thick Greek yoghurt and pecan nuts.

RICH RICE PUDDING

Serves 4

◆ 169

Although there is little time saved microwaving rice pudding the flavour is excellent and the rice fluffs up beautifully.
Use a deep container and reduce the setting once boiling point is reached to prevent ingredients from rising over the rim.
As there is no dry heat in the microwave the traditional crust that usually encases the rice does not form. The lemon zest and vanilla impart extra flavour to the rice and the butter and egg yolks help transform this into a delectable dessert. Alternatively serve cool in layers with a compote of fresh fruit and whipped double cream.

INGREDIENTS

3 oz/75 g pudding rice	**Container**
1 pt/600 ml Channel Islands milk	3½ pt/2 litre ovenproof glass casserole dish. Decrease timing by 3 minutes when using plastic microware bowl.
2 oz/50 g caster sugar	
½ split vanilla pod	
zest of 1 lemon	
1 egg yolk	
1 oz/25 g unsalted butter	

1 Put the rice, milk, sugar, vanilla pod and lemon zest in the deep casserole dish or bowl.

2 Cover and microwave on high for 8–10 minutes until boiling. Stir well.

3 Keep covered and microwave on defrost for 30 minutes until the rice is swollen and tender. Stir 3 times during cooking.

4 Beat in the egg yolk and butter. Cover and microwave on defrost for 2

minutes. Stand for 2 minutes, then remove the vanilla pod before serving.
Reheat: prepare the recipe to the end of step 3. Cover and microwave on high for 4–5 minutes until boiling. Stir once during this time. Complete the recipe from step 4.

IRISH COFFEE CREAM

Serves 4

Carrageen (or Irish Moss) is used to set this dessert; the flavour is rich while the texture is light and quite different from a similar combination of ingredients set with gelatine or agar agar.
Carrageen is a seaweed which has been used in Ireland for centuries to gel and set savoury and sweet dishes. It requires soaking in cold water before cooking to loosen sand, grit or other impurities.
Microwaving carrageen, when it is required to gel or set mixtures, shortens the cooking time considerably.

INGREDIENTS	
½ oz/15 g carrageen	**Containers**
½ pt/300 ml single cream	Large plastic microware jug.
¼ pt/150 ml full cream milk	Medium ovenproof glass bowl. Increase timing by 2 minutes when using
¼ pt/150 ml strong black coffee	ovenproof glass or ceramic jug.
3 oz/75 g good quality plain chocolate	
2 oz/50 g caster sugar	
2–4 tablespoons Irish whiskey	

1 Wash the carrageen quickly under cold running water, then cover with cold water and soak for 20 minutes. The seaweed will soften during this time and the water may gel a little.
2 Drain and put the carrageen in the jug with the cream, milk and coffee.
3 Microwave uncovered on high for 6–8 minutes until boiling point is reached. Stir twice during cooking.
4 Reduce the power to medium and microwave uncovered for 4 minutes. Stir twice during cooking. Stand, covered, while melting the chocolate.
5 Break the chocolate into pieces and put into the bowl. Microwave uncovered on medium for 2 minutes or until the pieces are just losing their shape. Stir until completely melted.
6 Strain the boiled carrageen mixture into a large bowl – use a wooden spoon to press all the liquid through. Scrape the underside of the sieve and beat this gelled liquid in.
7 Beat in the sugar and whiskey to taste. Mix half into the melted chocolate and beat well. Spoon into a pretty mould, smooth the top and press the mixture down well.
8 Spoon over the remaining mixture and smooth the top.
9 Cool and chill for at least 2 hours or overnight before serving.

TRUFFLES

Makes 20

Confectionery is easy to cook by microwave and one does not have to scour double boilers afterwards. Use very good quality chocolate to give these truffles a fine, rich flavour.

Melt chocolate on a medium setting otherwise it can overcook and turn gritty. Remove from the oven when the pieces are just beginning to lose shape and stir until completely melted.

Milk chocolate could be used for the filling and plain chocolate for the coating if preferred. Sieved cake crumbs could replace the ground almonds, and rum, Calvados or a coffee liqueur could be used in place of the brandy.

The truffles must be stored in the refrigerator until required.

INGREDIENTS

2 oz/50 g hazelnuts	**Container**
6 oz/175 g good quality plain chocolate	Medium ovenproof glass bowl
2 tablespoons double cream	(plastic microware is not suitable as the
2 tablespoons brandy	mixture reaches a high temperature).
1 heaped tablespoon ground almonds	Dinner plate.

◆ 171

1 Spread the hazelnuts over the dinner plate. Microwave uncovered on high for 2½ minutes. Chop finely.

2 Break up the chocolate and put half in the bowl. Microwave uncovered on medium for 2–2½ minutes until the pieces are beginning to lose their shape. Watch carefully; do not overcook. Stir until completely melted.

3 Add the chopped hazelnuts, double cream, brandy and ground almonds. Beat the mixture until all the ingredients are well mixed. Chill for 30 minutes or until the mixture is cool, thick and easy to handle.

4 Form into 20 small balls and transfer to silicone paper.

5 Microwave the remaining chocolate, following the instructions in step 2.

6 Using chopsticks or the prongs of a fork to hold the truffles, quickly dip each truffle into the chocolate and then put back on the silicone paper.

7 Chill well then place in pretty paper cases. Store in the refrigerator until ready to serve.

GREENGAGE AND GINGER COMPOTE

Serves 4

Greengages have a fine fresh flavour and good colour after microwaving and the stones are easy to remove. Score around each fruit before cooking to prevent the skins from bursting. It is important to choose fruit which is firm and just ripe; overripe fruit will disintegrate completely and the appearance of the dish will be spoiled.

The greengages can be replaced by other varieties of plums – the large, black Californian plums are particularly good.

Chill for at least 6 hours for the flavours to blend. Excellent served with Almond Shortbread (p.166).

INGREDIENTS

1 lb/500 g greengages, slit down from the top and all the way round with a sharp knife	4 pieces stem ginger, quartered
	2 tablespoons brandy
4 tablespoons dry white wine	**Container**
1 good tablespoon of acacia or lime blossom honey	Shallow plastic microware dish. Increase timing by 1 minute when using ovenproof glass or ceramic container.
1 tablespoon syrup from the jar of ginger	

1 Arrange the prepared greengages around the edge of the dish. Cover and microwave on high for 3–3½ minutes until just tender.

2 Using a slotted spoon, remove the greengages from the dish. Stir the wine, honey and ginger syrup into the juices.

3 Microwave uncovered on high for 3 minutes or until boiling. Stir once during cooking.

4 Stir in the pieces of stem ginger and brandy.

5 Remove the stones from the greengages and gently stir the fruit into the syrup. Cool, cover and chill for several hours before serving.

PLUM PUDDING

Serves 6

The flavour of this dark, moist pudding is exceptionally good
and the fruit plumps up beautifully.
I have devised quite a number of Christmas pudding recipes and this one
is the most successful to date. I use cake crumbs in preference to
breadcrumbs which improves and lightens the texture, although
breadcrumbs could be used if preferred. Wholemeal flour, cocoa powder,
black treacle, dark sugar, spices and Guinness all contribute to the
lovely black colour.
I used ready stoned prunes and citron peel bought in one piece. There
is no comparison with this and those ghastly tubs of mixed peel.
Unfortunately, microwaved Christmas puddings do not keep as well as
conventionally steamed ones, so it is best to make them close to the time
required and store in the refrigerator or freezer.
Cook partly on high and partly on medium to enable the centre to cook
through and prevent the outside edges hardening.

INGREDIENTS

1 oz/25 g plain wholemeal flour	3 oz/75 g slightly salted butter, chilled
2 teaspoons cocoa powder	1 tablespoon black treacle or molasses
3 oz/75 g plain cake crumbs	grated zest of 1 lemon and
½ teaspoon mixed spice	a good squeeze of lemon juice
½ teaspoon ground cinnamon	3 tablespoons Guinness
a good grating of nutmeg	1 tablespoon brandy
1 heaped tablespoon demerara sugar	1 large egg, beaten
2 oz/50 g candied peel	**Container**
6 oz/175 g prunes, stoned and chopped	1½ pt/900 ml ovenproof glass pudding basin,
4 oz/125 g raisins	lightly greased and base lined with greased
2 figs, chopped small	greaseproof paper.
1 oz/25 g pecan nuts, chopped	

1 Put all the dry ingredients, dried fruits and nuts into a large mixing bowl.
Mix together thoroughly.
2 Grate in the chilled butter and mix in.
3 In a small bowl beat all the liquid ingredients and lemon zest together then
stir into the dry ingredients. Mix thoroughly – the consistency should be
slack.
4 Transfer to the prepared basin, pressing the mixture down lightly with the
back of a spoon. Level the top and cover loosely with cling film, tenting this
up a little in the centre.
5 Microwave covered on high for 5 minutes, then reduce the setting to
medium and cook for a further 5 minutes. At the end of cooking the mixture
will be shrinking slightly from the sides of the basin and the centre should be
just set.

6 Stand, covered, for 5 minutes before carefully loosening around the edges with a palette knife and inverting onto a serving plate.
Reheat: covered on high for 2½ minutes.

FRESH FIGS WITH TIA MARIA, HALVA AND HAZELNUTS

Serves 4

This simple, sophisticated dessert is one of my favourites. The figs are cooked briefly with the coffee liqueur, hazelnuts and halva, which melts down a little but retains some of its crunchiness. Use firm, ripe figs and good quality halva. I prefer green figs in this recipe but if you use purple figs reduce the cooking time a little.
Chill well before serving; the figs will take on the most delicious flavour.
Serve with thick Greek yoghurt to balance the sweet rich figs.

INGREDIENTS	
4 ripe, firm fresh figs	**Container**
4 hazelnuts	4 plastic microware ramekins.
2 tablespoons Tia Maria or other coffee liqueur	Increase timing by 1½ minutes when using ovenproof glass or ceramic containers.
four 1 in/2.5 cm squares vanilla halva	
Greek sheep's milk yoghurt	

1 Cut a cross in the top of each fig to come two thirds of the way down.
2 Put the figs into ramekins or small individual dishes. Press a hazelnut into the centre of each and spoon over the Tia Maria.
3 Crush the halva slightly in your fingers and press lightly into the figs – half will protrude.
4 Cover and microwave on high for 2 minutes.
5 Using a teaspoon, press the halva down slightly into the fig and neaten up the shape (the figs open up like flowers during cooking).
5 Cover and cool, then chill for at least 2 hours (preferably overnight).
6 To serve, top each fig with a good dollop of thick Greek yoghurt.

MANGO ICE CREAM WITH PASSION FRUIT AND PISTACHIO NUTS

Serves 6

Simple to prepare and deliciously refreshing. Like all custard based ices, the freshest high quality ingredients will yield the finest flavour.
The mango can be prepared while the custard is cooling. Do not use a heavy ovenproof glass bowl or the mixture will take ages to cook.
Use a mild flavoured honey otherwise the ice cream will not have mango as the predominating flavour – caster sugar could replace the honey if preferred.

INGREDIENTS

½ pt/300 ml single cream	3 passion fruit
½ pt/300 ml Channel Islands milk	pistachio nuts, chopped
split vanilla pod	**Containers**
4 large eggs	Large plastic microware jug.
2 egg yolks	Large plastic microware bowl. Increase timing by 2 minutes when using
4 tablespoons acacia or lime blossom honey	ovenproof glass jug. Microware mould
1 large mango, peeled and puréed	

◆ 175

1 Put the cream, milk and vanilla pod into the jug. Microwave uncovered on high for 3½ minutes.
2 In a large bowl beat together the eggs, egg yolks and honey. Gradually whisk in the warmed milk.
3 Microwave on medium for 6 minutes, stirring after every 2 minutes, then cook for a further 2–3 minutes, stirring every minute until the mixture coats the back of a spoon. On no account allow the mixture to reach boiling point.
4 Leave to cool, remove the vanilla pod and stir in the mango pulp.
5 Pour into a shallow freezing tray and freeze until mushy.
6 Turn into a bowl and beat the mixture thoroughly.
7 Pour into an attractive mould and freeze until quite firm.
8 Microwave on defrost for 2–3 minutes, then stand for a further 2 minutes before serving.
9 Over each serving spoon the pulp from 1 passion fruit and sprinkle over a few pistachio nuts.

FIGS BENEDICTINE

Serves 4

Dried figs reconstitute quickly in the microwave; here they are cooked in red wine which imparts a refreshing tone and offsets their sweet flavour. Choose the largest, blackest figs for the finest flavour. The Benedictine combines well with the other ingredients and the syrup is delicious.
I would recommend that this dessert is prepared at least a day ahead so that a good full flavour can develop. The starfruit is best added near to serving time.
Grenadine could replace the Benedictine and pistachio nuts the almonds.

INGREDIENTS

12 oz/375 g dried figs, stalks removed, then rinsed in cold water	1 starfruit
	1 tablespoon slivered toasted almonds
seeds from 6 green cardamom pods	**Container**
1 in/2 cm piece cinnamon stick	Medium plastic microware bowl.
½ pt/300 ml dry white wine	Increase timing by 2 minutes when using
2 tablespoons Benedictine	ovenproof glass or ceramic bowl.

176 ◆

1 Put the figs, cardamom seeds, cinnamon stick and wine into the bowl.
2 Cover and microwave on high for 8 minutes. Stir once during cooking.
3 Stir in the Benedictine, then cover, cool and chill, during which time the figs should be stirred once or twice. (I find the flavour is at its best after 48 hours of chilling.)
4 Close to serving time: prepare the starfruit; shave off the dark brown strips and cut the fruit into ½ in/1 cm slices. Scatter the starfruit and slivered almonds over the figs.

QUINCE CREAM

Serves 6

This aromatic fruit has the subtle fragrance of evening scented flowers. Sour to taste, hard and often gritty, quince resemble large knobbly pears. After cooking, this fruit has the most delightful flavour and creamy texture which combines perfectly with the flaked rice in the recipe. Quinces are available during autumn and can be found in some supermarkets, country markets and from Middle Eastern grocers. Imported quinces have a finer flavour than those grown in England. Quinces should be stored in a dry cupboard and are ready for use when they smell sweet.
It is better to use a large plastic microware bowl than a heavy ovenproof glass dish for cooking the fruit as this shortens the cooking time.
Choose a deep container for the flaked rice to prevent it from boiling over.
Pear juice is not so readily available, but it does have an affinity with quinces.

INGREDIENTS

3 lb/1.5 kg quinces	**Containers**
¼ pt/150 ml pure unsweetened pear or apple juice	Large plastic microware bowl. 3½ pt/2 litre deep ovenproof glass casserole. Increase timing by 3–4 minutes when using ovenproof glass bowl; decrease timing by 2 minutes when using plastic microware casserole.
4–6 oz/125–175 g vanilla sugar	
4 oz/125 g white flaked rice	
pinch salt	
1 pt/600 ml boiling water	
½ pt/300 ml double cream	
2 pieces stem ginger, finely diced	

1 Peel, core and quarter the quinces. Slice into ½ in/1 cm thick pieces. Put the peeled quinces into cold water during preparation to prevent discoloration.
2 Put the prepared quinces and pear or apple juice into the large bowl. Cover and microwave on high for 12–15 minutes until the quinces are quite tender. Stir three times during cooking.
3 Transfer to a processor and blend until fairly smooth. Press through a sieve and put to one side whilst preparing the rice.
4 Put the flaked rice, 2 oz/50 g vanilla sugar, a pinch of salt and 1 pt/600 ml boiling water in the deep casserole or bowl. Stir well.
5 Cover and microwave on high for 4 minutes. Transfer to a processor and blend until smooth.
6 Mix the puréed quinces and rice cream thoroughly together. Stir in additional vanilla sugar to taste.
7 Pour into six individual pretty bowls. Cover with plastic film and allow to cool. Chill for at least 3 hours or overnight.
8 Close to serving time, whip the double cream and pipe a decorative border around the edges of each dish. Scatter the diced stem ginger over the quince cream.

◆ 177

BLACKCURRANT SAUCE

Makes 1 pt/600 ml

Microwaving draws out the fresh flavour of fruit, and the colours are always bright after cooking. Serve this sauce either hot or cold – it goes well with ice cream and poached fruits, or makes an excellent base for a red fruit salad.

INGREDIENTS

4 oz/125 g blackcurrants, fresh or frozen	**Container**
¾ pt/450 ml apple juice, unsweetened	3½ pt/2 litre plastic microware jug. Increase timing by 2 minutes when using ovenproof glass or ceramic jug.
1–2 tablespoons clear honey	
6 teaspoons arrowroot dissolved in 6 teaspoons cold water	

1 Place the blackcurrants in the jug and microwave uncovered on high for 1 minute. (Fresh blackcurrants will need an extra minute of cooking and stirring once.)
2 Add the apple juice. Microwave uncovered on high for 4 minutes. Stir once during cooking.
3 Liquidize then sieve. Return to the cleaned jug.
4 Stir in the honey and dissolved arrowroot.
5 Microwave uncovered on high for 1 minute, then whisk well. Continue to cook in this way, whisking every 30 seconds until the sauce thickens, clears and just reaches boiling point (this should only take approximately 2–2½ minutes). Stand, covered, for 3 minutes.
Reheat: uncovered on high for approximately 3 minutes. Stir once during this time.

CAROB SAUCE

Makes ¾ pt/450 ml

A healthy alternative to chocolate sauce. Serve over poached fruit and sponge puddings. Choose a good quality carob powder as some brands have a rather sickly flavour. I like the 'Kalibu' brand which has an excellent flavour and no unpleasant aftertaste. Carob powder is available from most health food shops.

INGREDIENTS	
¾ pt/450 ml skimmed milk	**Container**
1 tablespoon carob powder	3½ pt/2 litre plastic microware jug.
½ teaspoon vanilla essence	Increase timing by 2 minutes when using
1 tablespoon clear honey	ovenproof glass or ceramic jug.
3 teaspoons cornflour dissolved in 6 teaspoons cold water	

1 Place the milk, carob powder and vanilla essence in the jug. Whisk the ingredients together.
2 Microwave uncovered on high for 4–5 minutes until boiling. Whisk twice during this time.
3 Stir in the honey and dissolved cornflour.
4 Microwave uncovered on high for 30 seconds. Whisk well. Repeat and whisk again. Cover and stand for 5 minutes. Stir well before serving.
Reheat: uncovered on high for 3 minutes. Stir once during this time.

CUSTARDS

Custards cooked in the microwave have an excellent flavour and velvety texture. Use very fresh ingredients for the finest flavour. Take care when making custard with whole eggs. The power setting must be reduced to medium after the eggs have been added; this allows the custard to cook more slowly, and prevents curdling and toughening of ingredients.

For those who feel nervous at the thought of attempting real custard sauce, I've included a recipe using cornflour. This acts as an emulsifier, and, if the mixture should boil, a vigorous whisking is all that is needed.

Always cook custard in a large jug – the mixture rises up rapidly when boiling point is reached.

Richer custards can be made by using whole milk, perhaps adding a tablespoon of single cream. Vanilla sugar could replace the honey and vanilla essence.

1 REAL CUSTARD SAUCE USING WHOLE EGGS

◆ 179

Makes 1 pt/600 ml

INGREDIENTS

1 pt/600 ml skimmed milk	**Container**
4 size 3 eggs	3½ pt/2 litre plastic microware jug.
1½ teaspoons vanilla essence	Increase timing by 2 minutes when using
1–2 tablespoons acacia honey or caster sugar	ovenproof glass or ceramic jug.

1 Pour the milk into the jug and microwave uncovered on high for 2½ minutes.
2 Whisk the eggs lightly in a medium bowl then gradually whisk in the warmed milk.
3 Strain back into the jug. Stir in the vanilla essence and honey or caster sugar to taste.
4 Microwave uncovered on medium for 4 minutes, stirring well after every minute. Continue to cook in this way for a further 3–4 minutes until thickened. Do not allow the mixture to boil. Stand, covered, for 3 minutes before serving.
Reheat: carefully – don't allow the custard to boil. Uncovered on medium for 4–5 minutes until heated through. Stir twice during this time.

2 REAL CUSTARD SAUCE USING EGG YOLKS AND CORNFLOUR

Makes ¾ pt/450 ml

INGREDIENTS

	Container
¾ pt/450 ml skimmed milk	**Container**
1 teaspoon vanilla essence	3½ pt/2 litre plastic microware jug.
2 teaspoons cornflour dissolved in a little cold water	Increase timing by 2 minutes when using ovenproof glass or ceramic jug.
1–2 tablespoons acacia honey or caster sugar	
3 egg yolks, threads removed	

1 Place the milk, vanilla essence, dissolved cornflour and honey or caster sugar in the jug.
2 Microwave uncovered on high for 4 minutes. Stir twice during cooking.
3 In a medium bowl whisk the egg yolks lightly. Gradually whisk in the warmed milk.
4 Microwave uncovered on medium for 6–8 minutes until thickened. Stir well after the first minute and then every 30 seconds. Stand, covered, for 3 minutes.
Reheat: as for Real Custard 1.

ORANGE SAUCE

Makes ¾ pt/450 ml

A well flavoured sauce with a good fresh flavour that can be served hot or cold. Serve over fruit or ice cream, or in trifles, fruit flans and fruit salads.

INGREDIENTS

½ pt/300 ml pure orange juice	1 tablespoon medium sweet sherry (optional)
¼ pt/150 ml white wine	
2 in/5 cm piece cinnamon stick	**Container**
4 teaspoons arrowroot dissolved in 6 teaspoons cold water	3½ pt/2 litre plastic microware jug. Increase timing by 2–3 minutes when using ovenproof glass or ceramic jug.
caster sugar or light brown sugar to taste	

1 Place the orange juice, white wine and cinnamon stick in the jug.
2 Microwave uncovered on high for 4 minutes.
3 Stir in the dissolved arrowroot and microwave uncovered for 1–2 minutes until the sauce just reaches boiling point. Whisk well.
4 Stir in the sugar and sherry. Stand, covered, for 3 minutes.
5 Remove the cinnamon stick from the sauce once cooled. Serve hot or cold.
Reheat: uncovered on high for 3 minutes. Stir once during this time.

VANILLA SAUCE

Makes ¾ pt/450 ml

This makes a nice change from custard and a light honey such as acacia imparts a delicate flavour. Vanilla sugar can be used as an equally good alternative to the honey and vanilla essence.

INGREDIENTS

1 oz/25 g sunflower margarine	**Container**
1 oz/25 g plain white flour	3½ pt/2 litre plastic microware jug.
¾ pt/450 ml skimmed milk	Increase timing by 2–3 minutes when using ovenproof glass or ceramic jug.
1 teaspoon vanilla essence	
2 tablespoons clear honey	

1 Place the margarine in the jug and microwave uncovered on high until melted.
2 Stir in the flour and microwave uncovered on high for 1 minute, or until the mixture puffs up.
3 Gradually whisk in the milk, vanilla essence and honey.
4 Microwave uncovered on high for 1 minute. Whisk thoroughly. Repeat until the sauce reaches boiling point, whisking after every minute. Cover and stand for 2 minutes.
Reheat: uncovered on high for 3 minutes. Stir twice during this time.

◆ 181

POMEGRANATE SAUCE

Makes ¾ pt/450 ml

A pretty pink sauce that is excellent served over ice cream, or put a pool of sauce in individual shallow dishes while still warm, then chill and arrange fresh fruits such as lychees, kiwi fruits or guavas on top. Decorate with calendula, blue borage flowers or any other edible flower to add a very special finish to such a lovely dish.

When kuzu is not available, arrowroot can be used to thicken it; likewise, caster sugar could replace mirin, a traditional Japanese sweetener processed from fermented rice. It is used in both savoury dishes and desserts. Look for the completely natural product which can be found in oriental stores or ordered from Clearspring (p.209).

INGREDIENTS

8 tablespoons dry white wine, or half white wine and half sake	caster sugar
	lemon juice
3 pomegranates, sliced in half, seeds carefully removed, discarding all bitter pith	**Container** 3½ pt/2 litre plastic microware jug. Increase timing by 2 minutes when using ovenproof glass or ceramic jug.
2 tablespoons mirin	
2 heaped teaspoons ground kuzu or 3 teaspoons arrowroot, dissolved in a little cold water	

182 ◆

1 Put the wine, seeds from 2 pomegranates and mirin into the jug.
2 Microwave uncovered on high for 5 minutes. Liquidize, then pass through a sieve.
3 Put the diluted kuzu into the cleaned jug. Pour over the sauce, stirring constantly. When arrowroot is used, this is stirred into the sauce.
4 Microwave uncovered on high for 2½–3 minutes until well boiled for kuzu, and just boiled for arrowroot.
5 Stir in the remaining pomegranate flesh plus a little caster sugar and a squeeze of lemon juice to taste.
6 Cool, cover and chill well before serving.

COMBINATION COOKING

Combination ovens are often referred to as the new generation microwave ovens and have the advantage of shortening the cooking time whilst browning and crisping the food simultaneously. Food cooked in these ovens has the appearance of conventionally cooked food and items that would usually be cooked in a conventional oven but won't microwave successfully generally work well. The oven can be operated on the following modes: (a) microwave, (b) convection, (c) combination (microwave and convection).

Convection and microwave power level settings

If you are considering buying a combination oven, choose one in which the microwave power setting is variable. Many items will still be cooked on the microwave setting alone – soups, sauces, fish, vegetables, some meat and poultry, preserves and puddings.

Some combination ovens may have five microwave power levels which can be used when the microwave mode only is in operation. However, when the combination mode is used only one (usually medium) microwave power level can be set and this can prove to be a drawback. Avoid ovens that have only two microwave power levels – defrost (low) and cook (high) unless you plan to just use the oven for reheating, defrosting and occasional cooking.

The most practical combination oven is one with five power levels which can all be used on the microwave or combination modes.

The main snag is juggling around with the convection and microwave settings so that perfect results are obtained. It is very irritating to watch a cake burn on the outside yet still remain soggy in the centre. The problem in this case is that the convection setting was too high whilst the microwave setting was too low. It may take more than one attempt with a particular dish to estimate the exact convection and microwave setting and to calculate the necessary overall cooking time. It is a good idea to take notes of the oven setting, timing and observations. My first attempt at combination cooking was a complete disaster – a bakewell tart. I watched more fascinated than horrified to see the centre of the sponge split evenly into four, and then it rose up and down in rhythmic pulsation. It resembled a volcano about to erupt and I wondered whether the jam in the base would shoot out through the centre. This is an example of what a conventional cook would not be prepared for. My microwave setting was too high; when reduced to low, my second bakewell tart cooked to perfection.

Consider the following general rules: when determining the combination setting, put the convection setting a little higher than it would be normally if the dish was to be conventionally cooked. The microwave power levels should be set as follows:

MICROWAVE POWER LEVELS			
	Low	Medium	High
Cakes, breads, batters, casseroles, fish	●	●	
Sponge puddings, egg custards	●		
Meat and poultry (power setting depends on size)	●	●	●
Pastries (depending on the filling)	●	●	●
Vegetables		●	

I have managed to keep the phrase 'trial and error' out of this book yet for the cook diving straight into combination cooking from conventional cooking the problems may seem manifold at the beginning. As I have illustrated above, combination cooking can present many problems even to an experienced microwave cook. I would recommend using only the microwave setting at first – select simple recipes from the soups, sauces, vegetables and fish sections, and read over all the basic microwave cooking techniques required. With practice, you will understand why a food reacts in a particular way and then gradually reap the benefits that combination cooking brings.

The recipes in this chapter were tested on a combination oven with the following microwave outputs:
HIGH 650 watts, MED/HIGH 487 watts, MEDIUM 422 watts, MED/LOW 260 watts, LOW 130 watts.

I have listed the exact percentages for each power level I have used so that these can be compared with the different makes of ovens. I have used standard settings of medium, medium/low and low in the recipes, to simplify any conversions that may need to be made.

Check the microwave power wattages that can be used on the combination mode on your particular oven to ascertain equivalent setting and overall cooking time. If the wattage is higher than those listed, then decrease the cooking time slightly. If it is lower, increase slightly. Refer to the manufacturer's handbook for a breakdown on wattage percentages and if details can't be found, then contact the oven manufacturer.

Remember – the oven should never be operated empty on the microwave or combination mode. This will damage the magnetron.

Does combination cooking have the same advantages as microwave cooking?

Some of the advantages of microwave cooking are lost when a combination setting is used. The oven cavity and containers get very hot and preheating the oven is necessary for certain dishes, and considerably more electricity is consumed when the combination mode is used.

Cleaning a combination oven can be extremely difficult and some spills are almost impossible to remove. Food gets burned on and should never be removed with abrasive powders, creams or pads. Blot greasy patches first with absorbent kitchen paper, then wipe over with a soft cloth rinsed out in a mild solution of warm soapy water whilst the oven is warm. Never allow spills to build up – clean each time after cooking. When the microwave-only sequence is in operation, spills continue to be cooked on, and in a badly splattered oven interior, the overall cooking time is affected as these spills continue to absorb microwave energy.

◆ 185

Of course, if manufacturers had incorporated self-cleaning oven linings into the design of combination ovens, cleaning would be straightforward. (In the UK, to date, I know only of one, a Bosch, which is the size of a conventional oven.) A number of modifications are required to improve the design of these ovens. Manufacturers should be looking at the practical needs of users instead of steaming ahead, incorporating high tech features, some of which are un-necessary. When I hear of recipes being 'designed' with a bar code and ovens fitted with a special probe so that all that is required of the cook is to put the food into the oven, close the door and run the probe over the bar code on the recipe card, I despair! Cooking is an art; it should not be abandoned to technology. No wonder many serious cooks are highly suspicious of microwaves.

Can metal containers be used?

Read the instruction manual carefully (some ovens have three), and pay particular attention to any special instructions regarding metal containers when the oven is operated on the combination mode. In most ovens these are allowed but in one or two, metal cannot be used. In my oven, metal containers have to be placed on an upturned ovenproof glass plate which shields the magnetron. If metal containers were placed directly onto the metal turntable, the magnetron would become damaged and food would not cook properly. Of course metal containers can be placed directly onto the turntable when the convection only setting is used, but are absolutely banned when the microwave-only mode is in operation.

What type of food benefits most?

Microwaving meat successfully often presents problems, yet cooking meat by combination is very easy. Joints and smaller cuts of meat such as chops, steaks, gammon and poultry cook well in this way. The overall cooking time is considerably reduced, results are well browned and crisp, meat shrinks less and retains more moisture.

Shield thinner parts with small pieces of foil for half of the cooking time to prevent overcooking when the microwave setting is medium/high or high. (Check the manufacturer's instructions first regarding the use of foil.) Joints and whole poultry should be wrapped or tented in foil for at least 15 minutes after cooking.

Cakes have the usual crust which forms from the dry convection heat, unlike the microwave cooked cake which is soft throughout. The texture of cakes is very good, dried fruit plumps up nicely, and the fresh flavours of fruit zest and juices are more pronounced. Pastries and breads brown and crisp successfully – the texture of bread is wonderfully light. There is a limit though to the quantity that can be cooked at one time in the average sized combination oven. If more than 3 lb / 1.4 kg of dough is made it will be more convenient to cook it in a conventional oven. Continue to observe one of the basic microwave principles – as the quantity of food increases so does the cooking time.

Should the oven be preheated?

I recommend preheating the oven on the convection setting before baking cakes, pastries and breads by combination. I find that this improves the texture and also affects the way yeasts and raising agents react. It takes about 10 minutes for the convection setting to reach the required temperature in most ovens. If food is placed directly into a cold oven and then cooked on the combination mode, there will be no convection cooking until the oven has reached the set temperature. This affects the crust on bread, for example, and a perfect crust can only be achieved when the bread is baked in a preheated oven.

It is not necessary to preheat the oven for casseroles, meat, poultry, some fish and vegetable dishes. Cooked results are every bit as good whether the oven is preheated or not.

Does everything brown on combination?

Small portions of food will not brown on the combination mode as the cooking time is too short. The oven will not have had time to reach the convection temperature before the end of the cooking time. The preheating time varies with different ovens. There are times when it is necessary to think about the quickest and most successful way to cook certain foods. Take scones as an example. Here are three different ways:

COOKING SCONES		
	Total cooking time	Results
Microwave setting	3½ minutes Glaze, then brown under a preheated conventional grill	light and well risen, nicely browned.
Combination setting	15–20 minutes	risen and lightly browned, not as light as microwave setting; texture fair.
Convection setting	12–15 minutes	light and nicely browned and well risen, texture good but not as light as microwave setting.

◆ 187

Scones cooked by convection keep fresher than those baked by microwave or combination setting, both of which need to be eaten on the day they are made.

Conclusion – microwaving uses less electricity and is the quickest way to bake scones.

Roast potatoes can take almost as long to cook on the combination setting as they do in a conventional oven. There is a limit to the quantity that can be cooked and for 2 lb/900 g upwards, I would cook these in the conventional way. They brown and crisp better when cooked by convection.

Positioning of food

A metal trivet is often supplied with combination ovens and this stands on the turntable, enabling food to be cooked at two levels. Some ovens have a metal shelf. Larger joints, whole poultry, most cakes and pastry items are generally cooked on the turntable. Chops, steaks, poultry portions, fish steaks, fish cakes and sausages benefit when the cooking containers are placed on the metal trivet or shelf because they get nicely seared. Food close to the top of the oven browns and crisps faster.

Will the combination oven replace the conventional oven and hob?
That depends entirely on the number of people you cook for each day and the type of food you eat.

I have a large family and would probably need half a dozen combination ovens to cope with the enormous quantities of food I cook every day. To date, the size of domestic combination ovens is fairly small compared with an average conventional oven.

I find it quicker and more convenient to use a pressure cooker for grains, pulses and soups. Food that has been cooked in a wok has its own character; stir fried dishes cook faster in the wok than they do in the microwave. But for solo cooks, couples, the handicapped and where space is restricted, a combination oven may be the answer.

For the average family and where a number of different cooking methods are preferred, the combination oven will be complementary to the conventional oven. A final word of warning. Remember that when cooking on the combination mode is completed the oven will be extremely hot. If you next wish to cook on the microwave mode do not use plastic microware as this will melt. The cooking time will need reducing to take account of the residual heat in the oven.

188 ◆

ROAST CHICKEN

Serves 4

Chicken browns and crisps perfectly on the combination mode and is one of the easiest items for beginners to cook.

Most combination ovens have a splash shield which fits on to the turntable and the chicken is cooked on this. I have used a roasting bag for the first part of cooking to collect the fat and juices, which helps to keep the oven clean. The chicken is placed directly on the splash shield, uncovered, for the second part of cooking.

INGREDIENTS	
3 lb/1.4 kg chicken, trussed	**Container**
½ oz/15 g butter or margarine, melted	Roasting bag.

1 Brush the chicken all over with the melted butter. Place the chicken in a roasting bag and secure the top loosely with an elastic band.
2 Stand the chicken breast side down on the splash shield. Cook on combination 220°C microwave medium setting for 15 minutes.
3 Pour the juices and fat out of the bag then remove the chicken, stand it breast side uppermost on the splash shield.
4 Cook on combination 220°C microwave medium setting for a further 15–20 minutes until the juices run clear and the chicken is nicely browned and crisped.

MUSTARD RABBIT CASSEROLE

Serves 4

Rabbit cooks perfectly on the microwave only or combination mode.
This is a quick and easy casserole with a distinctive flavour.
Chicken could be used if preferred.
Use a large container so that the ingredients can be well spread out
and cook more evenly.

INGREDIENTS

1 medium onion, chopped	2 heaped teaspoons French mustard
2 shallots (optional)	black pepper
1 clove garlic, crushed	2 oz/50 g button mushrooms, wiped
1 tablespoon sunflower oil	4 teaspoons potato flour dissolved in a little cold water
2 lb/1 kg rabbit, jointed into 4	
1 bouquet garni	herb salt
¼ pt/150 ml dry white wine	**Container**
½ pt/300 ml hot chicken stock	Large ovenproof glass casserole dish.
1 stick celery, thinly sliced	
1 small carrot, grated or very finely chopped	

1 Place the onion, shallots if using, garlic and oil in the large casserole dish. Cook on combination 250°C microwave medium setting for 4 minutes.
2 Add the rabbit joints and cook on combination 250°C microwave medium setting for 10 minutes. Turn the rabbit over halfway through cooking.
3 Add the bouquet garni, white wine, hot chicken stock, celery, carrot, French mustard and black pepper. Stir well.
4 Cover and cook on combination 200°C microwave medium/low setting for 25 minutes.
5 Stir in the mushrooms and dissolved potato flour. Cover and cook for a further 5 minutes. Remove the bouquet garni, stir well and season to taste.
Reheat: covered on high for 6–8 minutes. Turn the dish once during this time.

BRAISED OXTAIL

Serves 4

Serve with baked potatoes, carrots and greens for a warming winter meal. As with many casseroles, the flavour is improved if the dish is made in advance, then reheated.
Make sure that the beef stock is unsalted and that salt is only added at the end of cooking, otherwise the oxtail will not tenderize.
A bulb baster is the ideal implement for removing fat from the dish during cooking.

INGREDIENTS	
1 large onion, chopped	1 stick celery, very finely chopped
1 clove garlic, crushed	½ pt/300 ml hot strong unsalted beef stock
2 rashers back bacon, derinded and cut into smallish pieces	¼ pt/150 ml red wine
3 lb/1.4 kg oxtail, chopped into joints	1 tablespoon tomato purée
2 bay leaves	salt
8 black peppercorns	**Container**
sprig of fresh thyme	Large ovenproof glass casserole dish.
1 medium carrot, very finely chopped	

1 Put the onion, garlic and bacon in the casserole dish. Cook on combination 250°C microwave medium setting for 10 minutes. Stir halfway through cooking.
2 Meanwhile, brown the oxtail on all sides in a frying pan.
3 Stir the bay leaves, peppercorns, thyme, carrot, celery, ¼ pt/150 ml hot stock, wine and tomato purée into the casserole. Mix ingredients together thoroughly.
4 Arrange the browned oxtail on top so that the larger pieces are towards the outside of the dish and the smaller pieces in the centre.
5 Cover and cook on combination 180°C microwave medium/low setting for 1 hour.
6 Remove the fat from the top of the casserole with a bulb baster. Turn the pieces of oxtail and spoon over the sauce.
7 Cover and cook for a further 30 minutes until the meat is tender. Remove fat from the top of the casserole and stir in the remaining hot stock.
8 Remove the bay leaves and sprigs of thyme and adjust seasoning to taste. Allow to cool completely, then remove any fat which may have settled on the top. Cover and refrigerate until required.
Reheat: covered on high for 6–8 minutes, depending on the starting temperature. Turn the dish once during this time.

EMPEROR BREAM

Serves 6

As an example of the approach to be used for cooking a large whole fish, I have chosen Emperor bream (capitaine blanc). This fish makes a spectacular centrepiece for a special occasion or dinner party. Using the combination mode, the overall cooking time is reduced. The flesh remains moist and tender and will have absorbed some of the flavours of the herbs and vegetables with which it is cooked. Use the fish head and trimmings for stock.

INGREDIENTS

5 lb/2.3 kg sea bream (capitaine blanc), ask your fishmonger to remove all the sharp fins	2 stalks of fresh lemon grass, crushed with a meat mallet or the end of a rolling pin
2 tablespoons sesame oil	few sprigs of fresh dill
1 medium bulb of fennel, sliced thinly	up to ½ pt/300 ml dry white wine
2 medium leeks, shredded	herb salt
1 medium red pepper, sliced into rings	**Container**
1 medium yellow pepper, sliced into rings	Cook directly on the turntable. If your oven has no turntable then cook the fish in a large shallow dish and turn the dish at least 3 times during cooking.
2–3 limes	
black pepper	Roasting bag.

◆ 191

1 Prepare the fish. Grasp by the tail and draw the back of a knife from tail to head until all the scales are removed. Do this in the sink or over a large bowl to prevent fish scales flying all over the place. (You could ask the fishmonger to do this.)

2 Remove the head and cut off part of the tail end so that the fish fits snugly on the turntable. Wash and pat dry with absorbent kitchen paper. Make 2 slashes through the skin of either side of the fish.

3 Brush the turntable with half the sesame oil. Arrange slices of fennel down the centre of the turntable, scatter over half the leeks and top with 4 rings of pepper.

4 Squeeze the juice of ½ a lime into the fish cavity and sprinkle liberally with black pepper. Place the fish on top of the vegetables on the turntable.

5 Fill the fish cavity with lemon grass, 3 rings of pepper, 3 slices of lime and some fresh dill sprigs.

6 Brush all over the top of the fish with the remaining oil. Arrange the remaining vegetables on top of fish and sprinkle with lime juice. Pour ¼ pt/150 ml wine over, then sprinkle with black pepper.

7 Cover with a split roasting bag tucked loosely under the fish. Secure with wooden cocktail sticks if necessary.

8 Cook on combination 200°C microwave medium/low setting for 15 minutes.

9 Baste with the juices, re-cover and continue to cook for a further 10 minutes.

10 Baste with the juices and 2 tablespoons wine. Continue to cook for a further 15 minutes.
11 Baste and add 2 more tablespoons wine. Cook without the cover for a further 15 minutes, baste and add a little extra wine once during this time.
12 Test to see if it is cooked by inserting the blade of a sharp knife through the thickest part of the fish; the flesh should just flake. Cover with foil, shiny side in, for 5 minutes.
13 To serve, season well with herb salt and black pepper. Remove the vegetables from the top and cut down through the middle of the fish from head to tail. Lift the first 2 fillets off the bone then ease the central bone out carefully – this should come out in one piece. Divide the underlying fillet into portions. Serve topped with the vegetables and juices.
Reheat: not recommended.

CHICKEN PIE

Serves 4

A quick, easy and tasty chicken pie. The pastry rises and browns perfectly over a creamy mixture of chicken and vegetables. Leave the chicken in large chunks and slice the mushrooms and celery thinly for the best results. The filling is cooked first using the microwave mode, then the pie is assembled while the oven is preheating on convection only, and finally baked by combination.

INGREDIENTS

1 tablespoon sunflower or corn oil	1 tablespoon finely chopped fresh parsley
1 small onion, finely chopped	herb salt, black pepper
1 stick celery, thinly sliced	8 oz/250 g puff pastry
4 oz/125 g sweetcorn kernels, defrosted if frozen	a little beaten egg for glaze
4 oz/125 g mushrooms, thinly sliced	**Containers**
1 oz/25 g plain white flour	Medium plastic microware bowl.
¼ pt/150 ml skimmed milk	Increase timing by 1–2 minutes when using ovenproof glass bowl.
½ pt/300 ml hot chicken stock	2½ pt/1.5 litre round pie dish.
12 oz/375 g cooked chicken, cut into large chunks	

1 To defrost 8 oz/250 g puff pastry, microwave on defrost for 2 minutes and stand for 10 minutes.
2 Place the oil, onion and celery in the microware bowl. Cover and microwave on high for 4 minutes.
3 Stir in the sweetcorn and mushrooms. Cover and microwave on high for 4 minutes.
4 Stir the flour into the juices then gradually blend in the milk and hot stock.

5 Microwave uncovered on high for 1 minute. Stir well. Continue to cook in this way until boiling point is reached.
6 Stir in the chicken, parsley and seasoning to taste. Transfer to the pie dish.
7 Preheat the oven on convection setting 240°C.
8 Roll the pastry out thinly into a large circle and cut a 1 in/2.5 cm strip from around the outside. Dampen the rim of the pie dish and press this strip firmly down. Lay the pastry over the chicken and vegetables and press down firmly onto the dampened pastry strip. Trim away excess pastry. Using a knife, flute the edges for an attractive finish.
9 Any leftover pastry can be rolled out and cut into leaves for decoration. Stick decoration to the pie with beaten egg, then brush over all the pastry with egg to glaze.
10 Cook on combination 240°C microwave medium setting for 15 minutes.
Reheat: uncovered on medium for 8–10 minutes. Turn the dish once during this time.

SPICED COD STEAKS

Serves 2–4

The spices give the finished dish a glorious colour; the top is lightly crisped and browned while the flesh remains succulent and moist. Cover the container for part of the cooking time to prevent the top of the fish steaks from drying out.

◆ 193

INGREDIENTS

2 tablespoons natural yoghurt	two 12 oz/375 g cod steaks
½ teaspoon turmeric	1 spring onion, sliced thinly on diagonal
½ teaspoon paprika	2 teaspoons sesame oil
½ teaspoon ground cumin	herb salt
½ teaspoon garam masala	**Containers**
1 clove garlic, crushed	8 in/20 cm shallow ovenproof glass dish.
good squeeze of lemon juice	Metal trivet.
black pepper	
½ teaspoon finely grated fresh root ginger	

1 In a medium bowl, beat the yoghurt until smooth. Beat in the spices, garlic, lemon juice, black pepper and ginger.
2 Arrange the cod steaks in the shallow dish. Spread the marinade over both sides of the fish steaks. Cover and refrigerate for 3 hours.
3 Preheat the oven on convection setting 250°C for 5 minutes.
4 Sprinkle the spring onion over the fish steaks, then drizzle the sesame oil over.
5 Cover with a piece of greaseproof paper secured to the fish with wooden cocktail sticks.

6 Stand the dish on the metal trivet and cook on combination 250°C microwave low setting for 15 minutes. Remove the greaseproof paper for the last 3 minutes of cooking. Adjust seasoning to taste before serving.
Reheat: not recommended.

YORKSHIRE PUDDING

Serves 6

For a successful Yorkshire pudding the oven and container must be hot before the mixture is cooked.
If you would prefer to make individual puddings pour the batter into 6 ramekin dishes and reduce the overall timing by approximately 5 minutes.

INGREDIENTS	
3 oz/75 g plain white flour	**Containers**
½ teaspoon salt	8 in/20 cm round shallow ovenproof glass dish.
1 large egg, beaten	Metal trivet.
½ pt/300 ml skimmed milk	
2 teaspoons corn oil	

1 Preheat the oven on convection setting 250°C.
2 Sift the flour and salt into a large mixing bowl and make a well in the centre.
3 Add the egg to the well and, using a wooden spoon, beat the egg vigorously while incorporating some of the flour.
4 Gradually add the milk and beat until all the ingredients are well combined. Stand for 5 minutes.
5 Halfway through the preheating time stand the empty shallow dish or ramekins on the metal trivet or on the metal shelf if your oven has one.
6 Remove the heated dish from the oven after 5 minutes (you will need oven gloves), and swirl the oil around the base and sides.
7 Pour the batter into the dish and place on the trivet or shelf.
8 Cook on combination 250°C microwave medium setting for 18 minutes until browned and well risen.
Reheat: not recommended.

PIZZA

Serves 4–6

The best pizzas I have made have all been cooked by combination.
The bread base is light and the vegetables retain more colour, flavour and
texture. All in all this really is a wonderful pizza, and, once assembled,
cooks in just 15 minutes.

INGREDIENTS

Base	
8 oz/250 g plain Farmhouse flour (p.207) or 4 oz/125 g plain white flour and 4 oz/125 g plain wholemeal flour	1 heaped tablespoon tomato purée
	herb salt, black pepper
½ packet easy blend dried yeast	2 oz/50 g mushrooms, sliced thinly
1 teaspoon salt	1 medium red or yellow pepper, sliced thinly
1 tablespoon olive oil	6 black olives, stoned
approximately ¼ pt/150 ml warm water	1 tablespoon finely chopped fresh parsley
Topping	4 oz/125g Cheddar cheese, grated
1 medium onion, chopped	**Container**
1 clove garlic, crushed	10½ in/26 cm ovenproof glass flan dish, greased.
1 tablespoon olive oil	Medium plastic microware bowl.
½ teaspoon dried basil	Increase timing by 1 minute when using ovenproof glass or ceramic bowl.
6 tablespoons chopped canned tomatoes	

◆ 195

1 First prepare the base. Mix the flour, yeast and salt together in a large bowl. Add 1 teaspoon of olive oil and warm water and mix to a stiff dough using a wooden spoon. (You may need to add a little more water depending on the type of flour used.)

2 Turn onto a floured surface and knead for about 5 minutes or until the dough is smooth and elastic. Don't over-flour the surface as dough becomes less sticky as gluten is developed during kneading.

3 Roll out and ease into the prepared dish. Cover with a dry teatowel or oiled polythene and put in a warm, draught-free place to rise.

4 Prepare the topping. Mix the onion, garlic, remaining olive oil and dried basil together in the medium bowl. Cover and microwave on high for 3 minutes. Stir once during cooking.

5 Stir in the chopped tomatoes. Microwave uncovered on high for 4 minutes. Stir once during cooking.

6 Stir in the tomato purée and season to taste with herb salt and black pepper. Put to one side until required.

7 When dough has almost doubled in size, preheat the oven on convection 250°C for 10 minutes.

8 Spread the tomato mixture over the base, leaving a 1 in/2.5 cm border of dough around the outside.

9 Layer on the mushrooms and pepper, top with the olives and parsley and sprinkle the cheese over.

10 Cook on combination 250°C microwave medium setting for 15 minutes. The pizza should be well risen and nicely browned.

Reheat: remove from the container and stand the pizza on a trivet or plate lined with a double thickness of white kitchen paper. It is best to cut the pizza into sections and space these out a little. This enables the centre to be reheated more successfully. Microwave uncovered on medium for 10 minutes.

LENTIL LOAF

Serves 4–6

A satisfying main course, lunch or supper dish. Just as good served cold, so it is ideal for packed lunches or picnics. Serve with soup and green vegetables or a mixed salad. A large sliced tomato can be pressed lightly on top of the mixture before baking.

It is possible to cook this dish entirely by combination but I have chosen to cook the lentils conventionally as it's quicker and easier. The onions can be microwaving while the lentils are being cooked.

INGREDIENTS

8 oz/250 g orange split lentils, rinsed under cold running water, then drained	2 teaspoons mushroom ketchup
	herb salt, black pepper
2 pt/1.2 litre cold water	**Containers**
1 large onion, chopped	Medium plastic microware bowl.
1 teaspoon dried oregano	Increase timing by 30 seconds when using ovenproof glass or ceramic bowl.
1 tablespoon sunflower oil	2½ pt/1.5 litre round ovenproof glass or ceramic dish, greased.
2 tablespoons natural yoghurt	
2 size 2 eggs, beaten	
5 oz/150 g Cheddar cheese, grated	
2 tablespoons finely chopped fresh parsley	

1 Place the washed lentils and cold water in a pan. Bring to the boil, partially cover (the lentils will boil over if completely covered), and simmer for 15–20 minutes or until tender. Strain, press lightly to remove excess liquid.

2 While the lentils are cooking place the onion, oregano and oil in the bowl. Cover and microwave on high for 5 minutes. Stir once during cooking.

3 In a large mixing bowl beat the yoghurt then beat in the eggs, 4 oz/125 g of the grated cheese, parsley, mushroom ketchup, herb salt, black pepper, onions and cooked lentils. Mix all the ingredients thoroughly.

4 Transfer to the greased round dish. Sprinkle over the remaining cheese.

5 Cook on combination 220°C microwave medium setting for 20 minutes. The cooked dish should be well risen, browned and set in the centre.

Reheat: covered on medium for 8 minutes. Turn the dish twice during this time.

ONION QUICHE

Serves 4–6

This flan has a light filling and a fresh flavour. The choice of herbs can be varied; my favourite mixture is oregano, thyme, summer savory and chives.

INGREDIENTS

Pastry	1 tablespoon finely chopped fresh parsley
4 oz/125 g plain Farmhouse flour	
pinch of salt	2 tablespoons finely chopped fresh marjoram (or other fresh herbs according to availability)
2 oz/50 g sunflower margarine	
cold water to mix	
Filling	herb salt, black pepper
1 lb/500 g onions, chopped	4 oz/125 g Cheddar cheese, grated
1 oz/25 g sunflower margarine	**Containers**
2 size 1 eggs, beaten	1½ pt/900 ml ovenproof glass casserole.
¼ pt/150 ml milk	8 in/20 cm ovenproof glass flan dish.
4 tablespoons natural yoghurt or single cream	

1 Mix the onions and 1 oz/25 g sunflower margarine together in the casserole dish. Cover.

◆ 197

2 Cook on combination 250°C microwave medium setting for 20 minutes. Halfway through cooking remove the lid and stir well. Continue to cook uncovered for the remaining time.

3 Make the pastry: mix the flour and salt together in a medium mixing bowl. Rub in the margarine lightly and stir in enough cold water to mix to a stiff dough. Use the blade of a knife for mixing. Wrap in polythene and chill for 5 minutes in the freezer or 15 minutes in the refrigerator.

4 Roll the pastry out lightly on a floured surface and line the flan dish. Try not to stretch the pastry as you are lining the dish. Press firmly into the base and prick all over with a fork.

5 Cook on convection 250°C for 10 minutes.

6 For the filling, beat the eggs, milk, yoghurt or cream, fresh herbs, salt and pepper together. Stir in the cooked onions and most of the cheese.

7 Pour the filling into the par-baked flan case. Sprinkle with the remaining cheese. Cook on combination 220°C microwave medium setting for 12 minutes. The quiche should be well risen, nicely browned and set.

Reheat: remove the flan from the container and place on a trivet lined with a double layer of white kitchen paper. Microwave uncovered on medium for approximately 6 minutes. Turn once during this time.

BRAISED VEGETABLES

Serves 4

Layered fennel, courgettes, and onions topped with sauce which sets to a soft
savoury custard. The oven does not require preheating for this recipe.
Use a deep round container and vary the vegetables according to season
and personal taste.
I have used thick Greek sheep's milk yoghurt and feta cheese as their sharp
flavours complement the sweet flavoured vegetables.

INGREDIENTS

1 large bulb of fennel, approximately 12 oz/375 g, thinly sliced, fronds reserved	¼ pt/150 ml Greek sheep's milk yoghurt
	2 large eggs, beaten
2 medium courgettes, sliced into ½ in/1 cm pieces	4 oz/125 g feta cheese, crumbled or grated
1 large onion, thinly sliced	8 oz/250 g beefsteak tomato, sliced
black pepper, herb salt	**Container**
1 teaspoon fennel seeds	3½ pt/2 litre deep round ovenproof glass casserole, lightly greased.
4 tablespoons chicken or vegetable stock or water	

198 ◆

1 Layer the fennel, courgettes and onion in the casserole dish. Season each
layer with black pepper, a little herb salt and fennel seeds.
2 Add the stock or water. Cover and cook on combination 180°C microwave
medium setting for 25 minutes.
3 In a medium bowl, beat the yoghurt until smooth. Gradually beat in the
eggs, then stir in the cheese and season well.
4 Spoon over the vegetables and top with the sliced tomato.
5 Cook on combination 180°C microwave medium setting for 20 minutes
until the centre is just set.
6 Season the tomato topping with herb salt and black pepper and garnish
with the reserved fennel fronds.
Reheat: covered on medium for 5–6 minutes. Turn the dish once during this
time.

POTATO AND HERB BAKE

Serves 4

This is a sort of variation of Lyonnaise potatoes.
I have used unsweetened soya milk in this recipe as I like its slightly nutty flavour, but ordinary milk can be used.
Use a deep container to prevent the milk boiling over during cooking.
This type of dish can take ages when cooked conventionally, and the vegetables have a much better flavour cooked on the combination setting.
Use all fresh parsley or half the quantity of dried herbs when other fresh herbs are not available.

INGREDIENTS

1½ lb/750 g (prepared weight) potatoes, peeled and sliced ¼ in/5 mm thick	black pepper
	¼ pt/150 ml unsweetened soya milk
4 or 5 shallots, sliced, or 1 small onion, sliced thinly	1 oz/25 g sunflower margarine
	2 oz/50 g Cheddar or Gruyère cheese, grated
2 tablespoons finely chopped fresh marjoram (or other herbs such as oregano, chervil, chives, thyme, tarragon)	herb salt
	Container
	3½ pt/2 litre deep round ovenproof glass casserole, lightly greased.
2 tablespoons finely chopped fresh parsley	

◆ 199

1 Layer the potatoes, shallots or onion, most of the herbs and some black pepper in the dish. End with a layer of potatoes. Pour over the milk and dot the top with margarine.
2 Cook on combination 180°C microwave medium setting for 25 minutes. During the last 5 minutes, sprinkle over the cheese.
3 To serve, sprinkle over the reserved herbs and season with black pepper and herb salt.
Reheat: covered on medium for 8 minutes. Turn the dish once during this time.

CHEESE SOUFFLE

Serves 4

This rises well and, like all soufflés, should be served immediately.

INGREDIENTS

1 oz/25 g sunflower margarine	½ teaspoon mustard powder
1 oz/25 g plain white flour	a little freshly grated nutmeg
¼ pt/150 ml milk	herb salt, black pepper
4 large eggs, separated	**Containers**
4 oz/125 g Cheddar or Gruyère cheese, grated	Large plastic microware jug. Increase timing by 1 minute when using ovenproof glass jug.
4 tablespoons finely chopped mixed fresh herbs – parsley, chives, marjoram, oregano	7 in/18 cm ovenproof glass soufflé dish, lightly greased.

1 Put the margarine in the jug and microwave uncovered on high for 1 minute or until melted. Stir in the flour. Microwave uncovered on high for 1 minute or until the mixture puffs up. Gradually whisk in the milk. Microwave uncovered on high for 2–2½ minutes until boiling point is reached. Whisk every 30 seconds during cooking. Cool slightly.
2 Beat in the egg yolks and stir in the cheese, herbs, mustard powder, nutmeg, herb salt and black pepper.
3 Preheat the oven on convection setting 200°C for 10 minutes.
4 Whisk the egg whites in a grease-free bowl until stiff peaks form. Beat 1 tablespoon of the egg white into the cheese mixture. Carefully fold in the remaining egg white and transfer to the lightly greased soufflé dish.
5 Cook on combination 200°C microwave low setting for 25 minutes, until well risen and set. Serve straight away.

QUICK BREAD

Makes 1 large or 2 small loaves

Easy blend yeast is obtained from supermarkets and it certainly simplifies yeast cooking. This loaf requires kneading once only, and cooks to a high rise and excellent texture.

Replace the Farmhouse flour with all wholemeal flour, or half strong plain white and half wholemeal flour.

Preheat the oven on convection before cooking by combination for a good crisp crust.

INGREDIENTS

1½ lb/750 g plain Farmhouse flour	**Container**
1 teaspoon salt	3½ pt/2 litre earthenware terrine or two 2 lb/1 kg loaf dishes, well greased.
1 packet (¼ oz/7 g) easy blend yeast	
1 tablespoon sunflower oil	
¾ pt/450 ml warm water	
a little beaten egg mixed with cold water and a pinch of salt for glaze	
1 tablespoon sesame seeds	

◆ 201

1 If flour has been stored in a cool larder or cupboard, warm first by tipping into a large mixing bowl and microwaving on high for 30 seconds.

2 Mix the flour, salt and yeast together in a large mixing bowl.

3 Stir the oil into the warm water then, using a wooden spoon, gradually mix this into the dry ingredients until a stiff dough is formed.

4 Turn out on to a lightly floured surface and knead for 5 minutes, or until the dough feels firm and elastic rather than sticky. Don't over-flour the surface during this stage.

5 Transfer to the well greased container and cover with oiled polythene or a dry teatowel. Place in a warm, draught-free place until doubled in size.

6 Preheat the oven on convection setting 250°C for 10 minutes.

7 Brush the loaf with the egg glaze and sprinkle over the sesame seeds.

8 Cook on combination 250°C microwave medium setting for 15 minutes. The loaf should be well risen and brown. To test whether it is properly cooked, remove from the container, turn upside down and tap the bottom – the loaf should sound hollow. Cool on a wire rack.

FRUIT CAKE

This is one of my favourite conventional cake recipes converted to combination cooking. The cake can be glazed immediately after cooking by brushing over a little warmed honey. A tablespoon or two of yoghurt improves the texture of all cake and scone mixtures.

INGREDIENTS	
8 oz/250 g self-raising Farmhouse flour	2 oz/50 g walnuts, roughly chopped
½ teaspoon mixed spice	zest of 1 orange
½ teaspoon ground cinnamon	3 tablespoons orange juice
a little grated nutmeg	2 tablespoons natural yoghurt
2 oz/50 g soft brown sugar	**Container**
5 oz/150 g sunflower margarine	7 in/18 cm soufflé dish.
2 size 2 eggs, beaten	Grease, line with greaseproof paper
½ teaspoon vanilla essence	then grease again.
8 oz/250 g mixed dried fruit	

202 ◆

1 Preheat the oven on convection setting 180°C.
2 Sift the flour and spices together on a plate.
3 In a large mixing bowl beat the sugar and margarine until light and fluffy. Gradually beat in the eggs. Stir in the vanilla essence. Stir in the dried fruit and walnuts then fold in the flour and spices. Add the orange zest and juice and enough yoghurt to mix to a soft dropping consistency.
4 Transfer to the prepared soufflé dish and level the top.
5 Cook on combination 180°C microwave low setting for 55 minutes. The cake should be browned, well risen and firm. Test by inserting a skewer or the point of a sharp knife into the centre – it should come out clean. Turn out and cool on a wire rack. This cake improves further after a week if stored in an airtight container.

CRUNCHY APPLE CRUMBLE

Serves 4

An ideal pudding for those who are trying to cut down on sugar.
My family and friends find the crumble sweet enough – but it may not suit all
tastes. For a sweeter crumble add 2 oz/50 g sugar to the crumble mixture
in addition to the coconut.

INGREDIENTS

1½ lb/750 g (prepared weight) cooking apples, peeled, cored and thinly sliced	2 oz/50 g desiccated coconut
	2 oz/50 g sesame seeds
½ teaspoon ground cinnamon	5 oz/150 g sunflower margarine
1–2 tablespoons clear honey or soft brown sugar	2 oz/50 g brown sugar (optional)
	Container
2 oz/50 g sultanas	3½ pt/2 litre deep round ovenproof glass dish.
zest of 1 orange	
6 oz/175 g plain Farmhouse flour, or 3 oz/75 g plain white flour and 3 oz/75 g plain wholemeal flour	

1 Preheat the oven on convection setting 200°C for 10 minutes.
2 Place the prepared apples in the base of the dish. Sprinkle with cinnamon, honey or sugar, sultanas and orange zest.
3 Mix the flour, coconut and sesame seeds together in a medium mixing bowl. Rub the margarine in lightly and, if you wish, stir in the optional additional sugar.
4 Spoon the crumble mixture over the apples, level the top and press down lightly.
5 Cook on combination 200°C microwave medium setting for 15 minutes. The crumble should be nicely browned and the apples tender.
6 Serve hot or cold with custard or natural yoghurt.
Reheat: microwave covered on medium for 5 minutes, depending on starting temperature. Turn the dish once during this time.

◆ 203

APPLE AND BLACKCURRANT PIE

Serves 4–6

The fruit is bright in colour, fresh tasting and topped with a crispy cinnamon
crust. The addition of cornflour to the filling thickens the juice from the
fruits and prevents a sloppy, watery sauce at the end of cooking.
Use a deep pie dish so there is plenty of room for the filling to expand
as it boils.

INGREDIENTS	
Pastry	**Filling**
4 oz/125 g plain Farmhouse flour	1 lb/500 g (prepared weight) cooking apples, cored and sliced thinly
1 tablespoon vanilla sugar or caster sugar	8 oz/250 g blackcurrants, defrosted if frozen
½ teaspoon ground cinnamon	1–2 tablespoons clear honey
2 oz/50 g sunflower margarine	2 teaspoons cornflour dissolved in 1 tablespoon cold water
1 egg yolk	
1–2 tablespoons cold water to mix	**Container**
a little beaten egg white and extra sugar for glazing	2½ pt/1.5 litre round ceramic pie dish.

1 Make the pastry: sift the flour, sugar and cinnamon into a medium mixing bowl.

2 Rub the margarine in lightly and, using the blade of a knife, mix in the egg yolk and enough cold water to form a stiff dough. Knead lightly, then place in a polythene bag and chill for 15 minutes in the refrigerator.

3 Preheat the oven on convection setting 220°C for 10 minutes.

4 Place the apples and blackcurrants in the pie dish. Drizzle over the honey and sprinkle with the dissolved cornflour. Dampen the edge of the pie dish.

5 Roll the pastry out carefully to fit the dish as a lid on a lightly floured surface and place over the fruit. Press the edge of the pastry down firmly. Make an impression with a fork along this edge. Slit a small opening in the centre of the pie for the steam to escape during cooking.

6 Brush with a little lightly beaten egg white, then sprinkle with about a teaspoon of vanilla or caster sugar.

7 Cook on combination 220°C microwave low setting for 25 minutes. The fruit should be tender, the pastry nicely browned and crisp.

8 Serve hot or cold with cream or yoghurt.

Reheat: microwave uncovered on medium for 6 minutes. Turn the dish once during this time.

CHERRY CLAFOUTIS

Serves 4–6

Fresh cherries are the traditional flavouring for this dessert, but peaches, apricots, apples, pears or other soft fruits can be used.

For a successful batter, the eggs should be at room temperature. Incorporate the stiffly beaten egg whites into the batter mixture at the last moment before placing in the preheated oven.

INGREDIENTS

1 lb/500 g cherries, stoned if fresh, defrosted if frozen	¾ pt/450 ml milk
4 oz/125 g plain white flour	a little sifted icing sugar for topping
2 oz/50 g vanilla sugar	**Container**
pinch of salt	3½–4 pt/2–2.3 litre deep ovenproof glass dish, well greased.
3 large eggs plus 1 extra egg white	

1 Preheat the oven on convection setting 250°C.

2 Place the prepared fruit in the dish.

3 Sift flour, sugar and salt into a large mixing bowl. Make a well in centre.

4 Separate one of the eggs and place the white with the extra egg white in a large grease-free bowl.

5 Gradually beat the remaining eggs and egg yolk into the dry ingredients. Gradually beat in the milk. Cover.

6 Whisk the egg whites stiffly then fold carefully into the batter. Don't worry if there are still a few lumps of egg white.

7 Pour batter over cherries. Place immediately into the preheated oven.

8 Cook on combination 250°C microwave medium setting for 20–25 minutes. The pudding should be well risen, browned and just set. Sift a little icing sugar over the top before serving. Serve hot or cold.

Reheat: not recommended.

BAKEWELL TART

Serves 6

A substantial pudding or cake which can be served hot with custard, cold with yoghurt, or simply on its own.

INGREDIENTS

Pastry	3 oz/75 g Farmhouse self-raising flour
4 oz/125 g Farmhouse plain flour (p.207)	½ teaspoon baking powder
pinch of salt	2 tablespoons natural yoghurt
2 oz/50 g sunflower margarine	2 oz/50 g desiccated coconut
cold water to mix	1–2 tablespoons milk
Filling	4 tablespoons red jam
4 oz/125 g sunflower margarine	**Container**
2 tablespoons clear honey	8 in/20 cm ovenproof glass flan dish, greased.
½ teaspoon almond essence	
2 size 2 eggs, beaten	

1 Make the pastry: sift the flour and salt into a large bowl, rub in the margarine and stir in enough cold water to mix to a firm dough. Chill in the refrigerator for 15 minutes.

2 Roll out the pastry and line the flan dish. Trim and flute the edge.
3 Preheat the oven on convection setting 220°C.
4 Beat the margarine, honey and almond essence together in a large mixing bowl. Gradually beat in the eggs. Sift in the flour and baking powder.
5 Using a metal spoon, carefully fold in the yoghurt and most of the coconut. Add enough milk to give a soft consistency.
6 Spread the jam over the base of the pastry and spoon the cake mixture over. Level top with a palette knife and sprinkle on remaining coconut.
7 Cook on combination setting 200°C microwave low setting for 20–25 minutes. Test by inserting the tip of a sharp knife into the centre – it should come out clean.
8 Serve hot or cold with custard or yoghurt.
Reheat: remove the flan from the container to prevent the base becoming soggy. Stand on a trivet lined with a double layer of absorbent kitchen paper. Microwave uncovered on high for 3½–4 minutes.

BREAD AND BUTTER PUDDING

Serves 4

A popular pudding with layers of creamy egg custard, plumped-up sultanas and a crisp, nutmeg scented crust.

INGREDIENTS

2 slices of bread from 1 large wholemeal loaf, crusts removed	3 large eggs, beaten
1–2 oz/25–40 g sunflower margarine	few drops of vanilla essence
3 oz/75 g sultanas	**Containers**
grated zest of 1 orange	2½ pt/1.5 litre round or oval casserole dish, well greased.
freshly grated nutmeg	Large plastic microware jug.
2 tablespoons soft brown sugar	Increase timing by 1 minute when using ovenproof glass jug.
¾ pt/450 ml milk	

1 Spread the bread with margarine, cut into triangles and place half in the base of the dish. Scatter the sultanas, orange zest, nutmeg and soft brown sugar over. Place the rest of the bread over the top.
2 Put the milk in the microware jug and microwave uncovered on high for approximately 3 minutes until hot but not boiling. Gradually stir the milk into the beaten eggs. Add the vanilla essence.
3 Strain the egg mixture over the pudding and grate nutmeg over the top.
4 Cook on combination 200°C microwave low setting for 25–30 minutes until just set. Test by inserting the point of a sharp knife into the centre, which should be almost set. The custard sets further after standing for 5 minutes.
Reheat: covered on medium for 5 minutes. Turn the dish once during this time.

GLOSSARY

Agar agar (Gelidium sp.)
A bland flavoured seaweed derivative used as a vegetarian alternative to gelatine in sweet and savoury dishes. It sets extremely rapidly and there is a slight difference in the texture of jellies made with this when compared to gelatine based jellies. Commonly sold as a powder but also available in a flaked form. Proportionally more flakes are required so read the instructions on the package as flakes can vary in strength; the powder is almost always the same.

Arrowroot
A fine white powder processed from the roots of tropical plants and used to thicken sweet and savoury dishes. Mix with cold water before adding to other ingredients. Sauces or mixtures made with arrowroot should never be allowed to boil after they have thickened and cleared.

Carob powder
Carob is an alternative to cocoa powder; it is the ground pod of the carob plant which grows prolifically in the Middle East. Although recommended as a healthy alternative to chocolate, there is a marked difference in the flavour. Kalibu brand is the best quality carob powder available; it is as well to avoid unbranded pre-packed carob powder as some of these have a sickly taste and are often pale in colour. Carob powder is also manufactured with other ingredients to resemble chocolate bars, again Kalibu carob bars are the best

choice and some of these are sugar free.

Carrageen
(Chondrus crispus)
Also known as Irish Moss. Carrageen has been used for centuries in Ireland to thicken and gel ingredients in many sweet and savoury dishes. It is essential to pick over the carrageen carefully before cooking, discarding any grit, broken shells and tougher fronds. Carrageen is rich in iodine and other minerals; it is said to be beneficial for respiratory disorders and the digestion. A fair sized portion is necessary to thicken a pint (600 ml) of liquid and the thickening ability will depend on its origin and the time of harvest. Purchase from a health food shop to ensure good quality.

Cold pressed oils
Processed at a low temperature which preserves their natural qualities, these are superior in flavour, aroma, colour and vitamins to chemically processed oils. More expensive but often thicker, so less is required.

Farmhouse flour
Sometimes described as 81% wheatmeal, or golden brown 85% flour. These flours are wholemeal flour that has had a small proportion of bran extracted. I consider this to be the most perfect flour for microwave baking. Half white and half wholemeal can be substituted although the results are not quite so successful. Available plain or self-raising from supermarkets, delicatessens and health food shops.

Herb salt
There are a number of herb salts on the market; some are not to be recommended as their flavour can overpower other ingredients. My favourite is Lane's Herb Salt; the ingredients are land and sea vegetables, horseradish, herbs and sea salt. Herb salt is an ideal seasoning for those who wish to reduce their salt intake. Available from health food shops and delicatessens.

Hiziki (Hizikia fusiforme)
Hiziki resembles a mass of thick black hair and has a stronger flavour than all the other sea vegetables used in the recipes. It is high in calcium and trace minerals and can be cooked with vegetables or simply soaked, sliced and mixed into salads. Hiziki is eaten in small quantities. Available from oriental stores and health food shops.

Kombu (Laminaria japonica)
A sea vegetable which is used principally for flavouring stocks, stews and casseroles. Kombu is rich in glutamic acid which helps to soften the fibres of many foods. A small piece cooked with pulses will impart a sweetness to the beans and resulting stock, it will also shorten the cooking time. Kombu comes in thick strips and a piece 2 in/5 cm is sufficient for a large pan/bowl of ingredients. It should be quickly rinsed in cold water or wiped before use to remove any salt crystals that may be clinging to the surface. Kombu is said to have strengthening

◆ 207

properties and contains many vitamins and minerals. Available from health food shops and oriental stores.

Kuzu
(sometimes called kudzu)
A white starch from a prolific leguminous wild vine which grows in the Far East. It is sold in chunks and should be ground in a mortar or grinder before dissolving in cold water. Warm or hot liquids should be poured on to the dissolved kuzu, not the other way round (as you would with arrowroot). It has alkalizing properties so is beneficial for digestive disorders. Available from health food stores, oriental stores and the Clearspring Grocer (p.209).

Laverbread
(Porphyra umbilicalis)
A delicious seaweed traditionally served with bacon for breakfast in Wales. It can be bought cooked in cans (Drangway brand) from health food shops and delicatessens, and in parts of Wales from market stalls and butchers. It has a rich flavour and combines well with vegetables, lamb, bacon/ham and fish.

Mirin
A traditional Japanese sweetener made from sweet rice and fermented rice. It is sold in identical bottles to soy sauce and is a pale brown colour. The Mikawa brand has the best flavour and is naturally produced. Used to sweeten savoury dishes and desserts and also as a glaze for vegetables and poultry. Available from Japanese stores and the Clearspring Grocer (p.209).

Miso
A fermented soy bean product, miso is a highly nutritious food, rich in protein, calcium and essential minerals and it is worth noting that it is a 'live' food. Mix with a little cold water before stirring into other ingredients and ensure that foods do not reboil once miso has been added as this destroys the active enzymes that are so beneficial.

I recommend naturally aged miso rather than the chemically aged product. Natural miso is aged for up to ten years in wooden kegs and is superior nutritionally and in flavour. Miso is a thick brown paste and the more common varieties are hatcho, mugi and brown rice; more unusual varieties, each having their own unique flavour, are red, white and buckwheat. It is probably best to avoid hatcho miso as this is rather strong and salty; the most popular miso is mugi which contains barley and has a most agreeable flavour.

All varieties of miso contain salt so use sparingly and in place of salt. The miso should not overpower the flavour of other ingredients. Miso is used to season soups, casseroles and pâtés and is most complementary to grains, vegetables, pulses, fish and some meat dishes; avoid adding to dishes that contain dairy products. Miso is definitely not meant to be spread straight on to bread in the same way as yeast extract. Available from health food shops and oriental stores.

Natto pickle
A traditional Japanese pickle with a sweet/sour flavour made from fermented soy beans, barley, ginger and kombu seaweed. Sometimes other vegetables such as carrots and burdock root are included. Natto should be eaten in small quantities and served with poultry, fish, vegetables, pulse and grain dishes. Available from Japanese stores and the Clearspring Grocer (p.209).

Nori seaweed
(Porphyra tenera)
A mild tasting Japanese seaweed, nori is very nutritious, containing iron, calcium, iodine and minerals. Usually sold pressed into paper-thin sheets, it is used as a wrapping for Japanese sushi or crumbled in soups and also as a garnish. Toasting before use improves digestibility; hold a single sheet over a gas flame for a few seconds until it crisps and the colour changes from black to green (the same effect can be achieved by putting the Nori under preheated grill for a few seconds but it must be watched very carefully). Available from health food shops and oriental stores.

Passata
Sieved canned or bottled tomatoes available from supermarkets and health food shops.

Potato flour
A bland starch extracted from cooked potatoes which is used to thicken soups, sauces and casseroles. Mix with cold water before adding to other ingredients. Available from supermarkets, delicatessens and health food shops.

Shiitake mushrooms
(Lentinus edodes)
Shiitake are one of the most commonly used oriental mushrooms; shii means oak, and in their natural habitat these mushrooms grow wild on fallen oak trees. Until quite recently only imported

dried shiitake was available, this has a strong distinctive flavour; cultivated fresh shiitake, now available, has a milder flavour. To reconstitute the dried mushrooms soak in plenty of cold water for 15 minutes, discard any tough, woody stalks. Slice the soaked mushrooms and cover with boiling water. Microwave on high for approximately 3 minutes. Stand covered for 5 minutes. The shiitake are now ready to use in the recipes; the cooking liquid can be used to flavour other dishes. 1 oz/25 g dried shiitake is equivalent to 4 oz/125 g fresh shiitake. Available from some supermarkets, delicatessens, health food shops, oriental stores and the Clearspring ¨rocer (p.209).

Shoyu and tamari
Naturally fermented soy sauce, which I use in preference to the chemically produced product which often has a rather 'harsh' flavour. Tamari is a double concentrated version of shoyu. Available from health food shops, delicatessens and oriental stores.

Takuan pickle
A traditional Japanese pickle, tan in colour, with daikon (mooli – long white radish), rice bran and salt. It has a strong sweet flavour and is delicious when thinly sliced and used as a garnish for vegetable and fish dishes. Available from Japanese stores or the Clearspring Grocer (p.209).

Toasted sesame oil
The sesame seeds are toasted before they are crushed and the oil has a rich, dark brown colour and concentrated nutty flavour. Toasted sesame oil should be mixed

with other oils; it is in the same class as high quality walnut and hazelnut oils. The unrefined Mitoku brand has an exceptionally good flavour. Available from the Clearspring Grocer (p. 209), oriental stores and delicatessens.

Tofu
Available firm, smoked and silken. Gourmet tofu is also being introduced; look out for marinated tofu and tofu with added herbs. Tofu is a set soy bean curd which is high in protein and calcium and fat free. Plain firm tofu is bland tasting but absorbs the flavours of ingredients with which it is cooked. Smoked firm tofu has a very definite flavour and might be perfect for those who are reducing or eliminating meat from their diets but long for a bacon sandwich. It is also delicious for kebabs. Silken tofu is a softer version and is packaged for long storage which makes it an ideal store cupboard ingredient. Use in salad dressings, for dips and to replace cream in flans and cheesecakes. Widely available in many supermarkets, health food shops, oriental stores and delicatessens.

Umeboshi
Whole pickled plums, also available as a paste. The paste is the most convenient as the whole plums need the stones removing. Umeboshi plums are pink and have a sharp, salty taste which complements many savoury dishes. The plums are aged in kegs for several years and the residual liquid is sold as umeboshi vinegar. The vinegar can be used as a wine vinegar in salad dressings and it is good for pickling vegetables. The plums can be used as an alternative to

mustard in dressings. Available from Japanese stores and the Clearspring Grocer (p.209).

Unsprayed citrus fruits
Ordinary citrus fruits have been sprayed and treated with wax and many people are unhappy about using these when the zest, in particular, is called for in recipes. Unsprayed citrus fruits are becoming more readily available in some of the larger supermarkets and health food shops. Scrub well before use.

Vanilla and almond essences
More expensive than the usual artificial flavourings but with a superior flavour and strength.

Wakame seaweed
(Undaria pinnatifida)
Wakame is a mild flavoured sea vegetable rich in iron, calcium and essential minerals. It needs rinsing quickly in cold water and then soaking for about 15 minutes, when it will swell up considerably. Sometimes there is a thick rib which is best removed after soaking as this does not always soften during cooking. Chop or slice the seaweed finely and use the soaking liquor in cooking as it contains valuable minerals and trace elements. Use in soups, casseroles and salads. Available from health food shops and oriental stores.

The Clearspring Grocer is both a retail shop and mail order service and will supply a number of the more unusual ingredients in this book. Their address is:
Clearspring Grocer
196 Old Street
London EC1V 98P
Tel: 01 250 1708

DEFROSTING AND COOKING TIMES

DEFROSTING MEAT AND POULTRY				
Type	Weight	Defrost setting time (minutes)	Method	Standing time
Beef joints boned on the bone	1 lb/500 g	8–10 10–12	Stand the meat on a trivet or upturned plate placed in shallow dish. Shield thinner parts with foil. Secure the foil firmly. Shield any bone ends. Ensure foil does not touch the sides of the oven. Overwrap the foil with cling film. Rest the joint if it becomes warm during thawing; rest the joint for 15 minutes halfway through the defrosting time. Mop up liquid as it accumulates so microwaves don't concentrate in it. Turn over 3 or 4 times during defrosting. Give the joint short bursts of microwave energy for best results, e.g. defrost 5 minutes, rest 5 minutes and so on. When meat is defrosted too quickly some of the flavour will be lost and it will cook unevenly. Remove from the microwave whilst still icy in the centre.	Stand for 30–60 minutes at room temperature until completely thawed. Meat is ready for cooking when a skewer can be inserted through the thickest part of the joint.
Lamb joints boned on the bone	1 lb/500 g	6–8 8		
Pork joints boned on the bone	1 lb/500 g	8 8–10		
Mince	1 lb/500 g	6–8	Use a shallow dish. With a fork, remove soft parts during thawing.	No standing time. Cook immediately.
Lamb chops Chump	2 × 4 oz/125 g 4 × 4 oz/125 g	3–4 8–10	Stand the chops on a trivet in a shallow dish. Separate as soon as possible. Arrange thicker parts to outside edges of dish and thinner parts towards centre. Cover with absorbent paper and mop up any liquid during thawing. Turn thicker chops over halfway through thawing time.	Stand 5–10 minutes. Wash and pat dry.
Loin	2 × 3 oz/75 g 4 × 3 oz/75 g	3–4 6–8		
Pork chops Chump	2 × 8 oz/250 g 4 × 8 oz/250 g	8–10 12–15		Up to 10 minutes or until completely defrosted. Wash and pat dry before cooking.
Loin	2 × 6 oz/175 g 4 × 6 oz/175g	6–8 10–12		

DEFROSTING MEAT AND POULTRY				
Type	Weight	Defrost setting time (minutes)	Method	Standing time
Sausages Pork/lamb thick thin	1 lb/500 g 1 lb/500 g	5–6 4–5	Separate as soon as possible, arrange in single layer in shallow dish. Turn and reposition once. Mop up any liquid.	Stand 5 minutes. Stand 3–5 minutes. Cook as soon as possible after thawing.
Kidneys Lambs Pigs	2 average 4 average 2 average 4 average	2–2½ 4–5 4 6–8	Defrost in a shallow dish. Separate as soon as possible. Mop up any juices during defrosting.	Stand 5 minutes or until completely defrosted. Wash, skin and remove inedible parts before cooking. Cook as soon as possible after thawing.
Liver	1 lb/500 g	6–8	Arrange in single layer on a plate or in a shallow dish. Remove from microwave whilst still icy. Mop up any liquid.	Stand approximately 10 minutes to complete thawing. Wash and pat dry before cooking. Cook as soon as possible after thawing.
Chicken, whole	1 lb/500 g	6	Slit the bag and remove the metal tie. Stand on a trivet or upturned plate in a shallow dish. Remove giblets as soon as possible. Shield the breast and wing tips and any parts that become warm during thawing. Overwrap foil with cling film for extra safety. Turn over 3 or 4 times during defrosting and allow a standing time of 15 minutes halfway through.	Stand immersed in cold water for 15–30 minutes until completely defrosted. Pat dry before cooking.
Chicken, portions	1 lb/500 g	5	Arrange in a shallow dish, placing thicker parts towards the outside edge. Turn over and reposition twice during thawing.	Stand immersed in cold water for 15 minutes. Pat dry before cooking.
Poussin	1 lb/500 g	6	Stand on a trivet placed in shallow dish. Turn halfway through thawing. Mop up liquid.	Immerse in cold water for 20 minutes.
Duck, whole	1 lb/500 g	6	As for chicken.	Immerse in cold water until completely defrosted, approximately 30 minutes. Pat dry before cooking.
Duck, portions	1 lb/500 g	5	As for chicken	Immerse in cold water for 15 minutes. Pat dry before cooking.

◆ 211

DEFROSTING MEAT AND POULTRY

Type	Weight	Defrost setting time (minutes)	Method	Standing time
Turkey	1 lb/500 g	10	Defrost large birds slowly. Stand on trivet placed in large shallow dish, slit the bag and remove metal tie. Remove giblets and wrapping as soon as possible. Shield parts that become warm during thawing. Halfway through thawing allow 20 minutes rest for the flesh to relax and heat to equalize. Turn the bird over a number of times during thawing and turn the dish. Defrost for 10 minutes then stand for 10 minutes and so on. Mop up any juices as they accumulate.	Rinse well in cold running water. Pat dry and stand away from all other foods at room temperature to complete thawing.
Chicken livers	8 oz/250 g	1	Stand in a shallow container, 30 seconds on each side.	Allow thawing to complete at room temperature and cook immediately after thawing.

COOKING MEAT AND POULTRY

Type	Weight	Setting (minutes) High	Med	Method	Approximate standing time
Beef rare medium well done	1 lb/500 g	5–6 7–8 8–10	11–12 12–15 16–18	Stand joints on a trivet or roasting rack and place inside a roasting bag to encourage browning. Cook larger joints for half the time on high and remaining time on medium setting, to prevent outside of meat toughening before the centre is cooked through. Pork is the only exception it should be microwaved on high throughout. Turn over halfway through the cooking time. Drain fat away during cooking. Boned and rolled joints cook more evenly. Those containing bones will cook slightly faster and any bone ends or thinner parts will need shielding at the onset of cooking. Remove this halfway through the cooking time for good, evenly cooked meat. Smaller joints can be cooked completely on a preheated browning dish.	Tent with foil, shiny side facing meat. The internal temperature of the meat will rise during this time. Joints: Beef 15–30 minutes. Lamb 20–30 minutes. Pork 20–25 minutes.
Lamb medium well done	1 lb/500 g	7–8 8–10	9–11 12–15		
Pork well done	1 lb/500 g	8–10			

COOKING MEAT AND POULTRY					
Type	Weight	Setting (minutes) High	Med	Method	Approximate standing time
Chops, lamb or pork loin chump	5–6 oz/ 175 g 6 oz/175 g	3 4	3½–4 4½–5	Trim chops of any excess fat. Cook in preheated browning dish, or cook on a plate and finish by placing under a preheated grill. Always cook pork chops on a high setting, and if kidney is attached, cover with greaseproof paper. Cook lamb chops on high for the first half of cooking time, then reduce to medium. Cooking time depends on thickness and shape of chops. Arrange thicker parts to the outside of the dish and turn over halfway through cooking time.	Stand covered. 2 minutes for 1 chop. 5 minutes for 2 or more.
Mince	1 lb/500 g	5		Use lean minced meat. Cover. Use a fork to break up any lumps; do this twice during cooking.	Stand, covered, 2 minutes.
Beef steaks, rump or fillet	8 oz/250 g	2–4		Add 1 teaspoon of oil to a preheated browning dish. Cook steaks uncovered for a minimum of 1 minute on each side. Further cooking will depend on desired result.	Covered, 2–3 minutes.
Gammon	8 oz/250 g	3½–4		Remove rind and excess fat, snip the edges to prevent curling. Cook on preheated browning dish, or on a plate. Cover with greaseproof paper. Turn the dish once or twice during cooking.	Covered, 5 minutes.
Bacon	8 oz/250 g	5		Remove rind and snip to prevent curling. Cook on trivet or in preheated browning dish. Arrange in a single layer. When a larger quantity is being cooked, slices can be overlapped but will need repositioning once or twice during cooking. Cover with greaseproof paper; remove this after cooking to prevent paper from sticking to food.	Uncovered, 2–3 minutes.
Sausages, beef or pork	2 average 4 average	2½ 4		Prick thoroughly. Cook uncovered on a preheated browning dish, turning once during cooking. Low fat sausages give better results.	Uncovered, 2 minutes. Pat with absorbent paper before serving.

◆ 213

COOKING MEAT AND POULTRY					
Type	Weight	Setting (minutes) High	Med	Method	Approximate standing time
Kidney, lamb or pork	8 oz/250 g	3½–4		Skin and trim away any inedible parts. Slice in half or cut in pieces before cooking. Arrange towards outside edges of dish. Cook covered.	Covered, 5 minutes.
Liver, lamb or calves	1 lb/500 g	6–8		Wash and dry, remove any inedible parts and slice thinly. Reposition once during cooking. Cover with greaseproof paper. Brown under a grill at end of cooking if desired, or cook in a preheated browning dish.	Covered, 5 minutes.
Chicken, whole	1 lb/500 g	6–8	9–10	Wash and dry. Stand on a trivet and place in or cover with a roasting bag. Start cooking whole larger birds breast side down, turn over halfway through cooking time. Remove fat as it collects. When cooked on medium throughout shielding is not always necessary. The best results are achieved when bird is cooked for half the time on high and remaining time on medium.	Tent in foil, shiny side in for 15 minutes to complete the cooking.
Chicken, pieces	1 lb/500 g	5–6		Arrange thicker bits to outside edges of dish. Turn over and reposition once or twice during cooking. Remove fat as it collects.	Stand covered for 5–10 minutes.
Poussin	1 14 oz/450 g 4	5 20		Follow procedure for chicken.	As for chicken but reduce standing time to 5 minutes for 1 15 minutes for 4.
Turkey	1 lb/500 g	10–12	12–14	As for chicken. Very large turkeys are best cooked conventionally. Large turkeys can be cooked for half the time by microwave and the remaining time conventionally. Turkey will need turning frequently during cooking and fat must be removed as it collects.	As for chicken but increase standing time to 30 minutes.
Chicken livers	1 lb/500 g	5–6		Slice in two and remove any gristly bits. Cook covered and remove from oven whilst still pink in the centre. Stir once during cooking.	Covered, 3–5 minutes.

COOKING MEAT AND POULTRY					
Type	Weight	Setting (minutes) High	Med	Method	Approximate standing time
Duck, whole	1 lb/500 g	7	10	Prick whole bird all over and shield wing tips and breast with foil. Stand on a trivet and cover with a split roasting bag. Start cooking breast side down. Turn over halfway through cooking time and remove foil. Remove fat frequently during cooking. Whole birds are best cooked on medium and larger birds on defrost for the second half of cooking time.	Drain away excess fat. Stand as for chicken. Place under preheated grill to brown and crisp the skin.
Duck, portions	4 × 12 oz/ 375 g	10 on high. Reduce to medium for a further 30 to 40 minutes		Wash and dry. Cook covered in a large dish. Turn and reposition once or twice during cooking. Drain off fat as it collects.	Brown under a preheated grill to crisp skin.

REMEMBER
• The starting temperature of meat and poultry affects the overall cooking time.
• Take the chill off meats before placing on a preheated browning dish.
• Stand the chilled meat on a plate and microwave for 1 minute or so. Pat meat dry with absorbent paper before cooking.
• Pork should always be cooked on a high setting.
• Poultry should always be thoroughly defrosted before cooking.

◆ 215

DEFROSTING FISH				
Type	Weight	Defrost setting timing (minutes)	Method	Standing time
Whole fish	1 lb/500 g	6–8	Place fish on a plate or in a shallow dish, arrange heads to tails. Cover with absorbent paper. Turn over and reposition halfway through cooking time. Shield any parts with foil that feel warm and continue until fish is almost thawed but still a little icy in parts.	Immerse in cold water for 5–10 minutes then pat dry.
Steaks	1 lb/500 g	5–6	Arrange thicker parts to outside of dish. Cover with absorbent paper and turn over once during thawing.	5–10 minutes. Pat dry.

DEFROSTING FISH

Type	Weight	Defrost setting timing (minutes)	Method	Standing time
Fillets	1 lb/500 g	6	Thicker fillets will take longer than thinner ones. Rest 2 or 3 times during thawing. Arrange and reposition as for steaks.	5–10 minutes. Pat dry.
Prawns, shrimps	8 oz/250 g	4 minutes	Defrost in a pierced plastic bag, or arrange in a shallow dish and cover with absorbent paper.	Immerse in cold water for about 30 seconds, then drain and pat dry.

- Fish should be cooked immediately after defrosting as it deteriorates rapidly.
- Test whole fish, after standing time, by inserting a skewer into the thickest part.
- Oily fish will defrost more quickly than white or smoked fish.
- Mop up liquid during thawing.
- Fish will defrost more evenly when it is exposed to short bursts of microwave energy i.e. 2 minutes defrost, 2 minutes rest, etc.

COOKING FISH

Type	Setting High	Method	Standing time
Whole fish – Dover sole, lemon sole, plaice, trout, mackerel, whiting, carp, bream, mullet	3–4 minutes per 1 lb/500 g	Wash and pat dry. Slash skin 2 or 3 times. Remove fins. Shield head and tail ends when cooking more than 2 whole medium fish (approximately 8 oz/250 g). Arrange heads to tails. Cook covered, reposition once during cooking. To prevent skins sticking together during cooking, separate with strips of cling film. Oily fish will cook slightly faster owing to their higher fat content.	3–5 minutes covered.
Steaks	4 minutes per 1 lb/500 g	Wash and pat dry. Cook covered in a large shallow dish. Arrange thicker parts to outside of dish. Turn over once during cooking.	3–5 minutes covered.
White fillets	3–4 minutes per 1 lb/500 g	Wash and pat dry. Arrange thicker parts to outside edges. Rearrange once during cooking.	3–5 minutes covered.
Smoked fillets	4–4½ minutes per 1 lb/500 g	Wash and pat dry. Arrange as for white fillets, adding 2–4 tablespoons water if a less salty flavour is desired. Cook covered, rearrange once during cooking.	5 minutes covered.

Note: cooking a whole salmon.
The skin is thick so a cover is not required during cooking.

COOKING FROZEN VEGETABLES

Vegetable	Weight	Water	Cooking time (minutes)	Cooking techniques
Asparagus	8 oz/250 g	1 tbsp	6	Arrange tips towards the centre of dish. Rearrange after 3 minutes.
Beans, cut	8 oz/250 g	2 tbsp	6–7	Stir once during cooking
Broad beans	8 oz/250 g	2 tbsp	7	Stir once during cooking
Broccoli	8 oz/250 g	1 tbsp	7–8	Arrange florets to centre of dish. Rearrange after 4 minutes.
Brussels sprouts	8 oz/250 g	1 tbsp	7–8	Stir once during cooking
Cabbage	8 oz/250 g	1 tbsp	4–8	Stir once during cooking
Carrots	8 oz/250 g	1 tbsp	6	Stir once during cooking
Cauliflower florets	8 oz/250 g	none	6	Stir once during cooking. Best cooked in a boiling bag.
Corn on the cob	1 medium 2 medium 4 medium	none none none	3–4 7–8 12	Wrap in pierced cling film or greaseproof paper. Arrange in shallow dish. Turn once during cooking.
Corn kernels	8 oz/250 g	1 tbsp	6	Stir once during cooking
Courgettes	8 oz/250 g	none	5	Stir once during cooking
Mixed vegetables	8 oz/250 g	1 tbsp	5	Stir once during cooking
Mushrooms	8 oz/250 g	none	6	Stir once during cooking
Onions, whole	8 oz/250 g	none	5	Stir once during cooking
Peas	8 oz/250 g	none	5–6	Stir once during cooking
Peas and carrots	8 oz/250 g	1 tbsp	6	Stir once during cooking
Peppers, diced	8 oz/250 g	none	8	Stir once during cooking
Potatoes, new	8 oz/250 g	2 tbsp	6–8	Best cooked in boiling bag
Spinach	8 oz/250 g	none	6	Best cooked in boiling bag
Swede	8 oz/250 g	2 tbsp	6–8	Stir once during cooking

◆ 217

Cook frozen vegetables from their frozen state on a high setting and always cover the container so that moisture is retained. Very little, and in some cases, no water at all is required when microwaving frozen vegetables. Cook in a shallow dish, spreading the vegetables out, or use microwave boiling bags, which give very good results. Reposition boiling bags once during cooking. Salt after cooking, as it will only prolong the cooking time and vegetables have more chance of toughening when it is added at the beginning.

COOKING FRESH VEGETABLES					
Vegetable	Weight	Preparation	Water	Cooking time (minutes)	Cooking techniques
Artichoke, globe	2 medium 4 medium	Wash and trim	2 tbsp 4 tbsp	8 15–20	Stand upright in dish. Turn dish once during cooking.
Asparagus	1 lb/500 g	Shave woody stems	2 tbsp	9–10	Position tips towards centre of dish. Rearrange after 5 minutes.
Aubergine	1 medium	Slice	1 tbsp	3–4	Stir once during cooking
Beetroot, whole	1 lb/500 g	Wash and leave whole. Prick skins.	4 tbsp	14	Turn dish once during cooking
Broad beans	1 lb/500 g	Remove from pods	4 tbsp	8–10	Stir once during cooking
Broccoli	1 lb/500 g	Shave woody stems	4 tbsp	8–10	Place florets to centre of dish. Turn dish once during cooking.
Brussels sprouts	1 lb/500 g	Trim, cut a cross through stalk end	4 tbsp	8–10	Stir once during cooking
Cabbage, shredded	1 lb/500 g	Trim, shred, remove hard core	4 tbsp	8–10	Stir once during cooking
Carrots	1 lb/500 g	Slice thinly	4 tbsp	12	Stir twice during cooking
Cauliflower	1 lb/500 g	Trim, break into florets	4 tbsp	9–12	Best cooked in boiling bag
Celery	1 lb/500 g	Trim and slice thinly	4 tbsp	10–12	Stir twice during cooking
Corn on the cob	2 medium	Remove silks when cooking in husk	none	6–8	Turn over after 3 minutes
Courgettes	1 lb/500 g	Wash and slice thinly	none	8	Stir once during cooking
Fennel	1 lb/500 g	Wash and slice	4 tbsp	10	Stir twice during cooking
Leeks	1 lb/500 g	Wash well and slice	none	8	Stir once during cooking
Marrow	1 lb/500 g	Peel and slice	none	7–8	Stir once during cooking
Mushrooms	4 oz/125 g	Wipe or wash and pat dry	none	2	Stir once during cooking
Onions, whole	4 medium	Peel	none	10	Reposition once during cooking time
Parsnips	1 lb/500 g	Slice thinly	4 tbsp	10–12	Stir twice during cooking
Peas	1 lb/500 g	Shell	4 tbsp	10	Stir twice during cooking

COOKING FRESH VEGETABLES					
Vegetable	Weight	Preparation	Water	Cooking time (minutes)	Cooking techniques
Potatoes					
old	1 lb/500 g	Peel and slice	6 tbsp	7–8	Best in boiling bag
new	1 lb/500 g	into 1 oz/25 g pieces	6 tbsp	6–8	Best in boiling bag
baked	1 medium	Scrub and prick	none	4	Stand on kitchen paper, cook uncovered
Runner beans	1 lb/500 g	Top, tail and slice thinly	4 tbsp	6–8	Stir twice during cooking
Spinach	1 lb/500 g	Wash	none	6–8	Best in boiling bag
Swede	1 lb/500 g	Peel, slice or dice thinly	4 tbsp	12–15	Stir twice during cooking
Tomatoes	1 lb/500 g	Wash, halve	none	4	Turn dish once during cooking
Turnips	1 lb/500 g	Peel, slice or dice thinly	4 tbsp	12–15	Stir twice during cooking

All fresh vegetables are cooked on high and covered, unless stated otherwise.
Cook in a shallow container or microwave boiling bag for best results. Salt at the end of cooking.

◆ 219

INDEX

ACKNOWLEDGEMENTS
Many thanks to Jill Norman for editing and coordinating the work on this book so thoroughly and to Gwen Edmonds. I
would also like to thank Neville Graham for his design work and Dave King and his assistant Jonathan for the care they
took over the photography. Also many thanks to Jenny Rogers who encouraged me to find a publisher in the first
instance. Thanks to Peter and my children for their patience, support and much valued criticism. They had their order of
eating fixed by my rhythm of writing. Finally, I would like to thank Toshiba for the loan of a combination oven.

Dorling Kindersley would like to thank Chinacraft, 198 Regent Street, W1, the China Reject Shop,
134 Regent Street, W1 and Neal Street East, Covent Garden, WC2 for the loan of china for the photography.